BEYOND DRUGS

THE PERGAMON TEXTBOOK
INSPECTION COPY SERVICE

An inspection copy of any book published in the Pergamon International Library will gladly be sent to academic staff without obligation for their consideration for course adoption or recommendation. Copies may be retained for a period of 60 days from receipt and returned if not suitable. When a particular title is adopted or recommended for adoption for class use and the recommendation results in a sale of 12 or more copies, the inspection copy may be retained with our compliments. The Publishers will be pleased to receive suggestions for revised editions and new titles to be published in this important International Library.

Books by Stanley Einstein

The Use and Misuse of Drugs :
A Social Dilemma

Methadone Treatment

Student Drug Surveys

Beyond Drugs

STANLEY EINSTEIN, Ph. D.

Executive Director
Institute for the Study of Drug Misuse
New York City

PERGAMON PRESS INC.

New York · Toronto · Oxford · Sydney · Braunschweig

PERGAMON PRESS INC.
Maxwell House, Fairview Park, Elmsford, N.Y. 10523

PERGAMON OF CANADA LTD.
207 Queen's Quay West, Toronto 117, Ontario

PERGAMON PRESS LTD.
Headington Hill Hall, Oxford

PERGAMON PRESS (AUST.) PTY. LTD.
Rushcutters Bay, Sydney, N.S.W.

PERGAMON GmbH
Burgplatz 1, Braunschweig

Library of Congress Cataloging in Publication Data

Einstein, Stanley.
  Beyond drugs.

   Bibliography: p.
   1. Drug abuse. 2. Drugs. 3. Drug abuse--
Treatment. I. Title. [DNLM: 1. Drug abuse--
Popular works. 2. Drugs--Popular works. WM270
E35b 1974]
HV5801.E42   362.2′9   73–7940
ISBN 0–08–017767–0
ISBN 0–08–017768–9 (pbk.)

Second printing, 1978

Printed in the United States of America

Contents

One of the most widely read books of all times is *The Decline and Fall of the Roman Empire* written in 1788 by Edward Gibbon. It sets forth five basic reasons why that great civilization withered and died. These were:

1. the undermining of the dignity and sanctity of the home, which is the basis for human society;
2. higher and higher taxes, the spending of public money for free bread and circuses for the people;
3. the mad craze for pleasure, sports becoming every year more exciting, more brutal, and more immoral;
4. the building of great armaments when the real enemy was within—the decay of individual responsibilities;
5. the decay of religion, faith fading into mere form, losing touch with life, losing power to guide people.

Preface

My involvement in the area of the nonmedical use of drugs was a happenstance. My continued involvement is a conscious effort. It raises problems for me as a therapist, teacher, lecturer, researcher, writer, and journalist for the following reasons: It doesn't deserve to be a separate field as it presently is; our concerns and energies would be better utilized if we mobilized them for the exciting challenge of coming to terms with living; my own biases, public health ones, are not necessarily more useful, in a predictive sense, than any other bias.

By training and inclination, my interest is going beyond drugs. Hence the title of the book. I owe much to my colleagues who stimulated my thinking about various aspects of man's drug-oriented behavior, to my students who constantly challenged me, and to my patients and research subjects who allowed me into their lives. In a strange way, I owe a lot to the "drug-abuse" empire builders and parochialists who upset and angered me enough to get me to sit and write a new book in a field that has become habituated if not addicted to information dissemination.

My personal indebtedness is to Rosalind Stein and Linda Bartolo, who typed the various versions of the manuscript, and to Lywanda Thompson for gathering the material on drugs and songs.

To my wife Sarah, daughter Tammy, son Josh, and father and mother-in-law, Abe and Fanny, thank you for your patience, understanding, and caring during the many hours that my writing took me away from active family life.

Stanley Einstein

The Author

Stanley Einstein, Ph. D., is Executive Director of the Institute for the Study of Drug Misuse in New York City which he founded in 1963. He has been Associate Director, Division of Drug Abuse, and Associate Professor of Public Health and Psychiatry at the College of Medicine and Dentistry of New Jersey at Newark, 1969–1973; Executive Director, New York Council on Alcoholism, Inc., 1967–1969; and Assistant Professor of Psychiatry at the New York Medical College, 1963–1967. He is also the Editor and Founder of the *International Journal of the Addictions Drug Forum*, and *Altered States of Consciousness*, was an Abstract Editor for the journal *Excerpta Criminologica*, Founder and Co-Editor of a monograph series entitled *The Non-Medical Use of Drugs*, and was also a journalist of a series of articles in the *Newark News* and the *Star Ledger* entitled *Drug Forum*, from 1971–1973.

He has organized and lectured at numerous workshops and symposiums on the topic of drug abuse, has been a consultant to the medical departments of many large corporations—the New York Telephone Company, General Motors Company, and Mobil Oil Company among them. Dr. Einstein is the author or co-author of over 50 drug-related articles that have appeared in scholarly journals since 1963 as well as of three previous books.

Introduction

[Puritanism is] "the haunting fear that someone, somewhere may be happy."

H. L. Mencken

By the time you begin reading this book, you will have, in all likelihood, been to some meetings about drugs, watched numerous TV documentaries and newscasts, been the victim of hysteria-producing films, and read articles and editorials in your local paper and in almost every popular magazine. In other words, this book is reaching a person who is surrounded by "the drug scene" and may already be sick and tired of drugs. So why another book? The answer to that is as complex as the contemporary American drug situation itself, with both rational and irrational elements.

The (hopefully) more rational reasons include:

1. offering useful insights to those concerned about the increasing drug problem which has either not been presented before or has not been presented clearly enough;
2. challenging a variety of drug-abuse myths and untested assumptions which continue to get many people into trouble;
3. serving as a catalyst which may cut through much of the hopelessness and despair experienced by both young and old concerning drug abuse;
4. offering some alternatives in place of the usual simplistic black and white reactions to a whole spectrum of colorful private and public behavior;
5. offering some guidelines and criteria that may prove personally useful in evaluating the consequences of dependence upon specific treatment, educational, preventional, and detectional techniques and programs;
6. pointing out the various roles that the use and misuse of all kinds of drugs have and continue to have in our daily lives;
7. challenging the reader to weigh the nondrug alternatives that already exist in his own life or are within reach;

ix

8. challenging those who feel most concerned about defining their own roles in the strengthening and/or weakening of the contemporary pattern of turning to drugs rather than to people to meet all sorts of legitimate and illegitimate needs.

Some of what you will read may upset or anger you. It's meant to! When traditional views are challenged, when some of our clearly dangerous—as well as silly—behavior is focused on, we often get angry and defensive. But better to be upset and angry at an author you may never meet than to continue what may be destructive behavior in relationships that have great meaning for you.

Some of what you will read may frustrate you. The book is meant to do that as well. Not only is it frustrating to turn to some authority in a society which prides itself on not turning to others (the pioneer image), but when no step-by-step blueprint is offered, you may feel that you have been taken. It is not the intention of this book to insult you. It is my intention to take a reader sufficiently concerned about drug abuse to read this book on a trip through contemporary life with drug abuse as a model, and to point out the general terrain and the possible dead ends. Getting stuck and getting lost will only be temporary incidents. As with many a well-planned trip, we each come with our own gear, our own needs, our own censoring mechanisms, and we may be doing ourselves a disservice by assuming that the meaning and consequences of such a venture can best be experienced only during the venture. Both the passing of time and what we do with whatever occurs in time are the crucial elements affecting any personal venture. Developing personally appropriate reactions to drug abuse is no different.

While the intention of this book is to focus on teen-age drug use, it is obvious that we must have an appreciation of adult drug use and the problems of growing up to better comprehend why the traditional sweets, alcoholic beverages, tobacco products, and sexual outlets apparently do not satiate the growing youngster.

Many of us do not comprehend the present drug scene because we feel it is alien to our values and way of life, and also because we feel that what was good enough for us should be good enough for the present generation. The term most often used to describe this is the *generation gap*. While the words are new, surely the concept isn't. The father of that prehistoric man who left the tree for a cave was certainly at a loss to understand this change in style of living. He was also most likely at a disadvantage in that he didn't know the word *sick*, so he couldn't blame the change on sickness, or perhaps feel guilty. It's hard for me to imagine him lying on a bed of rocks questioning where he went wrong.

In all likelihood, this is the major contemporary reason for the sale of so much material about drug abuse. Parents feel guilty about their children's actual drug use or frightened and anxious about potential drug use. In almost all cases, the parent feels inadequate to cope with "the drug problem," easily overlooking that for better or worse he has already faced a multitude of other guilt and anxiety-provoking problems during his child's development.

Youngsters often buy much of the drug-abuse material to be on top of new "facts," check out various issues, and to be prepared for the newest lecture that they will surely receive from some adult who bought the same piece of new material.

The unfortunate thing is that the new drug facts rarely serve to bring people together. Rather, the different meanings imputed to the same material become the newest ammunition to use during that phase called adolescence by what often appear to be enemies living in the same household.

Most parents understand that adolescence is the only time which American society permits active experimentation and testing to go on. From birth through the primary grades, growing up focuses on the attainment of basic language, motor and intellectual skills against a background of national, religious, ethnic, and family rites and rituals. During this period, the growing child's role is fairly clearly spelled out.

During late adolescence and early adulthood, his roles and behavior are again clearly spelled out. He is expected to utilize the primitive skills of childhood, which were tested and refined during adolescence, in the marketplace, the halls of academe, the armed services, or the various institutions we have developed for those citizens we deem to be failures.

Thus, most parents are prepared for how they will react to traditionally accepted types of adolescent testing or rebellion. What is often forgotten or overlooked is that a traditional form of rebellion is neither good nor bad; it is just traditional. In the second place, many, if not most, of our traditions are being sorely tested today. Lastly, and perhaps of most importance, whatever the particular parental attitude to an adolescent's tests—whether it be strict, tolerant, or ambivalent—it may not prove as helpful as expected if a real crisis arises. Drug abuse, as it is currently defined, is experienced as being exactly such a crisis. The increasing number of teen-agers experimenting with and frequently using a variety of drugs, whose parents actually know them instead of just reading about them, has been both mystifying and frightening to parents.

Adolescents' failure to understand the reaction of the adult population to their actual or pretended drug use derives from the same factor that is upsetting the adults. Although both youngsters and adults exhibit an excessive concern and interest in drugs and the drug scene, drug-oriented living is part of the fabric of daily life for the young, whereas it is perceived as being only a fad or style for the adult. When you grow up driving on the right side of the road, you generally don't question it, and it becomes part of your life style. When you are confronted with driving on the left side, you begin to question it and may perceive it in ways that are out of proportion to what it deserves.

Coupled to this difference in life styles is the fact that drug abuse has become a general smoke screen for both old and young to avoid dealing with some of the issues that seriously affect their daily lives and over which they feel they have little control.

When all of the major institutions of life are now once again being challenged—formal education, traditional patterns of marriage, communication, economics, theology, the arts, the actual extension of life, patterns of normal physical and mental health, the geography of the universe, patterns of warfare and nationalism, the level of noise, and the availability of space for privacy—drug abuse may seem to many to be a problem which is sufficiently circumscribed to focus on. It is the new straw man of our era. Unfortunately, using drug abuse as a smoke screen will in no way help us to deal appropriately with the issues mentioned above, nor with the many serious consequences of drug abuse itself. This smoke-screen approach will either tend to increase the many myths and bits of misinformation about the consequences and reasons for drug abuse that are already prevalent or will make it excessively difficult to distinguish between myth and reality in this field.

Exploiting the drug issues will not help us understand:

1. What are the real dangers of drug use and misuse?
2. Do only certain people become drug abusers?
3. Are there chemical solutions to people's problems?
4. Is the law, whether it is more punitive or less punitive, able to decrease significantly the present pattern of drug abuse?
5. Is taking drugs for other than medically approved reasons a sign of psychological illness?
6. If one assumes that drug abuse is indicative of psychological illness, can every drug abuser profit from the available kinds of treatment?

7. Is abstaining from drugs the single goal that should be sought after?
8. When is a chemical a drug and when is it a medicine?
9. Why are certain drugs socially accepted while others aren't?
10. What role do drugs have in recreational activities and why does this appear to be on the increase?
11. What can I, myself, do or say when it is *my* child, *my* friend, or *my* parent who is the drug abuser?

The inability to see beyond the "drug problem," to assess how a person—teen-ager or adult—is handling his life as a whole, is perhaps the greatest danger in taking a narrow view of drug abuse. From the parent's point of view, it is a great mistake to assume that if the teen-ager is staying away from drugs, he has his main problems licked, or that if he is experimenting with drugs or even using them on a regular basis, all is lost.

Likewise, from the youngster's point of view, it is dangerous to gloat over "parental hypocrisy" when the parent smokes, drinks, overeats, or even has great difficulty with any of these substances.

The parent and child who call each other "pothead" or "lush" are at best involved in attempting to score points. There are better games to play. At worst, this kind of communication may be a symptom of neither having anything else to say to the other—or being afraid to. Warm, loving human relationships—most necessary for that gregarious creature, man— are in no way helped by name-calling, insidious labeling, or poor communication.

It should be apparent to the reader by now that the intent of this book is to clarify what is actually known about drugs and drug users and to point out that the "drug problem" is not a phenomenon isolated from other facets of contemporary life. Where the facts are not known or where the data are still questionable (as in the cases of the physical effects of long-term or occasional marijuana use or the genetic effects of LSD use), this will be frankly admitted.

The emphasis will be on helping us to understand that decisions and behavior related to drugs are perhaps best understood by looking at these issues:

1. What are the available alternative solutions to the problems of living?
2. Why do people turn to *things*, including drugs, rather than to *people* in order to meet their basic needs?
3. How can a youngster learn—and how can adults help him learn—to express his individual values and needs through interactions with others rather than by reliance on chemistry or other types of object-oriented behavior?

In all likelihood, by the time you finish this book, you will feel that aside from a few facts which are new to you, you knew most of it. In fact, that is one of the messages of the book: At any point in time, anywhere in the world, given a few cultural variations, there are only a limited number of problems that man can and does experience and only a limited number of solutions to these problems.

Part of the challenge of life is to come up with our own appropriate variations of these solutions.

PROJECT

1. Note the concerns that you have about the use and misuse of drugs. Then relate these concerns or issues to particular people, note what you feel should or can be done, and why, and whom you can turn to for help.

Concern (What)	Particular People (Who)	Action (What and Why)	Resources (Whom)
(a)			
(b)			

2. After considering the various reasons that are given to explain drug use, note those that you think are the "real" ones. Decide whether you have any role in creating or eliminating these reasons or factors.

CHAPTER 1

Critical Issues and Definitions

If drugs did not simultaneously affect both private and public behavior and provoke value judgments about pleasure, and if they did not influence a gamut of social, legal and economic interactions, we would neither be as concerned nor as confused as we are.

Daniel X. Freedman, M.D.
Professor and Chairman
Department of Psychiatry
University of Chicago

WHAT IS A DRUG?

Not long ago Bill Cosby recorded this slice of American life: In a kindergarten, children are learning math by chanting, "One and one equal two." The chanting goes on smoothly until one child asks the teacher, "What's one?"

It may very well be that the same thing is going on with the present concern and effort to contain the misuse of drugs. With so many people so interested in this increasing activity and with so many people attempting to save so many of their fellow citizens, we may be overlooking exactly what drugs are.

The various kinds of drug use and the many different concerns about it easily make drug-related behavior one of the important issues of our time—so much so that the present focusing only upon the user of drugs permits us to overlook the obvious: People who spend time thinking about someone else's actual or possible drug use have an important drug problem also.

Before we get into what makes the use of drugs or the concern about drug use a problem, we had best come to terms with what a drug is. One might think that most adults, and certainly most children who are already

1

of school age, would surely know what a drug is. The same assumption is generally held for $1 + 1 = 2$. But it is important to define the term "drug," because there are consequences for the individual and his community that depend upon the definition used and the source of that definition.

Before we go any further, it would prove most useful if you would take this opportunity to think over and perhaps even write down what your own working definition of a drug is.

Some definitions may have to do with a drug's "medical" status, that is, whether or not it is used as a medicine. Many definitions relate to different pharmacological categories of drugs. The terms "stimulants," "depressants," "narcotics," "ups," "downs," and "hallucinogens" involve this type of categorization. Other definitions relate to judgments that are not really based on pharmacological properties. "Hard" drugs and "soft" drugs come to mind. Then, of course, one may think that drugs are something someone else who is involved in drug abuse takes, while what we take are medicines. The critical issue for defining drugs in this instance is who is using a particular substance and how we view him. Another general type of definition utilizes the actual or imagined consequences of a substance as the basis for defining it.

There are many different definitions and many frames of reference that people can use when considering drugs and their own reactions to the use and misuse of drugs. In a sense, it is because of this that many problems and misunderstandings exist, both for and between young and old. For example, the lead in a bullet is a chemical, and the consequences associated with it are dangerous, but it is highly doubtful that many people consider it a drug. When cyclamates were taken off the consumer market because of their effect on the kidneys of mice, they were categorized as food additives. When they were brought back, they were defined as drugs. Sounds confusing? Not really. This is just another example of man's attempt to adapt to the world he lives in. We define things in order to have a better grasp of our relationship to the given person, object, etc.

Historically, definitions of drugs have originated from four main arenas of life: social-religious, medical, legal, and scientific. Probably the oldest definitions are derived from social and religious activities. Most likely, alcoholic beverages of one form or another are man's oldest known drugs. It is unlikely that they were considered to be drugs in the past, although pharmacologically they have been classified as depressants. Most people today don't consider alcohol a drug. Rather, it is considered to be and is advertised and sold as a social beverage. For most of us, it is an ice-breaker, a source of conviviality. We make the guest in our home more at ease by offering him a drink. When holidays come, we often are concerned about having the right kind of "booze" for our special guests. We watch various sports on TV, nibbling something and drinking beer.

That infamous American tradition, the Christmas office party, would surely disappear without alcoholic beverages. Year in and year out, the same person attempts to play Don Juan and fails. He may have learned who he is as he grew up, but he never learned who he isn't. With a little alcohol, he acts out being the instant romantic. Thus, alcohol also has had a traditional effect in spelling out certain social roles. For the teen-ager or adult at a party, a glass in one hand and a cigarette in the other, with the backside on a chair or up against the wall, alcohol may readily relieve him of the anxiety of what to do with his hands or his body.

Alcohol, the beverage, is also closely associated by the general public with sexual behavior. We have learned in a variety of ways that sexual behavior, as well as the expression of certain feelings such as aggression, are more likely to be accepted if they are tied in with being high, tipsy, or drunk. Sounds almost like a cop-out. But that's the point: Socially accepted drugs have the distinct advantage of being associated with allowable behavior, while their relatives—the socially rejected deviant or disadvantaged drugs—don't hold such a position.

We see this more clearly, perhaps, in terms of substances that are part of religious rituals. Wine, an alcoholic beverage, has significance in the Mass for the Catholic. It is an integral part of the weekly Sabbath service for adherents of Judaism. Peyote, a hallucinogen which is derived from a cactus, has been considered to be a divine plant for centuries. Since 1964, American Indians who are members of the Native American Church have had the legal right to use it as a sacramental symbol in their services. Marijuana and hashish have been part of ritual life in India. Not too long ago, LSD was interpreted to mean League for Spiritual Discovery; its use was associated with spiritual strivings.

Since a variety of *objects* have been used in various religious services, it should not surprise us that various drugs have been included as well. The point is, however, that given a social, religious, or other institutionalized status, they are not considered to be *drugs*. One immediate consequence of this is that when difficulty is associated with their use, we don't consider that difficulty to be a "drug problem."

This issue is no minor one. When parents and teen-agers get involved in the marijuana-alcohol controversy, the attacking and defending are conceived of as being directed at significantly different things: a potentially dangerous drug and a social beverage. But it is important to understand that the social definition of a substance has little to do with its actual medical and psychiatric consequences. For the estimated 9,000,000 Americans who are the casualties of excessive drinking of alcohol, calling their substance of choice a "beverage" or a "drug" in no way changes their difficulties in day-to-day living. Calling LSD a basic ingredient of a religious ritual in no way makes the LSD experience more predictable. Nor does doing this guarantee a good trip or diminish the possibility of a bad trip or the future experiencing of flashbacks.

One of the consequences of social and/or religious definitions of drugs and man's various appetites is that certain behavior patterns become associated with their use and certain boundaries are established beyond which one is not expected to go. Another consequence is that if some difficulty does occur, we generally associate it with the substance and not with the person. "The drink was too strong." "The food was too rich." Each of us can surely add other similar sentences from our own experiences.

We usually focus our attention either on a particular substance or on the person using it, and we never really question whether the community has any role in either reinforcing or inhibiting drug-taking behavior. So the drug problem comes down to a certain person's using certain drugs. At this point, we still haven't defined the term "drug" and assessed who the drug abuser is. But one thing can be said: Which drugs are acceptable and which are not, at any given time or place, is not simply based on their pharmacological properties.

Medical Definition

Another place we look in an attempt to define drugs is in the field of medicine. From a medical perspective, a drug is a substance used to prevent illness, to maintain health, to treat illness, or to relieve pain. Drugs can be used to bring a person back to a certain level of functioning, to maintain him at that level, to slow down some process of deterioration, to prolong life, to ease death, to help birth, to prevent birth, etc. The important ingredient in this type of a definition is that drugs are conceived of as having a status called "medicine." Medicines are generally prescribed by people who have a special background (physicians), manufactured by specific institutions (pharmaceutical companies that employ pharmacologists) and are prepared for sale or are readily available for sale by the pharmacist in either a local drugstore or from an institution's pharmacy. Nurses and some other professionals may also administer the medicine. When you and I take a drug-medicine or give it to someone else, it is because someone else with training and authority has said it is okay to do so. This is another important factor which we shall return to in our attempt to understand the use and misuse of drugs. When someone takes a medicine on his own, with no medical authority to back up this behavior, or takes a substance which his community feels does not have (or no longer has) any medically approved status, he is generally considered to be taking a "drug" and perhaps even to have a drug problem.

From society's point of view and from the very personal position of child and parent, if one accepts only the medical definitions of drugs, some serious consequences may result. First, we might assume that the as-yet-undefined drug problem is best handled by the medical profession. Obviously, one should expect the medical profession to assume a major responsibility for medical and psychiatric conditions in any way associated with the use of or excessive concern over drugs. Their training, skills, techniques, tools, and facilities are necessary for certain consequences of the use and misuse of drugs. However, the *medical* consequences associated with today's drug scene are only one of the many facets of this complicated behavior pattern.

An equally important assumption which derives from a medical definition of drugs is that the youngster or adult should turn to the physician or other health professional with his concerns about drug use. While the logic is sound, the reality is quite different. It is a rarity for the physician, or any other professional, for that matter, to have been formally trained in all the facets of this condition or style of life. Studying pharmacology doesn't result in helping a concerned parent who wants to know what to do or say to her child to stop present or future drug use. Knowing how to treat syphilis doesn't help the physician alter the female street addict's major way of supporting her drug habit. Being a pediatrician is not necessarily sufficient to deal effectively with the youngster's statement: "If you haven't tried it, don't knock it." In an age of specialization, the cost of being a specialist may be the inability to intervene effectively in those specifics that are clearly related to the general problems of living.

Legal Definition

From the legal perspective, a particular substance is sometimes experienced as being so dangerous to the individual and/or his society that it must be controlled. Based on the assumption of danger, laws are passed and procedures developed to control the growth, manufacture, distribution, importation, sale, use, and possession of a given substance.

In spite of one's personal views concerning the effectiveness or legitimacy of any drug law, society has a tradition of attempting to control drugs and drug-related behavior and, no doubt, will continue to do so in the future. In fact, new laws being passed in every state of the Union relate to the teaching about drugs in school and spell out general content, who is to do the teaching, how many hours are to be spent teaching students and teaching teachers to teach students, and how much tax money is to be used for each student in this preventive effort.

We might assume that the law, with all its representatives and institutions, could effectively limit or do away with our present drug scene. But the last major American effort to dissuade rational adults from using a drug was an abysmal failure. It is well remembered in the annals of our history as Prohibition. Notwithstanding the various reasons given by Monday morning quarterbacks to explain its failure, its major reason for failure was no doubt related to the difficulties of changing man's appetites by laws.

Another consequence of defining drugs in legal terms is that confusing and even hysteria-producing drug categories, which are not scientific, are created. The *hard-* and *soft-drug* controversy is a significant example of this. Hard drugs mean opiates and their derivatives to some people, while soft drugs include everything else. Some people include LSD with the hard drugs, but call marijuana a soft drug. Alcohol is usually considered a soft drug, but many people today call "speed" a hard drug.

One assumes from the terminology that soft drugs are less dangerous than hard drugs. But the facts do not bear this out, and the chapter describing what drugs do and don't do will substantiate this. Then we are led to believe that one moves on from soft drugs to hard drugs. Implicit in this is the assumption that something in a drug propels a drug user to move on to try other drugs. The facts don't substantiate this contention either. Taking a particular drug, abstaining from drugs after taking them, or never taking a particular drug—all these activities are the result of personal and societal factors. The meaning of drug-taking behavior has to be considered, as well as the pharmacology of the drug itself.

It is questionable whether the training of any representative of law enforcement, like the training of doctors and nurses, is sufficient to handle adequately any but one facet of this multifaceted behavior.

What is a Drug?

So what is a drug? A broad, unbiased, scientific definition would be of great use in helping us to understand the extent of the drug problem and how better to cope with it. Such a definition is given by Modell (1967), who says that a drug is "any substance that by its chemical nature alters the structure or functioning in the living organism." This definition is not moralistic and not committed to a limited social arena. Its focus is on chemicals with active ingredients that affect behavior, physical or psychological.

This definition forces us to consider as drugs not only illicit substances such as heroin or marijuana, or legal substances used in unacceptable ways, such as amphetamines to get high on, but also alcohol, tobacco, coffee, tea, and even food. Each has active chemical ingredients, and each has both positive and negative consequences associated with its use.

This definition offers part of the key to understanding the present-day drug problem. Substances and reactions to substances are classified according to social usage during a given time. Whether a given substance is associated with serious or relatively minor medical, psychiatric, or social consequences is of relatively little importance in deciding whether it is in or out for this season of man.

One might conclude that this means that society's decisions about drugs are arbitrary. In a sense, this is so. In the same sense, almost any individual and community decision is arbitrary. A decision or behavior that is arbitrary is neither good nor bad—it just is. What concerns us and what should concern us are the consequences of the behavior, both personally and as a community. That alcohol is back in and marijuana is out is an arbitrary decision which may change again. The issue at stake for all of us is how best to live with these arbitrary decisions.

Accordingly, the drug problem and the answers to it occur only in the social arena among the whole community, not in the medical-legal arena, nor even in the scientific one. We must also consider temporal and geographical factors as we attempt to find solutions, since effective solutions, responses, and alternatives to drugs are generally useful only for a specific time and a specific place.

In practical terms, it may not be important if someone we are concerned about is having some difficulties with a substance and refuses to acknowledge that it is a drug. If that person refuses or is unable to see that his behavior is a problem for himself or for others around him, then a first step is to get him to see why such *behavior*, rather than the drug itself, can be a problem. Second, one has to be able to point out as best as one can what some of the consequences may be if the drug-related behavior is acknowledged as a problem or if it continues not to be acknowledged as a problem.

Table 1-1   Sources for definitions of drugs.

Socioreligious	Medical	Legal
For social rituals:	Medicines:	Natural and synthetic
Holidays	To prevent illness	substances considered
Festivals	To maintain health	to be dangerous to a
Birthdays	To treat illness	person and/or his
Special occasions	To relieve pain	society. Control of:
Rites of passage		growth,
		manufacture,
For religious rituals:		distribution,
		importation,
The Mass		sale,
Greeting of Sabbath		use,
Mescaline rites		possession.

Scientific
Any substance that by its chemical nature alters
the structure or functioning in the living organism.

Although implicit in problem solving is the assumption of set solutions, it is important to keep in mind that solutions to drug-related behavior must fit the needs and skills of all those who are concerned in a given situation. (See Table 1-1 for drug definitions.)

Drug Terminology

Adults sometimes attempt to dissuade youngsters from doing particular things by predicting terrible consequences.

In a sense, fairy tales were created to keep children in their places by frightening them. The message in most fairy tales is quite clear: If you don't do what you are told to do, you will survive only after experiencing some trauma.

Many of us may well remember being told of the association of insanity, blindness, and impotence with masturbation. It is questionable how many youngsters stopped or never began masturbating because of these "predictable" dire consequences. In fact, it's quite possible that these vivid tales helped to develop increased skepticism on the part of the child for some very valid statements made by adult parents and teachers on other issues.

Just a few years ago, a state official, much concerned about the increased use of LSD by youngsters, issued a statement that five university students had taken LSD and gone blind. Supposedly these students had lain down outdoors on their LSD trip, had diminished control of their eyelid reflex, and had gone blind while staring into the bright sun. Sounds reasonable—as do many other assertions in this field. The event, however, never occurred. The official, being blind himself and being legitimately concerned about the health of the youth of his state, had hoped to frighten them away from LSD use. One consequence, a personal and tragic one, was that he was hospitalized when it was discovered that the report was false. Every major newspaper carried the report, often as a front-page headline, and, of course, radio and TV gave coverage. All of this resulted in even more serious consequences. For quite a while, it became extremely difficult, if not impossible, to get young people in the State to listen to anything that was valid about the use and misuse of drugs. All of this emphasizes the point that the terms we use and the consequences we talk about should be reality-based, no matter how concerned we may be about drug abuse.

One term that immediately comes to mind is *addiction.* Most often, it is used inappropriately. Many times a concerned adult will tell his child, "If you use marijuana, you will become addicted." Not only is this not true in regard to marijuana, but the message implied is not an honest one. The message, more often than not, is that if you use a particular drug, you will fall from a state of grace and become an addict with all of the attributes that the image "addict" triggers off.

The characteristics and stereotypes related to drug abuse will be discussed elsewhere, but all of us do have particular images of the addict. It is these images that we don't want those we are concerned about to reflect.

Addiction, when removed from the hysteria of our times, is neither good nor bad. It is a scientific description of a process or condition related very specifically to the excessive use of addicting substances. This last sentence may sound like part of a contract written by a lawyer, but it's not so meant. At the present time, addiction is considered to be a physiological state that arises from the use of opium and its derivatives and synthetic narcotics (heroin, morphine, Demerol, methadone), alcohol, and barbiturates. It is the body's way of adapting to these substances. When a person begins to use one of these addicting drugs, he will discover that after a while, he needs more and more of the same substance to continue experiencing what he has been experiencing. Technically, this is called *cellular tolerance.* The cells of the body are adapting to the effects of these new foreign agents. Tolerance develops over different time spans for the same persons with different addicting drugs and develops differently from person to person. That's really why the term *excessive use* was used previously. The issue becomes the amount of the drug necessary for the body to adapt to.

Tolerance is only one criterion for addiction. The second criterion is the *withdrawal syndrome.* Just as the body has to adapt to the presence of an addicting substance, it must also adapt to its absence, once tolerance has been achieved. The physical and psychological symptoms associated with withdrawal differ again for the individual and among people as a function of the particular drug, as well as some important situational factors. The length of the withdrawal process also differs. With opiates, withdrawal symptoms reach a peak about 36 hours after abstaining from the drug, and after approximately 72 hours, withdrawal is generally completed, with the body returning to its "normal" nondrug, nontoxic state. With barbiturates, convulsions—one of the symptoms associated with barbiturate withdrawal—have been noted to occur up to seven days after cessation of this type of drug use.

Withdrawal is, however, not only a physical process. Where it takes place apparently has great influence upon its course. The environment of jail or other correctional institutions seems to produce the most difficult experience for the addicted person. The same seems to hold true for the person attempting to *kick cold turkey* by himself. In both instances, no substitutive drugs are used to ease the process.

In hospitals and other rehabilitation units, some discomfort is often reported even though medication is used. Surprisingly, in ex-addict directed programs, for example, Synanon, Daytop Lodge, etc., where medication is not used, there is the least amount of experienced and verbalized discomfort. It would appear that the addicted person learns that his symptoms will have a particular meaning and will be responded to only in certain settings. A dramatic example of this occurred a few years ago in New York City. A number of heroin addicts were arrested and jailed and manifested withdrawal symptoms. When the bags of heroin that they were arrested with were analyzed, it was discovered that they contained milk sugar and not narcotics. The addicts had assumed, however, that they were buying heroin, that they were addicted, and that when the drug was not available for them in jail that withdrawal symptoms were appropriate. Obviously, all of this wasn't thought out or planned on a conscious level. Sociologists call this process the *self-fulfilling prophecy.* We often experience that which we assume is appropriate in a given situation. We shall return to this useful concept again as we review the various facets of drug abuse.

The variability of the withdrawal process points up an important aspect of the contemporary drug scene: The pharmacological action of a given drug or combination of drugs may be the least significant aspect in a given situation. Related to this is the most obvious truism: The mind-body division may be useful for philosophy, religion, and cocktail chatter, but in this real world of daily living, we interact with totally functioning humans, and we are concerned about their daily functioning and not the separate categories of physical, psychological, and social behavior.

What concerns most of us about addiction is not the process, with its physical and psychological components, but the meaning we have learned to attribute to it. It is the psychological and social need for drugs that worries us. It is reading and hearing about a great number of individuals, young and old, who return to actual drug misuse or a drug-oriented way of living that concerns us. And perhaps of most significance, addiction challenges us when those we care about appear to have decided to live in a world peopled by objects and drugs and do not turn to a life space inhabited by potentially gratifying family, friends, and associates. We may feel rejected and helpless and then tend to blame this on a physiological condition.

The fact that a person has become addicted is in no way a valid predictor of his present or future style of life. Whereas medication is a useful tool for relieving the symptoms of withdrawal and for treating other facets or complications of the addiction process, there are no known chemical solutions or cute and clever slogans that can effectively change a person's life style. Self-defeat is built into using the term *addiction* as an "explanation" in the struggle against drug misuse.

Addiction is not the only term that has been blithely misused in this area. For some time now, both the scientific and lay communities have been attempting to differentiate among different kinds of drug misuse. Having arbitrarily decided that addiction is associated with physiological components, the terms *habituation* and *dependency* have been used as terms to describe behavior associated with nonaddictive drugs, that is, drugs to which the body does not become tolerant and which produce no particular physical effects upon withdrawal. Habituation has come to mean a psychological condition resulting from the use of addicting as well as nonaddicting drugs. The emphasis is on the psychological component of the behavior. We are concerned that the user "craves" the drug. Actually, the term habituation is not unique to drug use. Any behavior that we have engaged in over long periods of time will, in all likelihood, be continued. Indeed, if our daily lives didn't consist of many habits, if we had to think out everything we do, starting with which shoe to put on first, our total functioning would be significantly and adversely affected.

Thus, habituation as a behavior pattern is neither necessarily good nor bad. Rather, it is a description of a specific behavior process. It is important to recognize this, because associated with the contemporary feeling about habituation is the notion that a particular involvement with one drug or drug habit will somehow magically lead to other kinds of drug habits. This is often called the *stepping-stone theory* of drug use. Habits don't automatically lead to other habits. People get involved with a given habit for all sorts of rational and irrational reasons and give up and/or move on to other habits in the same complicated way that their first habit came about.

We may want someone to change, give up, or not develop a specific drug habit, but it is unlikely that simply by tagging or labeling the behavior that our goal will be achieved. Labels are convenient as a shorthand in categorizing and packaging, but it has yet to be demonstrated that they will significantly effect behavioral changes.

The term *dependency* completes the trilogy of words describing the general status of a person's drug use. Contemporary terms lead us to conclude that one is either addicted, habituated, or drug dependent. In one sense, habituation and dependency are the same: Continued use of any drug which hasn't led to or won't lead to the physiological state of addiction results in the person's being psychologically involved with that drug. There is, however, a major difference between the terms habituation and dependency. Dependency has associated with it moral and philosophical overtones. Obviously, if one is dependent, he or she is not independent, and we all have been taught it is better to be independent. The assumption is that the dependent person is under the control of the drug and the drug life, and that independent people are masters of their own destiny. Notwithstanding the question of how much control any youngster or adult has over any facet of his life, we do know that dependency of a particular variety is absolutely necessary if normal, healthy growing is to continue. We have to learn how to trust others and depend upon them. We all learn to depend upon various time-saving and pleasure-giving objects in our environment. That third of the American population which marries and then gets divorced may indeed have never learned how to appropriately meet their own healthy dependency needs and how to help meet such needs in their spouses.

The critical issue with dependency is not its inherent positive or negative value, but what its focus and meaning are, how it is achieved, and what its consequences are. As we continue to be concerned about the actual or potential drug-dependency behavior of people around us, we must begin to concern ourselves about the nondrug options for dependency that are available and how these are most effectively achieved.

The World Health Organization's expert committee on drugs has been aware for some time of the confusion inherent in attempting to distinguish between drugs and the consequences of their excessive use by using labels such as addicting, habituating, and dependency producing. A clear and important example of this is the status of amphetamines. Although continued use results in increasing the dosage, amphetamines are not classified as being addicting. The abrupt cessation of amphetamines most often results in irritability, depression, and a general feeling of being out of sorts. These are psychological symptoms. Addiction is related to the physiological effects of tolerance and withdrawal. Certainly for the person who has been using amphetamines to excess, it is of little solace to him when he stops that he is only habituated and not addicted. Likewise, for those concerned about his welfare, what is at issue is how and when most appropriately to intervene and where to turn for the needed and appropriate help—and not what is the correct label to describe the behavior.

The World Health Organization has suggested using the concept of "dependency," with or without physiological concomitants, in order to come to terms more effectively with the many different kinds of drugs and drug combinations that are presently being misused. Unfortunately, scientists and lay people continue to use terms that they feel more comfortable with and we all continue to read about and hear about addiction, habituation, and dependency. Apparently, it takes as much time to change the language appetites of man as it does to change many of his other appetites.

The consequences of the misuse of these terms may be as negative as the consequences of the misuse of the drugs themselves, both for individuals and their communities. The general semanticists noted this when they created the catch-phrase "the map ≠ territory"; the map is not the territory. Not only is a given drug-related term not necessarily an explanation of the issue; it may even serve to confuse the issue.

The following exercise is an example of this. It is based on the common-sense notion that how we perceive what we perceive significantly affects what we do with our perceptions. If we don't look critically at what we have learned about drug abuse, the answers to the following questions appear to be almost self-evident.

Questions	Answers
1. Treat an addict and what will result?	A treated addict.
2. Accept an addict into a methadone maintenance program and what will result?	An ex-addict.
3. Employ an addict and what will result?	A working addict.
4. Arrest an addict and what is a major consequence?	An addict with a police record who is temporarily out of the community.
5. Chemically test an addict for drug use and get a report noting no testable drugs are in his system that day and what do you have?	Possibly an inaccurate test or an addict who didn't use drugs today but will, in all likelihood, use drugs tomorrow.
6. Give a *junkie* a different socioeconomic classification and what do you have?	A drug abuser.
7. Categorize a drug-dependent person into the lower part of the socioeconomic scale and what will result?	A dope fiend, a junkie, or an addict.
8. Give a sick person drugs and what should be the result?	Hopefully, a healthier person using medicines.
9. Give a healthy person drugs and what should be the result?	More often than not, a sicker person.
10. Give a member of the NOW generation, particularly a youngster, a standard lecture on drug addiction and what will result?	A communication gap.
11. Lastly, express to the addict, or whatever else we choose to call him, some HOPE and what will very likely occur?	The development of a relationship with a peer who, while testing us, will most likely remain in the relationship.

Another important term which tends to confuse issues rather than illuminate them is *drug abuse.* Dr. Joel Fort, a California psychiatrist specializing in drug abuse, defines this term in his popular book *The Pleasure Seekers* (1969) in the following way:

> Properly used, drug abuse refers to the use of a drug, usually chronic excessive use, to an extent that produces definite impairment of social or vocational adjustment, or health.

A year later, in the same state, the California Medical Association defined drug abuse in the following way:

> Drug abuse is a complex constellation of related, but different problems. The boundaries are not distinct, and often coexist in the individual. Drug abuse has

been defined in many ways. A useful definition is: the use of any drug to the point where there is an adverse effect on an individual's health or on his ability to function as a responsible person. Some might restrict the term to narcotics, addictive dangerous drugs, or psychedelic drugs. Drug abuse, to some, includes all forms of drug intake, which may have an adverse effect on health. Cigarettes, coffee and alcohol are examples. Other than realizing this diversity of opinion, formal widely agreed definition is not needed.

It is, however, the diversity of opinion about key issues and terms such as drug abuse that makes it increasingly difficult not only to decide upon what can and should be done in the area, but also who should do it.

The World Health Organization defines drug abuse as "persistent or sporadic excessive drug use, inconsistent or unrelated to acceptable medical practice."[1]

A leading expert in this field, Dr. Jerome Jaffe, writes:

Drug abuse will be used in its broadest sense, to refer to the use, usually by self-administration, of any drug in a manner that deviates from the approved medical or social patterns within a given culture. So defined, the term rightfully includes the "misuse" of a wide spectrum of drugs, ranging from agents with profound effects on the central nervous system to laxatives, headache remedies, antibiotics and vitamins.[2]

Still another definition was developed by Dr. Jean Paul Smith for a government conference.

Drug abuse refers to the judgment that certain patterns of drug use are socially or medically disapproved due to harmful effects on the individual or society, the motivations of the giver and receiver which are inconsistent with accepted medical or social practice, the illicit channels of distribution or the unknown origins and quality of the compound.[3]

There have been numerous other attempts to define what appears to be a self-explanatory term, but really isn't. The most obvious source of such definitions is material gathered by people who do research or treatment with a "drug-addict population." Most often both writer and reader forget the context in which the material was gathered. Thus the definition of

[1]World Health Organization, Technical Report Series No. 407, Geneva, 1969, WHO Expert Committee on Drug Dependence, 16th Report, p. 6.

[2]Jaffe, Jerome, "Drug Addiction and Drug Abuse," in Louis S. Goodman and Alfred Gilman, Eds., *The Pharmacological Basis of Therapeutics*, 3rd ed. New York: Macmillan, 1968.

[3]Smith, Jean Paul, "What Is Drug Abuse?," presented at BNDD-FDA Conference on Methodology to Predict the Abuse Potential of Drugs, Washington, D.C., September 8–10, 1969.

drug abuse, which may have been created to better explain certain data, now may take on a more central role in explaining a person's life style as a social or national problem.

All of the definitions mentioned have one thing in common. They are arbitrary. Dr. Fort's common denominator is the effect of the drug. The World Health Organization focuses on medical practice. Dr. Smith adds the notions of motivation, channels of distribution, and the origins and quality of a given drug.

Implicit in these definitions is the notion of normal drug use. Although each of us may have a very logical definition of normal drug use, we'd find it somewhat difficult to get it accepted as a general rule in a heterogeneous group. It would be most useful to define abuse against a yardstick of normal use, but instead we define each in terms of the other, without really defining either. Interestingly enough, the concept of drug abuse is fairly new in the literature. Perhaps this fact can be used as a clue to help us better understand the term and whether it is of use to us in our day-to-day concerns.

The contemporary reality is that a drug abuse is not used to describe involvement with a wide range of substances. We don't call our overweight relatives and friends food abusers. We do call them lots of other things. Similarly, we don't call smokers abusers if they resort to cigarettes, cigars, or pipes.

When many Americans took comfort in their idea that it was mostly Negroes and Puerto Ricans on the East Coast and Mexican Americans on the West Coast who were taking drugs, the terms *addicts, dope fiends*, and *junkies* became part of our vocabulary. At the time these terms seemed sufficient. When we don't know someone, don't care to know him or perhaps go out of our way to avoid him, using denigrating terms is par for the course. When the person with the dreaded condition is a relative or friend, someone we not only know but want to protect and do something for, then denigrating terms are no longer sufficient.

In many ways, this may be the crucial factor that is necessary to understand the term drug abuse as it affects the individual and his community today. It is not what is being used, how it was obtained, or what its effects are that really count; *it is who is using the drug.* An important consideration in understanding our roles and responsibilities in relation to the drug user is that the term we use may appear to alter significantly the situation without substantially doing so.

In the early part of 1970 at an eastern university, I was a member of a drug-abuse panel which was top-heavy in establishment professionals—

13, to be exact. There were two student leaders, with long hair, keen minds, and sharp tongues. One of them attempted to rile the panel and amuse his fellow students by giving the following definition of drug abuse: "The next time you cut drugs and let some fall on the floor, you are abusing drugs! When you don't lick the knife clean after using it to cut drugs, you're abusing drugs!"

Drug abuse, at the very least, is an example of faulty English. We are not concerned about the *drugs* that are being abused. We are, however, much concerned about the increasing number of *people* who abuse themselves as well as others as they adapt to living through chemicals—when they really don't have to.

As with the soft- and hard-drug dichotomy, one might assume that the drug abuser is less in need of help than the "hard-core" addict. Whatever help a person needs or doesn't need should not be a function of a label, but rather the result of appropriate evaluation. One might likewise assume that drug abuse is just a phase, and addiction a commitment. In the same sense, one might view abortion as being retroactive contraception, or suicide as being the only sincere form of death. This last definition was given not to tie in drug-use terms with death, but rather to point out how one can endlessly and in a silly way define all sorts of behaviors that are part of our milieu.

Alice in Wonderland said it much better: "The question is whether you can make words mean so many different things." Obviously, we can, we do, and we shall no doubt continue to do so. It doesn't follow, however, that while we are playing games with words, we have to play games with the lives and/or specific behavior of people whom we feel, in some way, responsible for.

Whether we like it or not, drug abuse as a concept is here to stay. It has a role in books, conferences, films, lectures, etc. People whose lives are being affected by the use or misuse of drugs have more important and productive roles to play, both now and in the future, than to become the models of a labeling procedure.

Indeed, to the extent to which we label them *drug abuser* and isolate and keep them in that status, we may make it difficult, if not impossible, for them to change their way of life to a less drug-oriented one. Continue to respond to someone as if he is a drug abuser, addict, or what have you, and more often than not he'll soon be convincing in that role.

Perhaps one way to decide whether to use the term drug abuser is to determine whether this will help, hinder, or have no effect at all upon whatever intervention we plan.

FACTORS AFFECTING THE USE AND MISUSE OF DRUGS

As important as it is to define certain terms related to drug use and to understand some of the consequences of using these different terms, it is of even greater importance that we fully comprehend what the various factors that relate to drug behavior are.

The logic for this is quite simple. The fewer the number of factors included in this or any other social problem area, the greater the general conviction that the problem is circumscribed and associated only with particular people who need the help of experts in particular situations. The more open the boundaries are, the more certain one can be that the problem is going to be confused, complex, and in need of help derived from broad-based community intervention.

Traditionally, the drug problem has focused on only three factors: the *drug*, the *specific characteristics of people* using drugs for other than medically and socially approved reasons, and the *physical, psychiatric, and social consequences* of this kind of drug use. (There is a long history of presenting issues in threes, going back from Freud's oedipal triad to the Holy Trinity and forward again to that folksy notion that trouble comes in threes.)

One immediate consequence of viewing drug use from the perspective of this triad is that one is seduced into thinking that only special kinds of people develop the drug problem and that once they do, the consequences are predictable. The best way to discuss this type of contention accurately is to point out other factors that must be comprehended in order to respond more effectively and meaningfully to a given individual who is involved in his own unique way with a drug or a combination of drugs. Similarly, we need a broader framework to understand better the difficulties that a nondrug user may be experiencing in this day and age. One should not slight the fence-sitter either—of which there are many. Having experimented with drugs, or even using drugs regularly on an irregular basis, is still not a commitment to a drug-oriented style of life. If we want to influence effectively the overt behavior of these aforementioned individuals, then we must learn where they fit into today's drug scene. Table 1-2 is a schematic overview of these various facets.

Although one could begin with any factor, I choose to look at *scientific knowledge* first, because it tends to point up important sources of dispute and confusion. One could assume that science would by now have given us usable answers by which we could classify the heterogeneous group of drug users, as well as the variety of contemporary drugs. Theories should

Table 1-2   Factors affecting the use and misuse of drugs.

Drug Use	Characteristics of Users	Behavior of Users

Type
Frequency
Amount
Pattern
Manner
Meaning
	Age
	Sex
	Race
	Ethnicity
	Religion
	Educational status
	Vocational status
	Occupation
	Marital status
	Income
	Socioeconomic class
	Intelligence
		Physical, psychological,
		   and social functions
		   and dysfunctions
		
		Conventional, deviant,
		   and drug-oriented
		   social involvement

Drug Definitions	*Scientific Knowledge*	*Attitudes and Values*

Medical
Legal
Social
Religious
Scientific
	Classification of:
	   Drug users
	   Drugs
	
	Theories About:
	   Drug use
	   Drug action
		Stereotypes of drug users
		Stereotypes of drugs
		
		Economics

Treatment Programs	Research	Illegal facets Legal facets

Evaluation techniques
Goals
Treatment modalities
Treatment policies
   and procedures
Professional roles
Drug misuser roles
Follow-up systems
Early case finding
Prevention
	Public Policy
	
	Laws
	Policies
	Procedures
	Politics
	
	Mass Media
	
	People-oriented patterns
	   of living
	Object-oriented
	   patterns of living
	
	Treatment agent
	   and community
		Cultural Values
		
		Drug related
		People related
		
		Philosophy and Religion
		
		Nondrug-related social
		   rituals
		Drug-related social
		   rituals
		
		Education
		
		Nondrug-related alter-
		   natives to living
		Drug-related alternatives
		   to living

be available to help us understand why people begin to use and misuse drugs, why they stop, return or never return to the same behavior, or never begin it at all. Similarly, we should by now understand drug actions—how drugs work. Surely, the same national research abilities and efforts that have gotten us to the moon should be expected to get us into available man. But unfortunately there are more gaps in knowledge than hard data, more complicated scientific questions and issues than usable guidelines and answers.

Another major issue or area that concerns many is that of *treatment*. This area poses particular problems because we generally assume that the drug user is sick in order to explain his behavior. Since he is sick, he should be treated to get better. If he doesn't get better, there's no better proof of his having been sick to begin with. The key idea is that if the drug abuser gets better, it's because of the person and/or program treating him. If he doesn't get better or gets worse, it's because he was too sick, or insufficiently motivated. This kind of game is not unique in this area of behavior. If a student learns well, it's because of the teacher or general school program. If he doesn't, he is either unmotivated or an underachiever.

Treatment efforts must be understood for what they are and can be and should be if we are ever fully to understand what to make of the poor treatment results that we often hear and read about.

What we do and don't do about any facet of drug-related behavior is integrally involved with the *attitudes and values* of both the professional and lay community regarding drugs and drug abusers and the stereotypes held by people at a given period of time.

These attitudinal factors play a significant role in affecting the various ingredients of *public policy*. Indeed, the past and present laws, policies, and procedures practiced throughout the nation could not exist were it not for particular kinds of attitudes held by many regarding the use of particular drugs by particular people for certain alleged reasons. It is clearly no accident or chance occurrence that drug use has been a political football for nearly two decades, whereas smoking and drinking alcoholic beverages have not.

Economic considerations are often the battle cry for doing something. It is important to remember that drug abuse is not only related to illegal activities but that there are important drug-related legal-economic factors to consider which are by now basic to the American way of living.

The effects, both positive and negative, of the mass media, philosophy, religion, education, and the existent culture are also most potent forces that must be understood better if we are to get our bearings right and work out meaningful roles, relationships, and responsibilities for ourselves and those we care about.

The use and misuse of any drug or pattern of drugs do not occur and will never occur in a vacuum. Viewing the contemporary drug scene from the perspective of Table 1-2 and including other factors that you may feel are important will ultimately permit the development of viable alternatives that make best sense for us at this point in time.

THE HISTORY OF DRUG USE AS A PROBLEM

Since one type of drug or another has been with us since Homo sapiens became man and, no doubt, was also misused in the past, why is there such a turmoil today? Why has use become a "problem"? And a problem it is, for the individual, his community, and the nation.

The history of opium and its derivatives—and of society's reaction to their use—will help us better understand our present drug dilemma, which says that certain drug use by certain people in certain ways and for particular reasons is socially acceptable, but otherwise it is not acceptable. It is important to understand the process of accepting or rejecting a given drug and drug use, so we may make sensible decisions when the "drug problem" hits close to home.

Opium was known almost 8000 years ago to the Sumerians, who used the symbol *HULLGIL* to express "the power of opium to produce a sense of delight and satisfaction." It was later known to the Assyrians and the Hebrews, the Greeks and the Romans. During Roman times, opium was used in a liquid form, mixed with a number of other ingredients and known as *theriak*. It was considered a cure-all against many diseases. With the fall of Rome, the use of theriak was lost in the West but remained in the East. Dealers transported opium farther East where it was introduced to China. Beginning in the twelfth century, opium was grown in China, where its use became widespread two centuries later. Opium returned to Europe again during the Middle Ages, and in the sixteenth century, another opium preparation was developed.

The Portuguese physician Acosta noted in 1655 the difficulty that some patients had in giving up opium. During this same period, opium use was associated with prolonging one's life and was called a "heavenly condition." Concerns about the use of opium began appearing at about the same time. Psychological and physical problems were associated with its use in 1712 by the German traveler Kaempfer. Describing its use in Persia, he stated: "Many evils result from this abuse (opium), for the body wastes, the strength grows weak, the mentality becomes sad, the intellect dull." In 1729 Emperor Yung Chung of China prohibited the domestic sale and smoking of opium.

Descriptions of drug use in faraway countries began reaching Europe in the eighteenth century. From this point on, the concepts of habituation, physical dependence, tolerance, and euphoria began to be more delineated. *Nevertheless, addiction was not yet viewed as a problem necessitating social action.* It has been suggested that during this period, opium users may have been immune from the problems associated with addiction, because they did not know there was such a phenomenon as addiction (Hess, 1971). Perhaps the first serious warnings about opium appeared in 1763 when Awsiter, a London apothecary, predicted widespread habituation if the properties of opium became known. By 1791 the effects and uses of opium were already being noted in the United States of America.

DeQuincey introduced opium into our Western literature in 1821 and noted that although he had read about its dangers, he was caught up by opium's "fascinating powers." He described opium eaters as being "a very numerous class of men distinguished for talent and notoriety." During this period, opium was turned to from opposite ends of the social stratum—by workers whose income didn't permit beer or gin, and by poets, writers, and artists who popularized its use.

An interesting sidelight is that the first part of DeQuincey's book, *Confessions of an English Opium Eater*, was used, at times, as a model of English composition and for practicing translation into Latin in British schools. In a sense, the pleasures of opium use were thus introduced into the school setting for many youngsters and, oddly enough, no great uproar was heard in the community. Other writers, Coleridge, for example, wrote about the dreams and fantasies produced by opium.

With the discovery of morphine (1803), the use of intravenous morphine as a pain killer on a large scale during the Civil War, and the introduction of heroin in 1898, knowledge about the use and misuse of opiate drugs spread. Both medical and popular journals paid increasing attention to the increasing use of these drugs. It began to be felt that the patient should not be told that he was getting opiate medication, since such knowledge might contribute to his becoming addicted.

Addiction was not related to criminal or deviant behavior until the end of the nineteenth century. Obviously, this doesn't mean that actual criminal behavior, as related to opiate use, was unknown. Medical prescriptions were being falsified even then. The general community did not, however, experience such offenses as either threatening day-to-day living or as a major problem. The opiate of choice was legally and inexpensively available. The first deviant label noted was in 1896 when *The New York Sun* used the term "dope fiend."

It would appear that deviance began to be associated with opiate use when its traditional mode of use, by mouth or hypodermic needle, began to change over to opium smoking and when its traditionally accepted users—the Chinese laborers followed by white gamblers, prostitutes, and other underworld members—gave way to respectable young gentlemen and ladies. By 1875, the smoking of opium by "nice" young Americans was considered to be so prevalent that the first local ordinance was passed against it in San Francisco.

During the last half of the nineteenth century, American addicts could be divided into two groups. There were the law-abiding swallowers and injectors who received their opiate of choice from their physician or bought it legitimately for real as well as imagined ailments. There were the others, the unrespectable and their cousins, the preflappers, out for the kick of instant and temporary deviant status, who smoked opium. After a while, the latter group apparently became sufficiently flexible to alter its technique of opiate use.

It would appear, however, that the shady character of the first white opium smokers not only negatively colored opium smoking, but also all other narcotic use. Oddly enough, our ancestors overlooked the fact that the deviant status of the first opium smokers existed long before their initial use of opiates and that the vast majority of narcotic addicts during this same period were not criminals.

Although the seeds of drug stereotypy had been sown, there was still no concerted effort to control this behavior. The medical profession had not yet taken a stand on how to view what we may call *recreational drug use*, nor was it clear on weighing the negative versus the positive consequences of medical narcotic use.

Another factor that contributed to the deviant status of narcotic use was the powerful temperance movement, whose initial aim of moderate use of alcoholic beverages changed to that of prohibition as a goal. In various parts of the country, people began switching to opium in their own adaptation to the temperance movement (drug rehabilitation is not a new phenomenon!). We must keep in mind that during this same period there appeared to be an uncontrollable increase in available patent medicines that contained opiates.

To understand the final factors that led to the deviant status of narcotics, we must move into the international political arena. Whereas America appeared to be fairly unconcerned about opiate use during the latter part of the nineteenth century, a number of nations—Britain, Turkey, Persia, and Germany being perhaps the main ones—were significantly involved in the growth or processing of opium. These countries encountered the following dilemma: (1) the feeling that unrestricted opium trade was perhaps immoral, together with (2) an economic interest in continuing such trade, and (3) the assumption that if any of them moved out of the opium business, other nations would either continue or move into it.

During this same period, the United States, now "owner" of the Philippines as a result of the Spanish-American War, became concerned about reported opium use by American troops stationed there. An investigation did not substantiate this. The investigation did, however, lead, as a preventive measure, to restricted importation of opium to the Philippines for other than medicinal uses.

The Right Reverend Charles H. Brent, a key member of the Philippine Opium Commission which had made the recommendations leading to the restrictions, continued after the commission's work to urge President Theodore Roosevelt to control opium trade through international action. At about the same time, the House of Commons in Great Britain passed a resolution that opium trade was immoral and urged an end to it, and the emperor of China decreed that the growth and use of opium were to cease.

President Roosevelt proposed an international conference which finally took place in Shanghai in 1909. Each of the 14 invited nations was to report on the opium problem that it experienced. Turkey, a major opium supplier, did not attend the conference. A key issue growing out of this conference was that the focus of effort had changed from that of controlling opiate use in the Orient to international control. The meeting resolved to create greater measures of control on opium and its derivatives, to suppress gradually the smoking of opium everywhere, to support China's position on the cessation of opium use within her boundaries, and to foster research on the effects of opium and treatment of its use. The Shanghai Conference did not end in any treaties but rather in resolutions. A series of other conferences was held with more nations involved.

Vested interests colored each of these conferences. The First International Opium Conference was delayed by the British until 1911 because of their own private negotiations with the Chinese. At this meeting, the Germans, major manufacturers of morphine and cocaine, pushed for delaying treaty commitments until all conference participants had ratified the treaty and nonparticipants had signed a separate protocol. In 1913, the Second International Opium Conference was held. All of the participants of the first conference had not ratified the treaty, although the United States did so on December 10, 1913. A third conference was held in 1914 in which it was decided that if all the initial participants hadn't or wouldn't ratify the treaty, it should, nevertheless, become a meaningful reality by those that did ratify it. In response to this, the Harrison Narcotic Act was passed in 1914 as an American excise tax law. An interesting point was that this excise tax law was presented as a presidential proclamation to fulfill the United States' treaty obligations. The intriguing thing is that there was no compelling need to meet this treaty obligation until after World War I, when the initial proposals of the 1912 Hague Conference were finally agreed upon. The United States undertook to control American opium use, but was unable or unwilling to state that this decision was arbitrary—indeed, as arbitrary as that of the Chinese emperor.

Once the Harrison Act was passed, it laid the basis for the general American trend of a punitive approach to narcotics use. Enforcement of the Harrison Act led to arrests of physicians and pharmacists, the closing of 44 drug clinics throughout the nation, the definition of all addicts as criminals, and the evolution of a criminal underworld to supply a variety of drugs to what has evolved as an increasing number of drug misusers.

New laws and interpretations of old laws have tended to reify the notion that narcotics use, or indeed any drug taking, is a problem. What is often lost sight of is that behavior which may be perceived of, or interpreted to be, problematic for a nation, state, city, or other social institution may not be experienced as a personal problem. The laws, however, reinforce the stereotype of personal illness as the basis of drug taking.

While man's various appetites have always been controlled by laws and edicts and group pressure, any given appetite is neither inherently good nor bad. Why then is specific drug use considered to be deviant? Putting the information contained in the last few pages into both a sociological theory of deviance developed by Wilkens and into the framework provided by Table 1-2 may help us understand the process. The deviant status of drug taking results from:

drug definitions arising from moralistic positions against a background of the Temperance Movement;

drug use moving from opium smoking to an increasing number of drugs taken in every conceivable fashion;

characteristics of drug users being assumed to relate to the drugs they use;

behavior of drug users being perceived as a function of drug action;

scientific knowledge offering no reliable or valid data with which to classify drug users or why they use drugs, an inadequate knowledge of drug action and little or no appropriate research;

treatment programs which were hastily put together, often hastily disbanded, with inadequately trained staffs, insufficient resources, and no built-in evaluation;

public policy based upon vested interests of various groups, resulting in the channeling of legally available drugs into illegally controlled sources;

mass media offering the public yellow journalism in lieu of objective descriptions, because the facts that were needed for objectivity weren't available;

cultural values and education responsive to the powerful impact of the Temperance Movement;

economics which had, as its primary focus, the protection of national interests;

philosophy and religion which were, on the surface, strongly bound to morality and the holding onto traditionalism at a time when adjustments to the impact of the industrial revolution had to be made.

All of this tended to initiate and reinforce deviant stereotypes of drug users. Available information about drug use, drug action, and drug users became polarized. Information that didn't substantiate the stereotype was either censored, made unavailable, or treated as "no information." Other information was made quite available—and reinforced the tag of deviant. Those individuals who were so tagged tended to be isolated from the conventional mainstream of life as a function of the tagging process, and they, in turn, began to identify with and act out the deviant tag. Sociologists call this a *self-fulfilling prophecy.*

Paralleling this, the community at large, both professional and lay, became separated from the very populace they had labeled deviant, and this resulted in less information with which to check out the validity of the deviant label. One consequence continues to be that people using drugs for other than medically approved reasons not only are tagged as deviants and then behave like deviants but also are increasingly responded to by society in an inflexible manner, because we feel threatened.

The rigidity of institutional and personal responses to drug-related behavior makes it difficult, if not impossible, to offer presently available, as well as to create new, socially approved alternatives to such behavior.

This becomes the essence of the contemporary drug dilemma. It is easy to come down hard on someone else's behavior—a person we don't know and do not choose to know or associate with—but when drug behavior enters our own life space, via a child, spouse, friend, or other relative, our responses are based on meanings associated with the behavior which may indeed have little or no relevance to the given situation.

To ask someone to behave rationally and appropriately to the discovery of drug use by someone he cares about and/or is responsible for is asking him to be able to weigh the medical, psychiatric, social, and legal facets and consequences of such behavior, knowing full well what both he and society feel about drug use and without having a neutral sounding board to check out his concerns and tentative solutions.

PROJECTS

1. Out of your various appetites, select the one that gives you the most satisfaction and has significant meaning. Stop this behavior for a few days and keep a log of your thoughts, feelings, and overt behavior toward others. Consider those internal and external factors that apparently make it easier or more difficult to carry out this project. Given this short experience, consider whether man's appetites are easy to change and whether any single factor is likely to be instrumental in a change.
2. Select a simple everyday behavior pattern—such as putting on your shoes, brushing your teeth, picking up a cup or glass. Consider whether these behaviors have any meaning for you, significant or otherwise. Record the ease or difficulty with which you attempt to change these behaviors (e.g., if you usually put your right shoe on first or brush your teeth with your right hand, put on the left shoe first and brush with your left hand, etc.). The important issue to consider is whether all behaviors are easy to change and whether we know about and think about why we do the things we do.
3. Define *dependency*. Consider whom you feel you are dependent on at the present time. Does this raise any problems for you or for the other person? What kinds of problems? If you have concluded that you are not dependent upon anyone, does this raise any problems?
4. Analyze and note separately whether you feel that peer relationships and parent-child relationships can be built, strengthened, and maintained through drug use.
5. Select a drug-related concern of yours. Write it up as if it were a significant *problem* for you, including your thoughts about ways of responding to it. Write it up as if it were a significant *issue* for you, once again including your possible responses. Are there differences between both reports? Do you come up with more options, less options, or simply different options when you consider something to be a problem rather than an issue? At this point in time, how would you list drug use in your life style?

BIBLIOGRAPHY

Brecher, E. M., *Licit and Illicit Drugs.* Boston: Little, Brown, 1972.

Brown, C. C., and Savage, C., eds., *The Drug Abuse Controversy,* Baltimore: National Educational Consultants, 1971.

Cohen, C., "Multiple Drug Use Considered in the Light of the Stepping-Stone Hypothesis," *International Journal of the Addictions,* vol 7, no. 1, pp. 27–56, 1972.

Eddy, N. B., Halsbach, H., Isbell, H., and Seevers, M. H., "Drug Dependence: Its Significance and Characteristics," *Bulletin of the World Health Organization,* vol. 32, pp. 721–733, 1965.

Fort, J., *The Pleasure Seekers.* New York: Bobbs-Merrill, 1969.

Group for the Advancement of Psychiatry, *Drug Misuse—a Psychiatric View of a Modern Dilemma.* New York: Scribner, 1971.

Hess, A., "Deviance Theory and the History of Opiates," *International Journal of the Addictions,* vol. 6, no. 4, pp. 585–599, 1971.

Jaffe, J. H., "Drug Addiction and Drug Abuse," in L. S. Goodman and A. Gilman, eds., *The Pharmacological Basis of Therapeutics,* 3rd ed. New York: Macmillan, 1968.

Kalant, H., and Kalant, O. J., *Drugs, Society and Personal Choice.* Toronto, Canada: Addiction Research Foundation, 1971.

Kaplan, J., *Marijuana, the New Prohibition.* New York: World Publishing, 1970.

King, R., *The Drug Hang Up.* New York: Norton, 1972.

Kramer, J., "Controlling Narcotics in America, Part I & II," *Drug Forum,* vol. 1, no. 1, pp. 51–70, 1971; vol. 1, no. 2, pp. 153–168, 1972.

Modell, W., "Mass Drug Catastrophes and the Roles of Science and Technology," *Science,* vol. 156, 346, 1967.

Nowlis, H. H., *Drugs on the College Campus: A Guide for College Administrators.* Detroit: National Association of Student Personnel Administrators, 1967.

Smith, J. P., "What Is Drug Abuse?" presented at BNDD-FDA Conference on Methodology to Predict the Abuse Potential of Drugs, Washington, D.C., September 8–10, 1969.

Szasz, T. S., "The Ethics of Addiction," *Harpers,* April 1972.

Terry, C. E., and Pellens, M., *The Opium Problem.* New York: Bureau of Social Hygiene, 1928; Montclair, N. J.: Patterson and Smith, 1971 (reprint).

WHO Expert Committee on Addiction-Producing Drugs, *Third Report,* 1952, World Health Organization Technical Report Series, 57:9, and *Seventh Report,* 1957, World Health Organization Technical Report Series 116:9.

CHAPTER 2

Drugs : What They Do !

Not poppy, nor mandragora,
Nor all the drowsy syrups of the world
Shall ever medicine thee to that sweet sleep
Which thou owedst yesterday.

William Shakespeare
Othello (The Moor of Venice, Act. III, Scene III)

Much of what we do about people using drugs is related to our notion of
what the drugs themselves do. It is easy to conclude from what we hear
and read that certain drugs are dangerous and others aren't. The focus
always seems to be on the drug. And the natural conclusion is that dangerous drugs should be tightly controlled and removed from our reach; the
not-so-dangerous drugs, called medicines, must be made available, but
regulated; and "safe" medicines or drugs such as aspirin, nonprescription
sleeping aids, and relaxers should be available to almost anyone who has
the money to purchase them.

The supposed dangers of certain drugs are by now known to most
adults and youngsters as follows:

Physical dysfunctions	*Speed* (amphetamine) kills.
	Hallucinogens cause genetic deformity and chromosome breakage.
Psychological dysfunctions	*LSD* causes psychosis.
Social dysfunctions	*Hallucinogens* lead to turning on, tuning in, and dropping out of society.
Reinforced drug use	*Marijuana* leads to the use of hard drugs.
Deviant functioning	*Heroin* leads to violent crimes.
Sexual functioning	*Cocaine* enhances sexual drive and functioning.

29

Religious experiences   *Hallucinogens* cause religious, mystical
                             experiences.

Emotional reactions   Alcohol causes uncontrollable aggression.

The validity of each statement can be assessed only when we know what
drugs actually do and what they don't do. For certain drugs, such as
marijuana, the lack of data from scientifically based research makes most
statements anecdotal. Other drugs, which we really find hard to accept as
drugs, such as alcohol, tobacco products, coffee, and tea, we have difficulty in associating with dangers to the user and those with whom he
comes in contact. This, of course, is part of the contemporary drug dilemma.

As we review various drug and drug families, we shall be forced to
come to terms with the social reality that it is not simply what a drug does
to a person's mind and body that makes it acceptable and more easily
available, or unacceptable and less easily available. Rather, it is the way
we interpret and label the various behaviors which we believe are caused
by a drug that triggers our own reactions to specific drugs and drug users.

CLASSIFICATION OF DRUGS

Attempts to control the use of drugs rarely focus upon a specific drug.
Instead, they focus on an entire family. Implied in this is that all of the
drugs in that family are closely related and therefore act in the same way,
causing similar problems or having similar advantages. This common-
sense approach and its general acceptance by most of us have generally
added to the confusion in the field of drug use and misuse. Because it is
not simply the inherent qualities of drugs that place them in one group and
not in another; it is also who the classifier is and what his purpose is in
classifying that determines the various drug groupings.

The two major sources of drug classification are the law and medicine.
The law, responding to various segments of the population who consider
particular drugs dangerous at a given point in time, has as its goal controlling availability. With danger as its focus, the law has lumped together
opiates and their natural and synthetic derivatives, cocaine and marijuana, and has called them narcotics. From a pharmacological perspective, only the opiates are narcotics. Cocaine is a stimulant, and marijuana
is generally considered to be an hallucinogen.

The law has also created a fairly well-known and accepted two-
category system of drugs: *hard drugs* and *soft drugs*. Hard drugs are

opiates and their derivatives. Soft drugs are all other drugs we are now concerned about such as barbiturates, amphetamines, and hallucinogens, but not, for example, alcohol. Implicit in this classification system is that hard drugs are more dangerous than soft drugs and therefore merit greater concern and control. As we review what various drugs actually do, we may be forced to conclude just the opposite.

This is not to suggest that legally based classifications are wrong. There is no rightness or wrongness to a particular system if we understand and are willing to accept that the source and purpose of the particular system are sufficient for maintaining its existence. The critical issue becomes: What are the consequences to the individual and his society if we use one system rather than other available ones, or even create new ones?

Pharmacologists classify drugs according to their chemical nature, their effects on cellular functions, on physiological and biochemical systems, and on behavior. Working with experimental drugs or known drugs and medicines, the pharmacologists want to determine, as their purpose, both the utility and limitations of a given substance and to relate it to other known drugs. Their interest is in both major and minor effects and side effects of a specific drug at given doses and how that drug is affected by or affects other drugs or drug combinations. To them, drugs are neither good nor bad, neither dangerous nor not dangerous. Rather, it is the major responsibility of the pharmacologist to point out the most general drug effect at a particular dose when it is used in a specific way (orally, by injection, etc.) for a specific purpose.

The classification system used in this chapter is a pharmacological one. Drugs have also been classified in terms of their active ingredients. Groups such as the Christian Scientists and members of the Native American Church and the League for Spiritual Discovery have categorized drugs in terms of their own religious beliefs. Social movements such as the Temperance groups have likewise classified drugs in a particular way. Political groups have had a crack at drug classification. It is most interesting to note that Karl Marx called religion the opiate of the people, not the alcohol of the people.

The most formidable classifier of drugs is none of those already mentioned; it is society itself. We tend to classify drugs in terms of social usage, and thereby accept or reject a specific drug. As we review the various drugs in this chapter, we shall be forced to conclude that alcohol continues to be the most dangerous drug known to man. We generally classify it as a beverage, sometimes as a food, infrequently as a medicine, and rarely, if ever, as a drug. Cigarettes, which contain the active ingredient nicotine and which have, since the Surgeon General's report in 1954, been known to cause serious chronic ailments such as emphysema and cancer, are never considered to be drugs.

How we classify a drug and why we do so are obviously important aspects of the contemporary drug scene and the drug dilemma that many of us experience. To react to people as drug users and offer them the same kind of help, when their drugs of choice range from heroin, barbiturates, amphetamines, LSD, marijuana, or glue, is highly questionable practice. To hospitalize the heroin user and refuse hospitalization to the alcoholic—a fairly common practice—must be seriously reconsidered. To incarcerate the marijuana smoker when nutmeg is legitimately available at the supermarket is also questionable. For the lay and professional community to condemn the use of certain drugs, when as recently as 1968 more than 50 percent of the prison population were individuals who committed crimes while under the influence of alcohol, is a condemnation of questionable merit.

Obviously, we shall continue to develop new systems for classifying drugs, each with its own rationale. What is also needed is a classification system of reactions to drugs, drug use, and drug users which will point out the consequences of our own reactions.

THE CENTRAL NERVOUS SYSTEM AND DRUGS

While it is true that drugs affect a person's entire system, the drugs that we are presently most concerned about primarily affect the central nervous system. Pharmacological classifications are developed in terms of the particular part of the central nervous system that is most affected, or in terms of drug-related behavior that reflects a reaction by a given part of the central nervous system.

The *cerebral cortex* is the framework for our consciousness and houses information necessary for functioning. It is that area that serves to integrate our sensory and motor experiences, our memory and our perceptions. It is connected to the brain stem; an impulse to the brain stem will result in activating a specific part of the cerebral cortex. When the sensory areas of the cerebral cortex are activated, our perceptions are affected. When motor areas are activated, the message is for us to become active or more active. Excessive activation of the motor area may result in poor coordination and movement or even in convulsions. Our abilities to think, reason, be attentive, evaluate or judge, have illusions, and imagine are all associated with the site of activation and the kind of activation affecting us.

The *thalamus* functions as a relay station for messages to and from the cerebral cortex. It can activate specific areas of the cerebral cortex, or it can affect all of it. It also serves as a center of generalized sensation. Drugs that primarily depress the thalamus may serve to relieve pain. Drugs that stimulate the thalamus when their effects are relayed to and interpreted by the cerebral cortex may result in increased wakefulness, increased attention, or other mental action.

The *hypothalamus* is that area of the brain that controls the body's autonomic functioning, that is, gastrointestinal activity, body fluid balance, arterial blood pressure, and hormone secretions of the endocrine glands. It does this by affecting the *sympathetic* and *parasympathetic* systems. The experiencing of pain and pleasure is very much related to hypothalamic functioning. Activation of certain parts of the hypothalamus which relate to another important area, the *reticular formation,* can result in wakefulness, alertness, and a state of excitement, or drowsiness, sleep, and passivity. Stimulation of the sympathetic nervous system can lead to increased pupil size (pupillary dilation) and a general state of excitement.

The *reticular formation,* or reticular activating system, is that part of the nervous system that can excite or inhibit it. In a sense, it serves to integrate specific actions of the nervous system because of its relationship to specific cerebral areas, such as the hypothalamus. When the reticular formation is depressed, a person feels sedated, or may even become unconscious. When stimulated, the person becomes aroused, more wakeful and alert. This arousal reaction results from the reticular system's being stimulated by other areas. When affected, it can inhibit or stimulate sensory areas of the brain, as well as the spinal cord. Likewise, it plays an important role in motor activity. Diffuse stimulation can increase a person's muscle tone generally, or in only specific parts of the body. Stimulation of specific parts of the reticular system can result in specific muscular contractions or the inhibition of such contractions. Thus, body movement and equilibrium are very much a function of the reticular system.

The *cerebellum* is the body's center for muscle coordination, equilibrium, and muscle tone. Thus, a person's state of posture and sense of dizziness are affected by it. The cerebellum reacts to "information" from the reticular formation, the semicircular canals, and the cerebrum.

The *medulla oblongata* affects a person's respiration, vasomotor and heart action, coughing and vomiting. When stimulated, a person may breathe quicker; when depressed, he may breathe slower and slower, until he stops breathing and dies from self-asphyxiation.

The *spinal cord* is the body's center for reflex action, as well as the transmitter of "messages" to and from the brain's higher centers. When higher centers are being affected by drug action, it is indirectly affected.

DRUG ACTION

Chemical depressants act by inhibiting various mental and physical functions. Chemical stimulants serve to activate mental and physical functions.

While all of this is generally so, it is important to recognize that the reaction of a person to a specific drug or combination of drugs, even at a given dose, is unpredictable, since many nondrug factors affect both his internal and external behavior.

With all of the increased concern about drug use, it is ironic that we still are pretty much in the dark as to how drugs work. We know that their action is complex and involves various processes. We know that they are absorbed into the system at various sites and in different ways. After being absorbed, a specific drug is distributed in a particular way throughout the body and may be stored in tissues or accumulate in the bloodstream over various lengths of time. The original drug is generally transformed by a given bodily process into something else, which affects the body either generally or specifically. While being transformed, the drug, or its new derivative, may combine with various body cells and thus alter or affect their action. Finally, the drug, in whatever its final form or transformation, will be excreted primarily by the kidney or the liver.

The difficulty in predicting a drug's action arises from the fact that any given action is a function of its solubility, its concentration, the area of the surface from which it is absorbed, the blood circulation to the site of absorption, the route of administration, and the speed of absorption. What the drug interacts with, where it is stored, metabolized, transported, and redistributed, and into what it is transformed are significant factors. When we move from the actual biochemistry of the drug to the drug user's previous experience with a drug, his physical and mental condition, his expectations of its actions, and the actual physical and social milieu that he takes his drugs in, we can begin to appreciate why a drug's action, even at the same dose, may vary significantly from person to person, or in the same person from time to time.

A common example of this is drinking alcohol. Scientifically, we know that the liver of a person of average height and weight can metabolize approximately two ounces of whiskey every hour. If more than this amount is ingested in that period of time, the person, predictably, should begin to feel high, higher, act drunk, go into a coma, and ultimately die. There are, however, many drinkers whose psychological need for never losing conscious control of their behavior will often result in few overt behavioral changes, even though their blood alcohol level continues to rise. Similarly, there are drinkers, categorized as *pathological drinkers*, for whom one drink will result in behavior often associated with three, four, or five drinks. The examples have been related to alcohol rather than to other drugs because, as a socially acceptable drug, it is assumed that we are better acquainted with the many behavioral variations associated with its use.

It would be inappropriate to conclude that reactions to drugs are simply idiosyncratic at times for certain people. Rather, it is to be concluded that a person's internal and external reactions to drugs and drug use are unique to him. Our perceptions of and reactions to his drug use may serve to reinforce or inhibit this uniqueness.

DEPRESSANTS

Narcotics

Opium	black stuff, hop, ya-pen-yan, tar
Morphine	cube, dreamer, emsel, hard stuff, nocus, melter, M, Miss Emma, monkey, morf, morphie, tab, unkie, white stuff
Meperidine	Pethedine, Demerol, Dolanthol, Dolantin, Eudolal
Hydromorphine	Dilaudid, lords
Codeine	Schoolboy
Paregoric	bitter, blue velvet licorice, P.G., P.O., red water
Papaverine	red water
Methadone	Amidone, Butalgin, Diadone, Dolophine, dollies, dolls, juice, meth, Miadone, Physeptone, Polamidone
Heroin	Diacetylmorphine, big Harry, boy, coballs, dooje, duige, dope, H, hairy, hard stuff, Harry, horse, joy powder, junk, salt, schmeck, scot shit, slag, snow, stuff, thing, white stuff
Laudanum	

History

The opiates are not new to man. Their pleasurable effects were known by ancient man. Around 4000 B.C., the Sumerians used the ideograph HULLGIL (joy plant) to describe the opium poppy. In the *Iliad*, Homer referred to it as "inducing the sense of evil." During the third century B.C., Theophrastrus wrote about poppy juice. The Greek mythological character, Nepenthe, experienced pleasurable forgetfulness, which presumably was due to opium. The name *opium* is derived from the Greek name for juice, since it was obtained from the juice of the opium poppy. It is assumed that knowledge about it was passed from the Sumerians to the Babylonians to the Persians. Arab troops and traders brought knowledge of its medicinal use to Europe and East Asia, where it was primarily used to control dysentery.

In the fifteenth century, Paraclesus developed *laudanum*, which continues to be used. In 1803, the German pharmacist Serturner discovered *morphine*, which he named after the Greek god of sleep, Morpheus. *Codeine* was discovered by Robiquet in 1832 and *papaverine* in 1848 by Merck. *Heroin* was developed in 1898 by the Bayer Pharmaceutical Company in Germany, and soon afterwards was proposed as a cure for morphine addiction. *Meperidine* (Demerol) is a synthetic drug developed in 1939 by Eisleb and Schaumann. *Methadone* is likewise a synthetic nar-

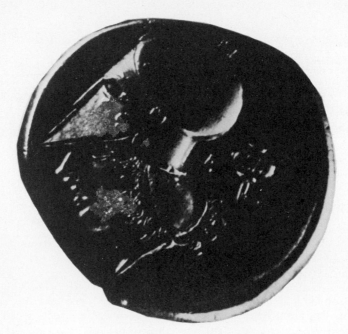

Fig. 2-1   A Sumerian clay tablet describes a "joy plant" which is believed to be the opium poppy. The opium capsule was worshiped by cults in ancient Greece, as noted by the capsule on this ancient Greek coin. (Courtesy of the U.S. Drug Enforcement Administration.)

cotic, developed by the Germans during World War II, when natural narcotics were not accessible to them.

As can readily be seen, the history of opiates and narcotics is both a long and an international one.

Sources

Opium and its various derivatives are obtained from the milky secretion of the opium poppy, *Papaver somniferum*, a plant which is indigenous to Asia Minor. This poppy grows well in areas of little rain and much sunshine. Although it is to be found in countries such as Yugoslavia, Egypt, Iran, India, China, Laos, Thailand, and in parts of Central and South America, most of the world's opium has been grown in Turkey.

When the plant's seed capsules are cut, the milky juice forms a brownish, gummy substance after drying in the air. The gummy material continues to be dried and is made into the powder we know as opium. This opium is either legitimately converted to various preparations, which have traditional therapeutic uses, or is converted into heroin for illicit use, in mobile factories in Beirut, Naples, Genoa, and Marseilles.

Fig. 2-2 As late as 1896, coca leaves and cocaine were being widely advertised as a safe product, in ads like this which appeared in *The Pharmaceutical Era* for 1896. (Courtesy of the U.S. Drug Enforcement Administration.)

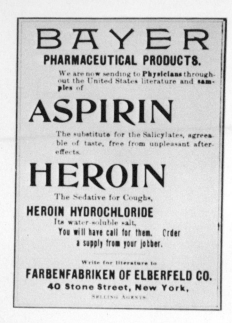

Fig. 2-3 In the nineteenth century, as in the early twentieth century, many of the most widely promoted and most respected patent medicines contained opium and morphine salts—such as Ayer's Cherry Pectoral, Jayne's Expectorant, Pierce's Golden Medical Discovery and Mrs. Winslow's Soothing Syrup—also heroin—as advertised here on trade cards. (Courtesy of the U.S. Drug Enforcement Administration.)

After the heroin is smuggled into the United States, it is generally mixed with other substances, such as quinine and/or milk sugar. A kilo (2.2 pounds) of smuggled heroin, which initially cost approximately $7000, may result in sales of almost a quarter of a million dollars when diluted. While it may be over 90 percent pure when smuggled into the country, by the time it is sold on the streets, it rarely contains more than 3 percent narcotics.

Therapeutic Uses

Excluding alcohol, the opiates are man's oldest known pain relievers. Morphine, Demerol, and methadone are used in conventional medicine for this purpose. Heroin, outlawed in the United States, continues to be used as a pain killer in Great Britain. Codeine is an essential ingredient of cough medicines, such as codeine terpin hydrate. Paregoric, a medicinal mixture containing opium, is used to treat diarrhea.

Morphine acts as an analgesic and causes drowsiness, mood changes, and a sense of mental clouding without the person's going to sleep. While some individuals may experience *euphoria*, others may experience the unsettling sense of *dysphoria*. Using it as an analgesic, the person may continue to sense the pain, but may feel it less and be more comfortable. Meperidine's major use is as an analgesic, although its derivatives are used in treating coughs and diarrhea. The primary uses of methadone are for analgesia, the medical treatment of narcotic withdrawal symptoms, and as a chemotherapeutic treatment for narcotic addicts (which is discussed in the chapter on treatment—Chapter 8).

Manner of Use

Depending upon which opiate is used, they may be smoked, *snorted* (sniffed), *skin-popped* (injected under the skin), mainlined (injected into the vein), swallowed, or put over an incision.

Opium and all of its natural derivatives and synthetic relatives are addicting. Their continued use will result in cellular tolerance, and discontinuing them results in specific withdrawal symptoms.

The opiate which is most often in the news and is of greatest concern to most people is heroin (Demerol continues to be the most misused drug by physicians and nurses.) Heroin is generally considered to be more potent than its relatives, morphine and codeine. Cellular tolerance can be achieved in a few weeks, using it daily. Once tolerance has been achieved and the drug is not available, the withdrawal or abstinence syndrome commences within a few hours after the person's last dose of this opiate. The person generally experiences his greatest discomfort between the 24th and 48th hour of withdrawal, and by the end of 72 hours, he is usually free of the severe withdrawal symptoms.

Heroin withdrawal affects all parts of the nervous system—both the autonomic and the somatic. The addicted person will often experience anxiety, generalized body discomfort, and aching, insomnia, yawning, eye tearing, runny nose, perspiration, dilation of the pupils, gooseflesh, hot flashes, nausea, diarrhea, an elevation of both body temperature and respiratory rate, abdominal and other muscle cramps, vomiting, dehydration, and loss of both appetite and body weight. Most of these symptoms are similar to those of a bad case of flu. It is important to remember this, because the dramatic TV or movie depiction of withdrawal is very rarely experienced. In fact, there are many narcotic addicts who learn that they are going through withdrawal because friends tell them that what they are feeling is just that, and not a cold. When decreasing amounts of a fairly low dose of methadone are given to the narcotic addict, he will experience few of these symptoms. (While the insomnia may have a basis in the chemistry of withdrawal, it surely is also the result of a way of life which usually fails to differentiate between night and day.)

During *cold-turkey* detoxification (withdrawal from drugs without the help of medication), the addict is more likely to experience a great deal of discomfort.

Consequences of Heroin Use

Heroin, relative to other drugs, does not deserve its dangerous reputation. Given our present knowledge, there are no psychiatric conditions that are directly caused by heroin, and the vast majority of medical consequences associated with its use either result from the manner in which it is used or the kind of life the user is living. Obviously, this doesn't mean that heroin is an innocuous substance that should be substituted for mother's milk at the 2 P.M. feeding.

It does mean, however, that many of its deleterious effects can be countered by education and do not necessitate acute medical intervention. If the person using heroin insists on continuing its use, irrespective of the reasons, and can be convinced to do so under sterile conditions, both he and his community will not have to direct their attention to serum hepatitis, skin infections, swelling of the hands and feet, abscesses of the skin and internal organs, fungus diseases of the skin, staphylococcal skin infections, tetanus, endocarditis, thrombophlebitis, bacteremia, septicemia, or malaria. These conditions occur when unsterile needles are used, when water from a urinal, or the street, is used to heat up the heroin, when dirty bottle caps are the receptacle for the mixture, and when the cotton that is used is dirty.

If we were more concerned about the drug user's health than his habit, we might educate him in the proper use of drugs, and then, from a public health point of view, we would be substantially diminishing many serious ailments around us. People, unlike theories, have their own minds and their own needs and therefore are not as easily educable. For example, in England, where registered narcotic addicts are offered not only pharmaceutically pure heroin, but also the necessary sterile tools of the trade for its use, only 20 percent of the addicts who request the heroin use the sterile paraphernalia.

The other medical conditions associated with the use of heroin are essentially derived from the addict's style of life, the conditions under which he is living, as well as the results of introducing aggravating foreign bodies into his system. The *junkie–dope fiend–visible street addict*, who lives the life of a ghetto or inner-city resident, is likely to suffer all the ailments of the ghetto nondrug user. Tuberculosis and bronchial asthma may be common. A common cold, if not taken care of, in a person whose resistance is already lowered because of significant weight loss and/or malnutrition, may lead to the complications of pneumonia. The already-mentioned weight loss, malnutrition, and periodontal diseases and dental cavities are likely to result if the person neglects himself and practices poor personal hygiene.

Venereal disease is also often associated with the use of heroin, as well as other injectable drugs, by the street addict. If one of his sexual partners doesn't give him venereal disease as a bonus, one of his fellow addicts who is sharing his unsterile set of works with him may very well do so. The unanticipated bonuses of street drug use are many and varied. For the female addict, venereal disease and cessation of her period are fairly common, since her major source of support is prostitution.

Other ailments or conditions which the street addict may experience are serious physical problems due to neglect of his health, failure to respond to pain because it is muted by the analgesic effect of the narcotic, and the violence that may occur when one addict attempts to shortchange another, resorts to behavior which is likely to result in violence (i.e., burglary, robbing a drug pusher, or attempting to silence an addict suspected of "ratting" to the police), or when the initial inhibiting effects of the drug are no longer operative and the person's preexisting rage spills forth.

Just as people react in less than hospitable ways when outsiders "invade" their neighborhood, the body finds it difficult to adjust to the introduction of foreign substances to its environs. Whereas the opium grower presumably knows what he is growing, the "deviant" chemist in Italy and France knows what he is refining, some smugglers know what they are delivering, and the various people cutting the heroin to its street strength know what they are mixing it with—it is really impossible to assume that the street addict knows what he is buying, sniffing, or injecting. Rarely is this advantageous for him, although since heroin began to be diluted with quinine, few addicts have suffered from malaria. The foremost result of the narcotic addict's use of pharmaceutically impure heroin is that he may be introducing foreign bodies into his circulatory system and other body organs that they can't handle. These substances may be sufficiently irritating to cause tissue scarring of the veins, thereby blocking them (venous sclerosis), increased pressure of the blood as it passes through the lungs (pulmonary hypertension), or cardiac failure because of the presence of talc granules, which interfere with the proper functioning of the heart, or embolic pneumonia, resulting from the same talc particles plugging up the lung, or the creation of scar tissue or tumors of the lung (pulmonary fibrosis) as a result of the presence of cotton fibers or granules of drugs or other materials.

In a sense, the narcotic addict is quite lucky that almost all of the conditions associated with his drug use are not directly related to the drug's action. There are enough medical conditions to keep him unhealthy without any new ones being added. Recently, two physical conditions, which are assumed to be directly related to heroin use, have been reported: a low-grade inflammation of the liver and withdrawal symptoms that may last up to 90 days. Also, death can result from narcotics being central nervous system depressants: As respiration continues to be slowed down, the person dies of self-asphyxiation—he stops breathing.

In interpreting the various claims that the "jail-the-addict," "hospitalize-the-addict," and "legalize-drugs" advocates present about the consequences of narcotic use, we must keep in mind what these drugs do and don't do. Opiates, like any other drugs, have psychological and physical effects. They do not, however, cause further drug use. The use of heroin, or any other narcotic, does not lead to crime or increased rates of crime. Street addicts, committed to "illegal" narcotics as their drug of choice—drugs which, by their chemical action, necessitate increasing dosages—will often engage in criminal activities. A perhaps not-so-odd phenomenon is the street addict, abstaining from narcotics or other drugs, who will continue to follow a criminal style of life.

Narcotics, in and of themselves, do not cause moral, spiritual, psychological, or social deterioration and degradation. Rather, it is the way the person has lived prior to and subsequent to his involvement with narcotics and the alternatives that they experience or are shown, which are meaningful, achievable, and acceptable to them, that will define the life they live. Narcotics are pain killers—no more, no less. They are not solutions for life's problems; no chemical is. Living in a community or household with others, or living alone, can only be meaningfully experienced through interaction with other people, not by interaction with any drug or any other object.

•

Barbiturates

Barbiturates	barbs, candy, goofballs, peanuts, sedatives, sleeping pills
Nembutal	*phenobarbitol sodium*, nemmies, nimbie, nimby, yellows, yellow jackets
Amytal	*amobarbital sodium*, blues, blue birds, blue devils, blue heaven

Seconal	*secobarbital sodium*, pink ladies, pinks, reds, red and blues, redbirds, red devils, seccy, seggy
Tuinal	*amobarbital plus secobarbital.* Christmas trees, double trouble, rainbow, tooies
Luminal	*pentothal, phenobarbital, sodium thiopenthal*, phennies, purple hearts, truth serum

History

The chemical source of barbiturates, barbituric acid, was discovered in 1864 by Adolph von Baeyer. Approximately 50 years later, in 1903, it was made into a therapeutic tool when two German scientists, Fisher and von Mering, developed Veronal. Within a few years (1912), phenobarbital or Luminal was developed. Since then, more than 2500 barbiturates have been synthesized. Fifty have been produced for clinical use, and approximately a dozen of these are presently being used. It has been suggested that our medical needs would be sufficiently met by relying on only five or six of them.

Therapeutic Uses

Barbiturates are central nervous system depressants. They serve to induce sleep, to sedate or tranquilize as an anticonvulsant for tetanus, epilepsy, and convulsions caused by other drugs, and as diagnostic and therapeutic tools in psychiatry. They can relieve pain, at the cost of impairing a person's state of consciousness. As general depressants, they act to depress the activity of the nervous system, skeletal muscles, smooth muscles, and cardiac muscles. Like all other central nervous system depressants, they can inhibit respiration. Their general depressing action is reversible.

Barbiturates are arbitrarily classified in terms of the duration of their action: long acting (Luminal), short-to-intermediate acting (Amytal, Nembutal, Seconal), and very short acting (Pentothal). Their degree of depression is a function of the particular barbiturate, the dose, route of administration, degree of excitability of the person's central nervous system at the time of administration, and the extent to which the person's previous experience with barbiturates has resulted in cellular tolerance.

Consequences of Barbiturate Use

The effects of barbiturates range from a sedated stage, through coma, to death from respiratory failure. The reactions to barbiturates are, as with other drugs, unpredictable. A dose that should and indeed has sedated a person may another time overstimulate him. Children and the elderly sometimes may experience excitement rather than sedation. This idiosyncratic reaction, seen when the supposedly sedated alcohol drinker becomes abusive and aggressive, is influenced by the individual's personality and environment.

Another aspect of barbiturate use is that whereas its major effect, sedation or drowsiness, may last only a few hours, distortions in the person's mood, in fine motor skills, and in judgmental abilities may extend for many hours.

When used appropriately, barbiturates can help a person achieve and maintain a more functional level of behavior. When misused, barbiturates can directly and indirectly lead to a variety of nervous dysfunctions. Unlike the opiates, these serious consequences are drug related and not generally related to the person's style of life.

As sedatives, barbiturates can create a sense of well-being, tranquility, and even elation. Used appropriately by an anxious person, his anxiety will become lessened and life more manageable. Since barbiturates are addicting, their chronic use may interfere with their therapeutic advantages in that cellular tolerance may lead to the use of increased doses, which results in upsetting the person's physical and psychological behavior. Such chronic use may lead to a state of intoxication difficult to distinguish from alcohol intoxication. This is so because both drugs are central nervous system depressants and, in many ways, act similarly. During this stage, the person's physical behavior is uncoordinated. He may feel quite confused and behave in an emotionally unstable way. At more moderate doses, the person may feel euphoric, as one may after a few drinks.

Allergic reactions to barbiturates can occur. This kind of reaction may result in a person developing swelling of the face, dermatitis, skin lesions, fever, delirium, anemia, certain degenerative liver changes, as well as feeling dizzy and nauseous.

There are even more serious and dangerous results from the misuse of barbiturates. One of the effects of barbiturates is to distort a person's sense of the passage of time, as well as his memory. When this occurs, he may not remember his already having taken barbiturates or how recently he took them. In either case, a fatal overdose may be the result. The term "drug automation" has been coined to describe this phenomenon. Upon recovery from a heavy sleep or coma, the person may not remember having taken the additional pills.

Since barbiturates and alcohol act similarly, the effect of their combined use can be dangerous. They tend to operate synergistically; the potency of each becomes exaggerated and may result in coma or death.

All too often an elderly person may take a sedative which does not put him to sleep as soon as he wanted it to. Feeling uncomfortable as he turns and turns in bed, he may get up and have a shot of cognac or another alcoholic beverage. When he still hasn't fallen asleep or hasn't slept as much as he feels he should have, he may take yet another barbiturate. The result can be tragic.

The same ending can occur for the chemical hedonists who purposely drink their alcoholic beverages with barbiturates and quaintly call this a *setup*.

During the 1940s, when the production of barbiturates had tripled, so did drug-related deaths. From 1957 to 1963, there were almost 8500 cases of barbiturate poisoning, nearly 1200 of them ending in death. Only half of these were suicides, less than 10 percent were due to accidental poisoning, and the remainder were due to accidental overdoses.

Many deaths and injuries may occur as a result of motor incoordination that is caused by the excessive use of barbiturates. It is indeed surprising that the press continues to focus on the effects of alcohol and marijuana in automobile accidents and rarely mentions the number that is directly related to barbiturate intoxication.

Since their initial development, barbiturates have been produced in endless varieties. They are available as powders, elixirs, syrups, drops, capsules, tablets, and in both sustained and delayed release form. During 1969, more than $80 million were spent on them. While this may seem like another useless statistic, we should perhaps spend a few minutes wondering why a nation that prides itself on its dynamism is having such great difficulty sleeping. Likewise, we might begin to question the meaning of the need to produce over 800,000 pounds of barbiturates annually since 1954. Using a standard medical dose of 60 milligrams, we are producing 6 billion doses annually—enough for each American to have 30 of them.

Compared to opiate withdrawal, the process of barbiturate withdrawal can be very dangerous. It should be done under medical supervision. Withdrawal symptoms begin after about 24 hours of abstinence, reach their peak in two or three days, and then begin to subside slowly, The barbiturate addict may experience anxiety, uncontrollable muscle twitching, hand tremors, a sense of general weakness, visual distortion, nausea, vomiting, sleeplessness, weight loss, a drop in blood pressure, convulsions, delirium, and at times temporary psychosis, which may be preceded by convulsions.

One of the dangers of barbiturate withdrawal arises from the relatively long time lapse for some of the symptoms to make their appearance. Convulsions have been reported occurring as late as seven days after withdrawal of the drug. The barbiturate addict, if he doesn't experience the symptoms he expects to at the time he expects to, may often feel a false sense of recovery—and be unprepared for the physical and/or psychological consequences he must still face. The probability of convulsions occurring is directly related to the amount of barbiturates taken.

Barbiturates are eliminated from the system by three processes: (1) redistribution from the brain to other tissues, (2) metabolic destruction, chiefly by the liver, and (3) excretion of the undestroyed material by the kidneys. The nature of the elimination process is dependent upon the particular barbiturate. Certain ones are stored in muscle and fat after redistribution from the central nervous system, and repeated doses may result in cumulative effects.

Nonbarbiturate Hypnotics

Perhaps the best-known substances of this group are the bromides, although as an entire group less is known about their pharmacology and toxicology than is known about barbiturates.

Therapeutic Uses

Bromides have been in use therapeutically for over 100 years. In 1857, they were begun to be used in the treatment of epilepsy. Although they proved to be an appropriate drug, their use was based on one of the scientific myths of that period. It was "known" that epilepsy was "caused" by masturbation. It was also "known" that potassium bromide acted as an anaphrodisiac, curtailing sexual interests. Using what must have been the nineteenth-century variation of new math, it was concluded that sexually induced epilepsy = sexually restricting bromide = successful treatment. Indeed, 13 of Locock's 14 epileptic patients were helped with his treatment. By the end of the century, bromides were the "in" medicine. Aside from their use in the treatment of epilepsy, they have been a basic ingredient of headache remedies, various nerve tonics, and other nostrums.

Consequences for Bromide Use

Bromides are addicting. Continued use can result in skin lesions and rashes, constipation, loss of appetite, and various gastric conditions. Chronic use may also lead to bromide psychosis and bromide intoxication. Individuals suffering from a minor state of intoxication are easily mistaken for being drunk. The psychological manifestations of their behavior are impaired thinking and memory, drowsiness, irritability, and emotional instability. Neurologically, the person may experience tremors, talk with thickened speech, and have difficulty with his motor coordination. More serious cases of bromide intoxication may result in delirium, delusions, hallucination, psychosis, lethargy, and coma.

Therapeutic use has decreased markedly with the availability of other sedatives and as we come to appreciate more and more the distinct disadvantages of bromides.

Doriden and chloral hydrate are other examples of nonbarbiturate sedatives. Doriden is addicting. Withdrawal from it may lead to hallucinations and grand mal seizures. Chloral hydrate, generally slipped to the good guy in that late late TV movie and known there as a *Mickey Finn*, is also addicting. Withdrawal from it resembles the delirium tremens (D.T.'s) of alcohol withdrawal.

Tranquilizers

Minor

Meprobamate	Equanil, Miltown
Diphenylmethanes	Atarax, Phober Suauitil
Chlordiazepoxide	Librax, Librium
Diazepam	Valium

Major

Reserpine	Serpasil
Phenothiazines	Compazine, Pacatal, Phenesgan, Sparine, Stelazine, Thorazine

Therapeutic Uses

Tranquilizers are used to dampen the types of feelings a person experiences that may interfere with his daily functioning. They relieve anxiety, tension, and apprehension, and, when used appropriately, result in the person's experiencing a sense of well-being. It is thought that the tranquilizers, and particularly thorazine, may somehow insulate the individual from the potential sources of stress and strain in his life by affecting his attentiveness to them.

Tranquilizers are arbitrarily classified into two groups: major and minor. The major tranquilizers are more potent and are generally used as antipsychotic drugs. They are not meant simply to take the edge off anxiety, but are used as a major contemporary psychiatric tool to treat the various symptoms of psychosis (hallucinations, delusions, excitement, agitation, and aggressiveness). Taken at the right time, in correct doses, a prepsychotic episode may never materialize.

Reserpine was the first major tranquilizer used in the treatment of psychosis. It is derived from a shrub, *Rauwolfia serpentina*, which is native to India and other tropical areas. It had been used in India for both the treatment of hypertension and psychotic behavior and was introduced to the United States in the 1950s. During this same period, the phenothiazines, synthetic major tranquilizers, were developed. Different companies have issued their own brands of this drug. The phenothiazines continue to be used as our major antipsychotic chemotherapeutic tool, with reserpine now being used less often.

Consequences of Tranquilizers

Whereas these two types of drugs can be dramatically effective in treating disturbed individuals, they can be quite dysfunctional when taken by "normal" people. One of the most serious consequences is that the drug can create a feeling of depression.

In assessing the merits of the major tranquilizers, we must take a hard look at some of the contemporary myths associated with them. Although "back-ward" patients of the past given these drugs can now be treated in an open ward in a psychiatric hospital, in a general hospital, or even be discharged back to their own communities in a short period of time, these tranquilizers do not *cure* mental illness. We are still at a loss to understand what triggers psychosis or what leads to its abatement. What these drugs are useful for is facilitating the management of the acutely disturbed individual and helping him be more receptive to other kinds of treatment. In recent years, thorazine has also been used in the acute treatment of LSD-induced flashbacks, which will be discussed in the section on hallucinogens.

The minor tranquilizers are not minor, but they do produce a sense of tranquility, which is their major therapeutic purpose. They are meant to affect anxiety, tension, restlessness, insomnia, irritability, and what we euphemistically call the psychosomatic tension headaches and gastrointestinal disturbances.

They do this essentially by taking the edge off these disorganizing feelings or conditions, and thus permit the individual to mobilize his available energies and strengths in a given situation. This may lead to one of the more serious dangers associated with the misuse of tranquilizers. The implicit promise of tranquilizer-based living is that life will be beautiful and that one will be able to manage and live it effectively and joyfully.

The reality is that there is a lot about life that is not, and will never be, beautiful and that to manage effectively—let alone to experience it without being overwhelmed—necessitates the development of various social skills, a sense of trusting others, and a group of friends and relatives who are a dynamic part of one's style of life. Tranquilizers do none of this.

The minor tranquilizers have increasingly replaced the barbiturates which, as was previously noted, have some tranquilizing effects. They tend to be more expensive than the barbiturates, and many practitioners are not at all convinced that they are any more effective. Two of the factors that may have led to this switch-over is the addictiveness of barbiturates and their association with planned as well as accidental suicide. As the minor tranquilizers have been used more and more, we now know that Librium and Miltown (Equanil) are addicting when taken to excess. The withdrawal symptoms from Librium include depression, agitation, nausea, and grand mal convulsions. These symptoms do not appear until approximately 48 hours after the last dose is taken. The withdrawal from Miltown includes vomiting, tremors, anxiety, hallucinations, and grand mal seizures.

As for fatalities, it should be quite clear by now that death is a possibility with the misuse of any substance. The critical issue that tranquilizers raise for all of us is whether we want to adapt ourselves to the increasing tensions and problems of the community and world we live in (and we can do this with various degrees of success through drug use and misuse), or whether we want to adapt our surroundings to our human needs, in which case tranquilizers would have limited use.

Since the "drug problem" is often viewed in terms of illicit drugs, it would be easy to think that tranquilizers present a problem only for the "addict personality" or drug-dependent person. But when we consider that millions of Americans use tranquilizers, that the sedative-tranquilizers account for approximately 20 percent of all physicians' prescriptions, and that a person is as likely to use a drug in the way and for the period of time it has been prescribed as not, it is clear that it would be foolish to minimize the American tranquilizer problem.

STIMULANTS

Cocaine

Cocaine   *benzoylmethlecgonine*, Bennie, Bernies, C, Carrie, Cecil, Cholly, coke, Corine, dynamite, flake, gin, girl, gold dust, happy dust, heaven dust, joy powder, paradise, snow, speed ball (when mixed with heroin), star dust, the leap, white girl

History

Cocaine is a central nervous system stimulant which is derived from the leaves of the *Erythroxylon coca*, a small plant which is native to the slopes of the Andes. The plant was considered to be sacred both by the Incas and the Aztecs and was used in their religious rites.

It was the first local anesthetic to be discovered, Although it was known to produce numbness of the tongue and skin and had been recommended as a local anesthetic by 1880, it wasn't until 1884 that it was extensively studied. Sigmund Freud was the researcher. While researching and describing its properties, he managed to accomplish two other things: (1) he weaned one of his colleagues from morphine with it and thus produced what is probably the first case of medically induced cocaine dependence, and (2) he reinforced the myth of the aphrodisiac value of cocaine, particularly in letters to his fiancée.

One of his colleagues, Dr. Koller, began using cocaine as a local anesthetic in ophthalmology. Soon after, it was used in dentistry. In 1905, a synthetic substitute, procaine, was developed by Einhorn.

Therapeutic Uses

Traditionally, the leaves of the plant have been chewed in Peru, Bolivia, Columbia, and Argentina by the Andean Indians in order for them to endure their cold climate and their way of living. Chewing little balls of coca, they can better tolerate fatigue and hunger. Cocaine is no longer used in religious services.

The value that cocaine had as a local anesthetic is a thing of the past. Newer and more effective local anesthetics, medically valuable in that their action is reversible with no damage to either nerve fibers or cells, are available. Nor is cocaine now used in solution form to treat oral and nasal lesions. Even its use as a flavoring agent by the Coca Cola Company has changed, with the active ingredients being removed from the leaf.

Whereas the coca leaf is chewed, cocaine is either sniffed or injected. It is not used orally, because it is poorly absorbed by the gastrointestinal tract. It is not physically addicting, and there is no evidence that it leads to the development of tolerance. There are no known withdrawal symptoms related to it, although abrupt cessation of its use has been associated with severe depression and persisting delusions.

Consequences of Cocaine Use

When coca leaf is chewed, the taste buds become stimulated, the person experiences a tingling sensation which soon changes into a feeling of numbness as the drug's anesthetic action begins. The person may then feel a general sense of well-being and at least temporarily may no longer feel physically or mentally fatigued.

When cocaine is sniffed or injected, the person may feel a sense of restless excitement and as if he has unlimited energy. This, of course, is one of the serious consequences of cocaine use: The person may overestimate his actual capabilities at the time. For periods of time, he may indeed be able to work more, but this is not because he has more energy, but rather because he does not experience his fatigue. Sherlock Holmes presumably got his instant energy this way.

The toxic effects of cocaine use include anxiety, confusion, paranoid delusions, delirium, auditory, visual, and tactile hallucinations, convulsions, digestive disorders, vomiting, headaches, nausea, emaciation due to loss of appetite, sleeplessness, and exaggerated reflexes.

Cocaine is often used in combination with heroin, the *speed ball*, to extend the length of the heroin high. Since its drug action is of fairly short duration, and since it is not an inexpensive "street drug," the use of cocaine by itself is relatively rare. Aside from the economics of cocaine use, it is rarely used by itself because its stimulating effects may so overexcite a person that he will turn to a sedative or another depressant to bring him down.

Death can result from respiratory arrest. Cocaine poisoning can be a serious problem. One form of it, acute cocaine intoxication, can result in almost immediate death before a proper examination and diagnosis can be made. When this does occur, it is usually due to the abnormally rapid absorption of high concentrations of the drug into the system, which adversely affects the heart.

Amphetamines

Benzedrine	*amphetamine sulphate*, beans, bennie, benzies, cartwheels, hearts, peaches, roses
Dexedrine	*dextroamphetamine sulphate*, dexies, footballs, hearts, oranges, browns
Methedrine	*methamphetamine hydrochloride*, Desoxyn, Norodin, syndrox, bambitas, crystal, Doe, meth, speed, splash
General	A's, coast to coast, co-pilots, eye openers, greenies, ellie babies, jolly beans. LA turnabouts, lid poppers, pep pills, sweets, truck drivers, uppers, wake-ups

History

Amphetamines are powerful central nervous system stimulants, particularly of the reticular formation and the cerebral cortex. Unlike cocaine, which is a naturally derived stimulant, the amphetamines are synthetic drugs. They were first developed in 1927 in the United States and belong to a class of drugs known as sympathomimetics—the mimics of the stimulated sympathetic nervous system. These drugs, including amphetamines, have the following actions:

1. excitatory action on smooth muscles (such as those in blood vessels supplying the skin and mucous membrane) and on secretion of the salivary glands;
2. inhibitory action on other smooth muscles, such as those in the intestinal wall, the bronchial tubes, and blood vessels supplying skeletal muscles;
3. excitation of heart action, resulting in increased heart rate and force of contraction;
4. metabolic actions, such as an increase in the conversion of glycogen into sugar in the liver and muscles, and the liberation of free fatty acids from fatty tissues;
5. an excitatory action on the central nervous system resulting in respiratory stimulation, increased wakefulness, and a prevention as well as reversal of fatigue;
6. a reduction in appetite.

Therapeutic Use

Amphetamines have been used to relieve nasal congestion (from hay fever, colds, and other respiratory infections), to counteract the drowsiness caused by some drugs in the treatment of epilepsy, to treat Parkinsonism, a variety of depressive states, petit mal epilepsy, and certain toxic reactions caused by central nervous system depressants. The widespread contemporary use of various amphetamines can be mostly associated with their action as psychic energizers (giving temporary extra energy and a feeling of alertness), as appetite depressants, and for their supposed value as aphrodisiacs.

Going backward:

1. There is absolutely no evidence that amphetamines serve as aphrodisiacs. In all likelihood, any increased or more satisfactory sexual behavior is a function of the self-fulfilling prophecy.
2. Amphetamines have little effect in suppressing the appetite of indi-

viduals whose major substance misuse is food. Dietary restrictions and frequent rapid movement away from the table and the refrigerator continue to be the best therapeutic tools for them. Some of the weight loss associated with amphetamine use may be due in part to some loss of smell and taste, as well as the increase in physical activity. Exactly how amphetamines reduce appetite is still unknown.

3. There is a vast difference between feeling energetic and actually being energetic. Whereas appropriate doses can aid a person to feel alert, less fatigued, elated, self-confident, and perhaps even more prone to be engaged in some physical activity (even at times accomplishing more actual work), as the drug dose is increased or becomes extended in time, the quality of the work may suffer.

This, of course, is another example of one of the dilemmas of living in a technologically advanced society. With more and more boring, fatiguing, and personally meaningless tasks engaging our energies, it is easy to be seduced into an amphetamine-based approach to them.

Consequences of Amphetamine Use

Indeed, it is easy to be seduced by amphetamines. In the first place, the "scare" of addiction can't easily be used. By now, many people know that amphetamines are not, in the strictest sense, addicting. They do differ from other central nervous system stimulants, primarily because excessive use leads to drug tolerance. The development of tolerance is a slow process. Often the user can tolerate doses many times greater than a therapeutic dose. Since all parts of the nervous system do not achieve tolerance simultaneously, the user can continue to feel nervous and have great difficulty sleeping as he takes more and more amphetamines.

Even though amphetamines are not addicting, when these stimulants are withdrawn suddenly, the fatigue and need for sleep that have been masked during the high now become exaggerated. The person often feels depressed both psychologically and physically. If the amphetamines had been taken as self-medication to combat psychological depression, the "crash" that occurs will generally result in the person's experiencing an even more pervasive depression. In order to escape the fatigue and depression, the person may sleep for inordinate periods of time, or begin to take more amphetamines.

Amphetamines can be taken orally or by injection. Mainlining creates a more potent effect because the absorption occurs more rapidly.

The serious effects of excessive use are both psychiatric and physical and are related directly to the action of the drug, as well as to the consequences of injecting any drug under less-than-sterile conditions. The false sense of unlimited energy may also result in the person's not taking proper care of himself, which may create or reinforce medical and psychiatric problems.

Along with depression and fatigue, the excessive user may experience headaches, irritability, palpitations, dizziness, insomnia, agitation, panic, confusion, apprehension, and delirium. Other toxic effects include circulatory collapse, nausea, vomiting, diarrhea, and abdominal cramps.

Both the toxic and lethal doses of amphetamines vary from person to person. Given these variations, it is important to note that amphetamines in large doses can lead to psychosis. Amphetamine psychosis is characterized by vivid visual and auditory hallucinations, delusions, and mood changes. These effects are more likely to occur following intravenous injection rather than oral ingestion. A serious form of hepatitis—hippy hepatitis—has been related to methedrine use.

Another behavior rather recently associated with amphetamines is the yo-yo phenomenon or the ups-and-downs syndrome. It is a fairly common occurrence, not only among the visible A-heads, but among many conventional amphetamine misusers, as well. Feeling tired or needing that extra energy, the person pops a few amphetamines. If the result is too much "up," he takes a barbiturate to bring him down. If life is now too tranquil or too much "down," the person can take some more amphetamines. Drug tolerance will increase, with more of each drug being needed constantly. The person is now a living yo-yo. From a perverted perspective, this yo-yo cannot even enjoy whatever pleasures are available from the use of either drug.

Amphetamines have also been used in combination with heroin, known as bombita, to extend the length of the heroin high.

The slogan "speed kills" is an accurate description of one of the irreversible hazards associated with amphetamine misuses. It is ironic that the slogan began with drug users and not with drug educators. As a result of the communication of this slogan, it appears that there has been a significant decrease in the intravenous use of high doses of methedrine. From the community's point of view, the fact that this slogan caught on has great significance. It reinforces the contention of this book, that drug misuse can be altered only if information that is meaningful and acceptable to the audience it is being communicated to is used. Whereas "speed kills" has caught on, the information concerning deaths from barbiturates or alcohol has not, and the deleterious effects of smoking have not either.

In the hurly-burly of contemporary American life, it would prove an advantage to most of us if we could begin to live a life based on "speed is not enough."

HALLUCINOGENS

The hallucinogens are a class of substances that have been arbitrarily grouped together because one of their major effects is to produce types of changes in perception, mood, and thinking that are not ordinarily experienced except in dreams or during deeply felt religious experiences. Under certain conditions or at certain dose levels, similar behavior can be experienced with other drugs such as bromides, narcotic antagonists, cocaine, and amphetamines.

During the hallucinogenic drug experience, the user will often experience a heightened awareness of himself and his environment, over which he has little control. Boundaries among the objects he perceives, himself, and the environment may be diminished, at the same time there is an increased sense of being part of mankind and the cosmos. "Insights" and "true meaning" are readily experienced, but they may have little effect on the person's usual style of life.

The various terms we have created to describe this category of drugs belie the fact that we are most uncertain as to how we should view them. The term *hallucinogenic* implies that the major drug action is causing hallucinations. True hallucinations are experienced during psychosis, when the disturbed individual hears voices, sees objects as people, feels things crawling on him, and smells various odors which, although nonexistent, for him really exist. The perceptions and misperceptions experienced by the hallucinogen user are generally known by him to be a result of the drug he has taken, but he can't do very much about what is happening. The term *mind-expanding* has its own limitations. The person may be inundated with myriad stimuli, which he attempts to put into some sort of meaningful order at the time, but it is rare for the insights of the drug experience to be integrated into his own life style. When used as psychiatric tools to investigate the relationships between states of consciousness, the brain and biochemistry, these substances are called *psychedelics* or *hallucinogenics*. It would appear that the meaning of the drug's *use* actually determines the family's name.

The confusion over the names and the hysteria related to the use of these various substances once again point up an important issue: When inadequate information is available or is communicated under conditions of ambiguity, and when such behavior becomes a prime focal point for political and social forces in the community, little good can result for anyone concerned.

Hallucinogens

LSD	*D-lysergic acid diethylamide*, LSD-25, *lysergic acid diethylamide*, acid, blue acid, Big D, cubes, heavenly blue, instant Zen, pearly gates, royal blue, sugar, sugar lump, the Chief, the Hawk, wedding bells, Zen, 25
Mescaline	*trimethoxyphenylethylamine*, an halonium, a moon, bad seed, Big Chief, cactus, half moon, hikori, hikuli, huatari, Mesc., mescalene, mescal beans, mescal button, P, peyote, seni, the button, tops, wokowi
STP	*2,5-dimethoxy-4-methyl-amphetamine*, dom, serenity-tranquility, peace, syndicate acid
Psilocybin	*tryptamine, psilocin*, mushrooms, sacred mushrooms
DMT	*dimethyltryptamine*, businessman's special, 45-minute psychosis
DET	*diethyltryptamine*
Cannabis	*tetrahydrocannabinol*, Acapulco gold, bhang, boo, bush, butter flower, *cannabis indicia, cannabis sativa*, charas, ganja, grass, griffo, giggle-smoke, hashish, hash, hay, hemp, herb, Indian hay, J, jive, joint, joint-sticks, kif, khif, loco weed, love weed, marijuana, Mary Jane, Mary Warner, mu, muggles, mutah, pod, pot, reefers, roach, rope, sative, smoke, straw, splim, sticks, tea, Texas tea, THC, weed
Atropine	
Bufotonin	
Datura	
Harmine	
Ibogain	
Kava	
Khat	
Morning glory seeds	Heavenly blue, pearly gates, flying saucer, summer skies, blue star, wedding bells
Nutmeg	
Phencycledine	
Peperdil benzilate	

LSD

History

LSD is a powerful hallucinogen which was initially synthesized by a pharmacologist, Hofman, as recently as 1938. Five years later he accidentally discovered its potent psychological effects.

> In the afternoon of 16 April 1943, when I was working on this problem, I was seized by a peculiar sensation of vertigo and restlessness. Objects, as well as the shape of my associates in the laboratory, appeared to undergo optical changes. I was unable to concentrate on my work. In a dream-like state, I left for home, where an irresistible urge to lie down overcame me. I drew the curtains and immediately fell into a peculiar state similar to drunkenness, characterized by an exaggerated imagination. With my eyes closed, fantastic pictures of extraordinary plasticity and intensive color seemed to surge toward me. After two hours, the state gradually wore off.

Although LSD is a recent arrival, ergot, the substance from which it is derived, has been with us for centuries. Ergot is a parasitic fungus that is found on wheat rye and other grasses, as well as in the morning glory. As early as 994 A.D., its toxicity had been noted. In that year, 40,000 people died in France from ergot-infected flour or feed. In the form of morning glory seeds, ingested in a tea or chewed, South American Indians used it hundreds of years ago to achieve religious hallucinations. In this form, it is approximately one-tenth as potent as LSD.

Therapeutic Uses

LSD is not addictive, although both tolerance and *reverse tolerance* do occur. Reverse tolerance is a phenomenon in which less, rather than more, of a drug is needed in order for previous effects to recur. Tolerance both develops and disappears rapidly. Individuals tolerant to either LSD, mescaline, or psilocybin will be tolerant to the other two drugs as well as to other LSD derivatives. There are no systematized withdrawal symptoms.

Miniscule amounts of LSD, measured in micrograms, can be either ingested or, infrequently, injected into a muscle. The LSD comes in the form of liquid, capsule, or pill and has often been ingested on a sugar cube. It is odorless, colorless, and tasteless.

At the present time, LSD is not being used therapeutically. Sandoz Pharmaceutical Company turned over all of its pharmaceutically pure LSD to the United States Government a few years ago, in the midst of the

LSD hysteria. Thus, the present LSD user suffers the same consequences as users of other illicit drugs: He never knows what he is buying and what extra "bonuses" come with his purchase.

In the very recent past, LSD has been used in the rehabilitation of criminals, the treatment of sexual disorders, mental retardation, schizophrenic children, psychotic adults, alcoholics, drug addicts, personality disorders, and for the relief of distress in terminal cancer patients. With the cessation of evaluative research, it is quite difficult to know what acceptable therapeutic value LSD has. This, of course, becomes one of the hazards faced by any chemical substance which, having achieved the status of a drug, still has not achieved the status of medicine.

Consequences of LSD Use

The mood and perceptual changes arising from LSD use can occur within 45 minutes or less of its ingestion. Doses as low as 25 micrograms can produce psychological effects in susceptible people, with the average effective dose being 150 micrograms. The potency of LSD is dramatized when one considers that an aspirin is 300,000 micrograms.

The site of action and how LSD affects man are still unknown. Oddly enough, animals appear to be resistant to its effects. There are no uniform or predictable effects among people or in the same person at different times. The effects are dependent not only on the dose, but also on the person's physiological and psychological state, the setting in which it is taken, the reasons for taking it and the expectations of LSD experience, the tasks set for and by the individual, previous experience with the drug, whether someone else is with the LSD user, and what his expectations are. Given these factors and the variety of ways in which they may interact, it becomes quite clear why an LSD trip—good or bad—is unpredictable and must be considered a very individual and personal experience.

The user, or *acid head*, as many LSD users are called, will generally experience the following effects. There may be marked and frequent mood changes, ranging from extreme pleasure to extreme anxiety. Laughing and crying may occur with only slight provocation. This emotional lability, over which he has no control, can be terrifying for a person who has poor emotional stability to begin with.

Perceptual distortions frequently occur and are known as synesthesia. The person may experience one type of sensory experience in another— hearing color, feeling smells, etc. Perhaps the most dramatic effect of LSD use is the perceptual experiences which have been described in the introduction to this section. Visual, tactile, olfactory, kinesthetic, and, to a lesser degree, auditory, perceptual changes occur. Distortions in space and time are experienced, as are changes in body image. Frequently the person may experience part of himself being out of himself, observing himself, a "spectator ego" observing an "active ego," which is the focus of the ongoing sensory experiences. Again, this sense of depersonalization can be frightening, as can experiencing one's internal organs and body processes. Colors appear to be more vivid and forms more fluid.

While illusions and delusions do occur, true hallucinations are rare. The person is generally aware that what he is experiencing is drug induced. The person may feel as if he is more emphatic and has a sense of an almost unlimited ability to communicate with others. The reality of this is difficult to assess.

Intellectual processes may become impaired, although recall or memory may be enhanced. The LSD user may experience difficulty in thinking, keeping up with his thoughts, or making something meaningful out of them. One scientist writing about this has noted, "Indeed, 'meaningfulness' seems more important than what is meant, and the 'sense of truth' more significant than what is true." Confusion often occurs as a result of LSD use, although the general public, not using LSD, also experiences confusion about it.

The physical effects associated with LSD use are dilation of the pupils, sweating due to increased body temperature, and an increase in blood pressure.

Claims continue to be made that LSD produces psychosis, suicide attempts, homicide attempts, panic episodes, and deep depressions—even death. LSD psychosis is generally brief and limited, with the person having insight into its cause, which is unlike natural psychosis. It is more likely that the psychosis, when it occurs, comes about in a less than stable individual, or a borderline psychotic, who is unable to cope with the overwhelming stimulation and perceptual distortions that can go on for 8 to 10 hours, and over which he has no control. Suicide attempts, panic reactions, and depression are also most likely related to the inability to end or effectively control an experience that seems timeless for an already disturbed individual.

Obviously, more research is necessary to verify whether these dysfunctional behaviors are directly related to the action of LSD. Regarding suicides, which are rapidly communicated, particularly if the person is a well-known American's child, such as Art Linkletter's daughter, we must remember that this is the third most common cause of death in young adults, regardless of drug use. For the person experiencing these feelings, it makes little difference if they are directly caused by LSD or are related to his own psychic makeup. The consequence of taking mood-altering drugs lightly is to open a Pandora's box. Sometimes the findings are treasures—the *good trip*; sometimes they are horrendous—the *bad trip* or *bummer*.

The good trip reveals man's ability to experience more than he can explain, describe, or functionally integrate. The "good tripper" is able to experience the meaning he attributes to each sensation with interest, awe, even with reverence. He is not upset by having to integrate his experience of the moment with reality as he has experienced it and learned it in his lifetime. He is not overwhelmed by the temporary loss of his ability to attend selectively to the world of internal and external stimuli.

The bad trip occurs when, in a sense, the person's moorings or anchors to his familiar world are markedly loosened. If the person begins to be overwhelmed by the LSD experience, and if his initial reaction is panic, which easily escalates, the bad trip is more likely to occur. For the individual who is already unstable or who does not have a set pattern of life, with established patterns and habits, vulnerability to bad trips is increased. High doses of LSD, uncertain reasons for taking it, and ambiguous anticipations, as well as the irregular quality of the black market, may also result in bad trips.

As we have come to understand more and more about the bad trip, even though it remains unpredictable, it has become more manageable. The effects of bad trips are generally of short duration (24 to 48 hours). Sedatives, or tranquilizers, used by knowledgeable and patient physicians, in conjunction with emotional support and reassurance, are generally all that is needed. The panic reaction of the LSD user is most often "talked down" by his friends.

Another consequence of LSD use is the *recurrent trip* or *flashback*. Days later, or even months after his last use of LSD, the person, without taking it again, may begin to experience a bad trip. Theoretically, it should be possible also to reexperience a good trip. Not one of these good trips has been reported. More than likely, this is so because the person wouldn't seek help during an unsolicited enjoyable experience, whereas he would for a frightening bad trip. At the present time, we don't understand why the flashback occurs, not can we predict when it will occur or when it will go away. There is no known treatment specifically for it, although various medications may be administered, to take the edge off the person's panic or anxiety.

One theory suggests that some people, during an LSD experience, may begin to pay attention to stimuli that they normally ignore, and once this happens, they may continue to be sensitive to these stimuli. It has also been suggested that the flashback phenomenon may be similar to the recurrent bad dream about a trauma. The person continues to dream about it or be obsessed about it in an attempt to master it or put it into a manageable perspective.

There are some other behavior patterns associated with LSD use which neither the proponents of LSD nor the general community pay adequate attention to. Very often the person who has experienced a good trip and returns to his real world, the world where he has to function in some way, is caught up in confusing emotions, because the contrast between the chemically induced world and his own is so great. Attempts to integrate LSD-induced insights into everyday living may be futile, and the person may begin to drop out more and more from his surroundings. He may not necessarily turn to drugs. His dropping out and our inability to attract or mobilize his energies, talents, and interests are a tragedy for everyone concerned.

There will obviously be other LSD users who appear to profit from their drug-induced experience. Recreational use, a temporary escape, an attempt at enlightenment are not mistaken for being anything else. And yet, even among this group, particular difficulties may ensue. The casual user may, after a while, become a chronic user, just as for some, casual social drinking may turn into everyday constant drinking and even problem drinking. Chronic LSD use, in a sense the result of too many good trips, may for all intents and purposes serve to limit the person's involvement with others and his community.

Another source of confusion regarding the effects of LSD is the claim that its use leads to birth defects and chromosome breakdown. Fetal malformation has occurred in experimental animals, but the data regarding humans remain conflicting. Although we generally are aware that extrapolating certain findings from one species to another is dangerous, LSD-induced hysteria often blinds us to this fact in this area. In the few cases in which malformed infants have been born to mothers who used LSD either prior to their pregnancy or during its early stages, the purity of the LSD was unknown. The mothers were often multiple-drug users, and since the number of cases is so small—six—the malformations could have been coincidental.

Two larger recent studies only add to the confusion. In one, with 127 infants, there was an increase in birth defects; in the other, with 121 infants, there was no such increase. Both studies suggested that there might be an increased risk of spontaneous abortion among LSD-using women.

Regarding chromosomal damage, the results are as confusing. Seven studies report chromosomal damage; seven report no chromosomal damage; and two additional studies claiming chromosomal damage are being criticized for their statistical analysis. The damage, if and when it does occur—and we know it occurs with other drugs such as antihistamines—may be related to the person's multiple-drug use, as well as to adulterants mixed with the LSD. Obviously, we must also be careful that we don't fall into the trap of assuming that a preceding event (taking LSD) is necessarily the cause of what follows. It should be equally clear that the threat of damage to oneself or one's offspring will not necessarily result in the diminution or cessation of LSD use. Using scare techniques, whether the facts are valid or not, will work only with people who can be scared. The results of fear and anxiety are as unpredictable as the consequences of LSD use. Some individuals may actually turn to LSD or other drugs in their attempts to cope with these feelings.

As difficult as it may be to step back and assess the entire situation when someone about whom we are concerned is using or plans to use LSD or other drugs, for that matter, this is the only realistic course open to us. Experimentation with LSD, to find oneself or for any other reason, is in a sense no better or worse than the myriad other paths of experimentation that have occurred in the past and will surely continue in the future.

The challenge to those of us who are both concerned about drug experimentation and are willing to commit time and energy to finding alternatives to it is to discover or develop the options or alternatives that make sense to the drug user and challenge his attention and commitment. As for the committed user, we should continue to be available to meet his physical, psychological, and social needs, and attempt to engage him, if it is possible. We must face up to the harsh reality that some people can't be reached or effectively helped by us at a given time. This doesn't mean that we give up. It does mean that we keep them in mind and keep them in sight. Under new circumstances, both for ourselves and for the committed user, new satisfactory answers might result.

Mescaline

History

Mescal and mescaline are derived from the peyote, a small spineless cactus, *Lophophorawilliamsii*, which grows in Mexico and parts of the southwestern United States. The drugs affect the central nervous system, as do other hallucinogenics, and are chemically related to *epinephrine,* a natural substance in the body. This cactus has been used in religious rituals and considered to be a divine plant, nourishment for the soul as well as food for the body. Its religious use spread from the Indians of Mexico to the Apaches, Omahas, Kiowas, and Comanches in the United States.

Mescaline was named after the Mescalero Apaches of the Great Plains, who had developed a religious peyote rite. The Western world originally became aware of these cactus derivatives when the Spaniards discovered that the Aztecs in Mexico worshiped a variety of cactus. Mescaline and the peyote cactus from which it is derived were the more potent of them. Indians claimed that God put some of His Holy Spirit into the peyote, and that it brought them closer to heaven. As part of its divine status, peyote was also considered to be a cure-all. Used for religious experiences, it was eaten.

The religious rite was most often group oriented, which consisted of a ceremony of hymns, dances, and prayers. It is unfortunate that a misconception has arisen that these religious rites are orgiastic in nature. As peyotism spread in the United States, missionaries attempted to get its use outlawed by federal legislation. It wasn't until 1964 that Indians in America were finally given the legal right to use peyote as a sacramental symbol in their Native American Church. At that time, the Supreme Court of California stated that "to remove the use of peyote is to remove the theological heart of peyotism." It was felt that peyote was eaten as a sacramental object in the same way as sacramental bread and wine are used by other religions, and that carrying mescal buttons was analogous to wearing a crucifix. At the present time, only members of the Native American Church can legally partake of the peyote ritual.

Therapeutic Uses

The first introspective studies of the effects of mescaline were made by Havelock Ellis in the 1890s. In 1896, the active ingredient of peyote was isolated; in 1913, its psychological effects were first studied; and in 1918, its pharmacological structure was defined. Thus, from a therapeutic potential, mescaline has been with us for a longer period of time than many other drugs, and yet it has been used sparingly. Its major use has been as a psychiatric tool to study schizophrenia and other psychotic states, as well as to study visual hallucinations.

Neither mescal nor mescaline is physically addicting, nor are there

Fig. 2-4   The earliest known illustration of peyote cactus (shown here) appears in a Mexican Herbal composed in 1552 (the Badianus manuscript). (Courtesy of the U.S. Drug Enforcement Administration.)

specific withdrawal symptoms associated with them. Tolerance is slowly developed to mescaline. Once tolerance is achieved, the person is also tolerant to LSD and psilocybin. Mescal is generally eaten, although it has been taken as a brew, as well as in a capsule. Mescaline, because of its bitter taste, is usually ingested with some liquid.

Consequences of Mescaline Use

The drug action results in unusual psychic effects and visual hallucinations. The individual may perceive brightly colored lights, geometric designs, animals, and at times even people. Although one's sense of color and space perception may be impaired, insight generally is not. At times, anxiety may occur, while at other times there is a sense of euphoria. The effects usually last from 10 to 12 hours.

The toxic effects include dilation of the pupils, as well as unusual and bizarre color perception, flushes, vomiting, cramps, increased pulse rate, elevated blood pressure, and at times muscle twitching. Some individuals have reported experiencing a sense of depersonalization. As with LSD, once psychological, social, and environmental factors significantly determine the drug experience, and once it begins, it runs its course, one should not be surprised that adverse reactions occur.

STP

STP is chemically related to both mescaline and to amphetamines. A number of other "alphabet" hallucinogens are also chemical modifications of amphetamines: MDA, MMDA, DMT, DET, and DPT. STP is not addicting. With small doses an individual may experience mild euphoria; large doses may result in hallucinogenic effects. Doses of about 5 milligrams will cause marked hallucinogenic effects, their intensity and duration being related to the dose that is ingested.

STP neither has a history of use as a sacramental substance to enhance religious rituals and experiences, nor has it been used therapeutically. STP has been found to be 100 times more potent than mescaline. Its hallucinogenic actions have been recorded as lasting up to 72 hours. Its toxic effects include nausea, sweating, tremors, blurred vision, multiple images, vibration of objects, visual hallucinations, disturbed shapes, enhancement of details, and time distortions.

Since its drug action can last longer than any of the other hallucinogens, and since, like them, the person has no control over the drug experience, STP can be a terrifying drug for its user.

DMT, DET

DMT is a synthetic derivative of tryptamine. It has also been found in the seeds of some West Indian and South American plants. Its drug effects are similar to those of LSD. They last a relatively short time— about half an hour. DET is a synthetic derivative similar in drug action to

DMT. Although many psychogenic drugs are derivatives of tryptamine, tryptamine as a substance does not have drug effects similar to any of its derivatives.

Psilocybin

Psilocybin is the active ingredient of a "magic" mushroom, *psilocybe mexicanie*, which is native to Central America. It was known as "the flesh of the gods" and was used for hundreds of years prior to the Spanish conquest of Mexico and Central America by the same Indians who used peyote. A major goal for its use was to communicate with supernatural powers. Its drug effects are practically indistinguishable from those of mescaline and LSD. It is not addicting, and its hallucinogenic effects generally last from five to six hours. Psilocin is derived from the same source as psilocybin, and its drug effects are similar.

Cannabis (marijuana and other derivatives)

History

Cannabis and its various derivatives have been known to man and have been used legally and illegally for approximately 3000 years. The natural source of its hallucinogenic properties is the hemp plant, *Cannabis Sativa*. The plant grows like a weed in almost any climate or soil condition, although the potency of its derivatives appears to be related to the place where it is grown. Plants grown in warmer climates produce more potent derivatives.

Until quite recently, there have been only male and female forms of the plant, and most texts describing it have attributed its hallucinogenic properties only to the female plant. A hermaphroditic variety has been cultivated, which seems most appropriate, given the recent styles in unisex apparel or, as one author has noted, "The mescal plant of the unisex generation." Recent chemical analysis of the plant's active ingredients has shown that they are equally present in both the male and female plants.

Together with alcohol and opium, cannabis is one of man's earliest known drugs. Its first medicinal use was noted in 2737 B.C. by the Chinese emperor Shen Nung, who included it in a pharmacy book. He prescribed its use for "female weakness, gout, rheumatism, malaria, beri-beri, constipation, and absentmindedness." Mixed with wine and called mo-yo, it was used by the Chinese physician Hoa-Gho as a surgical anesthetic. A few years later, cannabis extracts were introduced to India and used as part of their native medicine. The Pharaoh Ramses recommended in a papyrus its use for washing sore eyes. During the Middle Ages, a European folk remedy utilized the kneaded dried leaves of the plant, in combination with butter, for treating burns. Cannabis extracts were also used in treating earaches, to prevent inflammation of ulcers, and for straightening out the posture of women suffering from a uterine disease. It was claimed that after they inhaled smoke from the plant, they no longer stooped.

Paralleling its ancient therapeutic uses, cannabis also was used for religious and recreational purposes. The Chinese referred to it as "the delight-giver," as well as the "liberator of sin." It appears that even in the past, cannabis could stir up ambivalent reactions to its effects.

Cannabis began to be used for its hallucinogenic value about 1000 B.C., when it became part of Hindu culture. It was used as an aid in meditation and is frequently described this way in Indian folk literature:

"To the Hindu, the hemp plant is holy. A guardian lives in bhang."
"No god or man is as good as the religious drinker of bhang."
"The supporting power of bhang has brought many a Hindu family safe through the miseries of famine."

Oddly enough, cannabis never caught on in the religious practices of China, a neighboring nation which was quite willing to use this substance medicinally.

One of the cannabis derivatives and names, hashish, is thought to have been derived from its use by Hasan-i-Sabbah, prior to the First Crusade. The name marijuana is Mexican-Spanish for the hemp plant and had at one time been used as a name for cheap tobacco. Other derivatives of the cannabis include Ganja and Charas. Ganja is derived from the tops of a specially cultivated and harvested grade of the female Indian hemp plant and includes the resin. Charas is the pure, unadulterated resin from the tops of the finest female Indian hemp plants, usually those grown for Ganja. Hashish is a powdered and sifted form of Charas. Marijuana is the least potent and includes the leaves and stems of the uncultivated plants, sometimes including the seeds, and chopped up into a crude tobacco consistency. In India, where it is legal, it is known as bhang, used in liquid form for socializing and/or prescribed by physicians as a medicine.

Hashish is at least twice as strong as marijuana, Ganja two to three times as strong, and Charas about ten times stronger than marijuana. Since it is the resin that houses cannabis' psychoactive qualities, and Charas is the pure resin, it is the only derivative with which hallucinogenic reactions are fairly regular.

Marijuana came to the United States of America around the beginning of the century from Mexico. It was brought in by American and Mexican sailors, who paid $10 to $12 a kilo and then sold it wholesale in New Orleans at $35 to $40 a kilo. At that time, it was generally smoked by either the poor or the Negro population. During Prohibition, concern about its use became evident, and 16 states passed laws against its use and/or sale. The New Orleans *Morning Tribune* published a series on the "marijuana menace." The major focus of concern was the claim that many teen-agers were smoking marijuana. Oddly enough, little was done about marijuana use, and the laws created to control it were hardly enforced. (The major effort at this time was directed toward controlling alcohol use.)

During the 1930s, a major crime wave occurred in New Orleans. It was blamed on marijuana use. In 1936, Louisiana state narcotic officers reported that "60 percent of crimes committed in New Orleans were by marijuana users." Newspapers throughout the country picked up this theme, which resulted in a renewed national concern about its use. Again, law enforcement authorities did little about this. The Treasury Department, parent body of the Federal Bureau of Narcotics, noted that "this publicity tends to magnify the extent of the evil (of marijuana) and lends color to an inference that there is an alarming spread of the improper use of the drug, whereas the actual increase in such use may not have been inordinately large."

None of the reasons for controlling its use was in any way valid. Claims were made that it caused addiction (which it doesn't), caused crime (which was not adequately demonstrated, and which no drug does—only people do, and which in no way explained the crime and violence that has long been part of our national heritage), caused loss of reproductive powers (which it doesn't), and that it was increasingly being used by youngsters (although no valid data were ever presented to substantiate this).

One serious consequence of the manner in which marijuana was controlled, unlike the opiates, was that it was also made unavailable as a medicine. The drive to control marijuana occurred against a background of Prohibition, the Depression, and other significant American social phenomena.

The point of all this is that, while it is the prerogative of any country to reinforce or inhibit the use of any substance, to focus on the purported actions of a drug rather than the social, political, etc., needs of a nation at that time may ultimately create more problems than are ever solved by controlling the drug. Surely, controlling marijuana or not controlling its use ultimately has little effect upon the quality of life that people live.

At the present time, marijuana is no longer used therapeutically in the United States, and its recreational use is illegal. People continue to become involved in silly discussions and arguments about whether it is more or less dangerous than alcohol. These drugs cannot be compared for a number of reasons. They belong to different drug families; alcohol is a depressant, whereas marijuana is an hallucinogen. Alcohol is addicting, and marijuana is not. Alcohol is legally available, and marijuana is not. The marijuana experience has to be learned; drunkenness is a usually unavoidable effect of the excessive consumption of alcohol. Rigorous scientific research has permitted us to learn about the many physical and psychiatric consequences related to alcoholism, whereas the era of marijuana research has still to come.

Therapeutic Uses

Prior to the last century, cannabis was relatively unknown to Western medicine. In 1839, Dr. W. B. O'Shaughnessy, a British physician in India, became interested in it. He reviewed the 900 years of literature describing its use in Indian medicine and began to conduct his own experiments with it. He found it to be safe in animals; increasingly large doses did not kill his mice, rats, or rabbits. He then began to use it in humans to treat seizures, rheumatism, tetanus, and rabies, and noted that it relieved pain, was useful as an anticonvulsant and as a muscle relaxant.

Cannabis has been used therapeutically as an antibiotic, an analgesic, to relieve headaches (reducing the frequency and severity of migraine headaches), menstrual cramps, excessive menstrual bleeding, to relieve labor pains in childbirth, to treat illnesses having a psychosomatic basis such as cystitis and asthma and insomnia, to control coughs, relieve tremors and paralysis, and to treat chorea. It has been used as both a diagnostic tool and as a treatment for some psychiatric illnesses. Early in its therapeutic use, it was suggested as being a useful diagnostic tool to safely ascertain whether an early, natural abortion may or may not have occurred. It had been suggested as the most effective drug for treating loss of appetite, as well as mild depression in the elderly. It was used to withdraw opiate addicts, since it was noted as appeasing their desire to use opiates at the same time that it increased the person's appetite. Lastly, it has been used experimentally in its form of THC to control epilepsy.

The development of other drugs, the stereotyped and often hysterical attitudes, the political factors that formalized its illegal status, and the lack of the research needed to assess its usefulness have prevented its continued use as a medicine.

Cannabis and all of its derivatives are not addicting. There is no empirical evidence for the development of either a state of tolerance or a characteristic abstinence syndrome. In the United States it is generally smoked. In Asia and Africa, it is consumed as a food or beverage.

Consequences of Marijuana Use

Marijuana's primary use is as a recreational drug. Individuals using it often experience and exhibit hilarity for no discernible reason, and may feel euphoric, which in turn may result in increased sociability. Distortions in time and space are fairly common, and it is immature if not plain dangerous to drive under its influence. (Obviously, the same must be said about any drug that affects a person's driving ability.) The person's judgment and memory can become impaired. He may feel confused, and other aspects of his emotional behavior may become distorted. Aside from the many nondrug factors which may affect the person's cannabis reaction (factors which affect all hallucinogenic experiences), increases in the active ingredient of a drug will obviously alter the person's behavior.

Increased doses and/or use can result in an intensified appreciation of sounds, form and colors, hallucinations and illusions, as well as delusions of a paranoid type that may result in antisocial behavior. The person may experience increased anxiety and exhibit abusive and aggressive behavior, which may be a function of the acute intellectual and sensory changes. Sleep may be disturbed as well. The intoxicated person may become quite active, with little, if any, impairment in his coordination; he will often develop an increased appetite, and his mouth and pharynx may become sore. Higher doses that are also high in THC, the active ingredient, may result in vivid hallucinations, the content of which is related to the individual's personality, as well as a drug-induced psychosis.

Recent reports of cannabis psychosis are often misinterpreted. When an American GI in Vietnam is smoking marijuana by himself and becomes psychotic, it is often overlooked that the native source of his drug is more potent than that generally available in the United States, and that one result of his solitary rather than group use is his inability to *titrate* or control its effects. Many of the effects of marijuana become controllable for the individual as it is passed from person to person at a social gathering.

A traditional symptom of marijuana use, blood-shot pupils, has been discovered to be related to the circumstances under which it is generally taken and not simply the drug's action.

As we react to marijuana and its use, we must remember that prior to 1968, Americans had conducted and reported only three studies with human subjects. Also, prior to 1964, when Dr. Raphael Mechoulam, in Israel, first synthesized its active ingredients, delta-1-tetrahydro-cannabinol, or THC, most reports of its effects were generally scientifically deficient and limited to anecdotal material.

Since the discovery of THC, it has been possible to conduct dose-related studies. The early American studies were not dose related. The first study was conducted in the Canal Zone with 34 soldiers. The study reported the following results:

1. physical—hunger and overeating (hyperphagia), increased pulse rate, with unchanged blood pressure and a tendency to sleep;
2. psychological—loss of inhibitions and unchanged performance on various psychological tests;
3. neurological—unchanged performance on neurological tests.

The doses, type, and quality of the marijuana were unspecified, and no control subjects were included.

The second research study, known as the LaGuardia Report, was done with 72 prisoners, 48 of whom were previous marijuana users. The drug was given as an oral extract, and these results were reported:

1. physical—body steadiness decreased, particularly after high doses for nonusers;
2. psychological—basic personality structure unchanged, feelings of relaxation experienced, loss of inhibitions and a sense of self-confidence experienced;
3. intellectual—intellectual functioning impaired.

As with the previous study, doses and quality of the drug were unspecified, and no controls were used.

The third study also used prisoners, but they were chronic marijuana users. The primary purpose of this study was to investigate the effects of the long-term smoking of marijuana on psychological functioning. The findings noted:

1. physical—minimal dysfunctions in manual dexterity;
2. psychological—initial feeling of exhilaration and euphoria, which changed within a few days to indifference and lassitude, minimal dysfunctions in memory.

Like the other studies, no controls were used, and the doses and quality were not specified. From a scientific point of view, one would have to conclude that these studies could offer no conclusive evidence concerning the consequences of marijuana use. Unfortunately, people hear, become selectively deaf, use, and don't use material without regard to the data's scientific validity or limitations.

Not only is much of what has been written about marijuana anecdotal, but since a good deal of the substance that has been used for research has generally been collected from arrests and kept for varying periods of time as evidence, its potency is either unknown or nonexistent. Researchers have become increasingly aware of these and other factors that must be more adequately controlled. Route of administration, potency of the material being used, use of placebos and appropriate control groups, the development and use of tests that are sensitive to the effects of marijuana, reasonable and meaningful control of the subjects being studied, as well as the physical setting of the study and control of the social, ethical, and legal factors related to the subjects being studied are just some of the more obvious factors.

A recent study is an example of the new type of research being conducted. The sample was a relatively small one—17 volunteer males, ages 21 to 26—and was done in Boston. Eight of them were chronic marijuana users; the nonusers were cigarette smokers. The setting was a comfortable office, which was well lighted. The marijuana was supplied by the Federal Bureau of Narcotics and consisted of finely chopped cannabis leaves and was free of seeds and stems. Both low and high doses were used. The tests given were felt to be sensitive to a number of psychological and physiological effects which have often been reported as occurring from smoking marijuana. The placebo consisted of the chopped outer covering of mature stalks of the male plant, which contained no THC. The contents of both the active and the placebo cigarettes were not visible, and the rooms were sprayed with a scent to mask the odor of marijuana. The data collected from this study led to the following conclusions concerning the effects of marijuana:

1. physical—heart rate increasing moderately, respiratory rate appearing to remain unaffected, no discernible changes in blood sugar levels, pupil size not changed with short-term use, although the conjunctive blood vessels are dilated;
2. psychological—performance on simple intellectual and psychomotor tests impaired, this impairment appearing to be dose related for non-marijuana users, but less so for chronic users.

Perhaps the most important result of this study from a contemporary American perspective was that marijuana research can be safely conducted with human volunteers.

Marijuana is being grown for research purposes in various parts of the country. Although the necessary future dose-related research will help us to understand what marijuana actually does and what it doesn't do, it may have little effect on the present emotional polarization that has taken place regarding its use. Under federal impetus, the availability of natural and synthetic THC will finally permit us to do the research. Synthetic THC, administered to chronic users, both by mouth and by cigarette smoke, has indicated that at low doses the effects are similar to those of marijuana, while at high doses they are similar to more potent hallucinogens.

Part of the difficulty in reacting to marijuana and its use relates to the fact that much of its effect has to do with the user and not the drug itself, as well as a variety of sociopsychopolitical forces. The subjective or psychological effects of marijuana, particularly at low doses, are related to the user's personality, his expectations, the circumstances under which he takes the drug, and the route of administration.

The user must learn how to use the drug in order to achieve the best results, how to recognize and categorize the drug effects, and how to be sensitive to these effects. This type of learning experience is generally not considered to be part of acceptable American behavior, even though by teaching our citizens how to drink, we surely have held down the enormous serious alcohol problem that we do have.

As a rule of thumb, low doses generally lead to pleasurable experiences and high doses to unpleasant ones. The psychotic episodes that have been recorded, lasting from a few hours to a few days, have been associated with high doses. When they as well as other psychiatric conditions arise, more often than not they occur with the unstable, predisposed person. Since the effects of marijuana, more than any other drug, vary so from person to person, as well as in the same person at different times, its "unpredictability" may create anxiety, as well as other reactions related to handling the anxiety, in a population to whom marijuana is essentially an alien substance, or is perceived as a threat to the traditional values of a given population.

It is in this sense that marijuana has often become the focal point for the misuse of available energy and concern.

Perhaps of most significance is that the energy consumed by these discussions is then not available for personal and community issues that can and must be resolved. How an individual and/or his community works out the various solutions to life's challenges at best will be affected only minimally by its control of marijuana. The decision to control marijuana, as with other substances, is an arbitrary one and, once made, should interfere as little as possible with other more important concerns.

Vapors

Vapors   Carbon tetrachloride, chloroform, gasoline, glue, ether, kerosene, lighter fluid, paint thinner, refrigerants, shellac

The world of chemical substances is, in many ways, more flexible than the world of people who use them. While they permit themselves to be used and misused in a variety of ways, attitudes toward their use are, at a given point in time, rather more limited and fixed. The vapors are a clear example of this. Having clearly enunciated functionally accepted uses, many commercial and some medicinal, they became the cheap and often unasked-for entrance into the world of hallucinogen experiences.

They can be categorized as depressants, because many of them have a depressant action on the central nervous system, similar to barbiturates and narcotics. Their experienced effect is, however, of an hallucinogenic nature. The psychological effects of these inhalable substances are generally inebriation, exhilaration, euphoria, and stupor. These feelings may be associated with colorful hallucinations. Some writers in the field of drug misuse consider inhalable substances to be the poor man's LSD.

Perhaps the most misused of these substances is glue, which has toluene as its major component. It is this latter substance that is considered to be responsible for glue's hallucinogenic effects, as well as its toxic effects. It is an irritant to the mucous membrane and inflames the nostrils, lips, and eyes. Glue sniffers may experience nausea, vomiting, and dizziness. Although many assertions have been made about glue sniffing resulting in serious psychological and physical problems, including death, the evidence for these assertions is disputable. The various deaths that have been attributed to its use have most often been found to be caused by the individual's suffocating while getting high. Putting one's head into a cellophane or plastic bag and inhaling the vapors of a substance to get high may obviously result in death if the plastic cuts off the air supply to the nose and mouth.

These various vapors and volatile substances are not addicting. It is uncertain whether their use results in tolerance or characteristic withdrawal symptoms. All of them are easily and legitimately accessible. In a sense, they become another model for our contemporary drug dilemma.

They point up the fact that an almost infinite variety of substances, which are part of our daily style of living, can be misused. Attempts to control their use serve to demonstrate how we play games, both institutionally and individually.

In my own neighborhood in New York City, stores that sell airplane glue exhibit the following signs: "Airplane glue can only be bought with model airplane kits." I have known numerous youngsters who have huge collections of unused kits in their homes. They are amused by the silliness of having to purchase a kit in order to get the glue that they sniff. They are confused by the fact that their parents see mounting piles of kits and react to this infrequently by chiding their child to complete the airplane model, never asking any questions. They are likewise confused because no one has helped them understand that drug use is not limited to certain licit and illicit medicines, but includes an almost unlimited source of natural and synthetic substances, many of which are sold to make living easier. They are confused because they are told by well-meaning and, at times, not so well-meaning adults that the drug user is a particular deviant individual.

In a very significant sense, our contemporary drug problem is increased rather than diminished when we fail to recognize the various factors that go into a person's decision to use or not to use a particular substance, and the meaning he attached to his decision. The drugs and their effects are only a minor part of today's drug problem. The people who use and misuse them and our formal and informal reactions to these drugs and their users continue to be the major part of the problem. Unless we accept and understand this and act in a meaningful and appropriate way, based upon this important insight, we shall surely continue to confuse further an already confusing part of man's behavior.

Alcohol

Alcohol   Booze, bubbly, blind tiger, cane corn, canned heat, coffin varnish, corn mule, dago red, dog's nose, Durth corage, eye opener, fire water, gargle, giggle water, hair of the dog, hooch, hooker, ink, juice, jungle juice, King Kong, lightning, monkey chaser, moonshine, mountain dew, mule, nanny-goat sweat, nose paint, paint remover, pick-me-up, pig sweat, poison, real McCoy, red eye, red ink, ruin, sauce, serum, shamrock, shicker, shine shot, slam, slug, snake oil, sneaky Peter, stiffener, suds, third rail, torpedo juice, vino, white lightning, whoopee water

History

Alcohol can be said to be man's oldest drug. In ancient times, alcoholic beverages were used to treat many disorders. In one medical papyrus dated about 3500 years ago, beer and wine were included in 39 prescriptions. Since ancient times, alcoholic beverages have been used as food, drink, medicine, euphoriant, intoxicant, as a catalyst for conviviality, as a reinforcer for joy at such important social occasions as weddings, as a psychic pain reliever at such occasions as funerals, and as part of many religious rituals as a sacramental substance. Its uses and misuses continue to be defined by each society, culture, and community. In the Middle Ages, alchemists viewed distilled alcohol as the elixir of life.

Therapeutic Uses

Alcoholic beverages have been used clinically to tranquilize and sedate, to stimulate appetite, as an emergency energy source, to treat iron-deficiency anemia, diabetes, cardiovascular disease, anginal attacks, hypertension, arteriosclerosis, kidney ailments, a variety of infectious diseases, the common cold, fainting spells, nausea and vomiting, arthritis, premenstrual tensions, and as an antiseptic for topical use.

Prior to the introduction of intravenous narcotics during the Civil War, alcoholic beverages were used as pain killers. Battlefield surgery often consisted of having the patient drink himself into passing out, at which point surgery commenced. During World War II, the Russians used alcohol as a major anesthetic when they no longer had other anesthetic supplies. Since the anesthetic dose and the lethal dose are so nearly the same, the patient often died. Alcohol is therapeutically used these days as an astringent, a cooling agent, a counterirritant, and as an antibacterial agent. It is also used as a potentiating agent for narcotics, barbiturates, and tranquilizers.

Applied topically, alcohol dehydrates and hardens cells, cools skin by evaporation, prevents sweating, and irritates the mucous membranes. Inhaled, alcohol increases the absorption of medications into the lungs and improves the exchange of oxygen by changing surface tension. Applied locally, at high concentrations, it can block conduction in peripheral nerves. When ingested, it is absorbed very rapidly from the stomach, small intestines, and colon. After entering the body, alcohol is oxidized in the liver. It is fairly uniformly distributed throughout all body tissues and all fluids. The person of average weight and height can generally metabolize one 2-ounce shot of liquor an hour with no deleterious effects of any consequence. Drinking more than this leads to feeling high, drunkenness, and even death.

Consequences of Alcohol Use

Alcohol intake, which increases the alcohol level in the blood, has been described as creating the following conditions:

Percent of Alcohol in Blood	Behavior
0.00–0.05	dull and dignified
0.05–0.10	man—dashing and debonair; woman—delightful and desirable
0.10–0.20	daring and devilish
0.20–0.30	dangerous and disheveled
0.40	delirious and disgusting
0.50	clearly drunk
0.60	dead drunk
0.70	DEAD

There are, however, a small group of individuals, called pathological alcoholics, who are so sensitive to alcohol that even ingesting a small amount will lead to dysfunctional behavior.

For most people, drinking more than their bodies are able to metabolize can lead to serious immediate, as well as long-range, psychological and physical problems. Such problems are a result of alcohol's action as a drug. Numerous other problems may arise if the person's life style is such that he does not take adequate care of himself.

One can literally go from the head to the toes and point out serious toxic effects related to excessive drinking. A number of these conditions are not reversible (see Fig. 2-5).

Drinking can be a recreational and/or escapist activity with serious end results. There are many social and economic problems that are directly related to the psychological and physical consequences of ingesting alcohol.

Alcohol is a depressant of the central nervous system. Its drug action results in releasing man's inhibiting control mechanisms. This explains why some people react as if they have been stimulated—the shy person becoming aggressive and abusive, the quiet person behaving boisterously. Alcohol exaggerates who a person is once his inhibitions are gone or loosened, so that behavior and fantasies that are normally under control are less controlled or not controlled at all.

Alcohol is an addicting drug. Unlike other addicting drugs, such as opiates and barbiturates, the addiction process may take 3 to 10 years to develop.

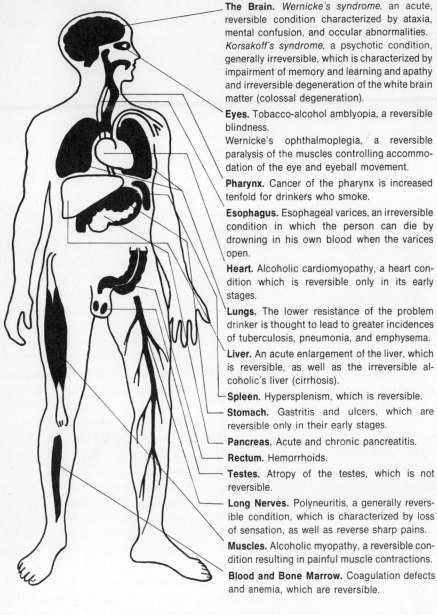

The Brain. *Wernicke's syndrome*, an acute, reversible condition characterized by ataxia, mental confusion, and occular abnormalities. *Korsakoff's syndrome*, a psychotic condition, generally irreversible, which is characterized by impairment of memory and learning and apathy and irreversible degeneration of the white brain matter (colossal degeneration).

Eyes. Tobacco-alcohol amblyopia, a reversible blindness.
Wernicke's ophthalmoplegia, a reversible paralysis of the muscles controlling accommodation of the eye and eyeball movement.

Pharynx. Cancer of the pharynx is increased tenfold for drinkers who smoke.

Esophagus. Esophageal varices, an irreversible condition in which the person can die by drowning in his own blood when the varices open.

Heart. Alcoholic cardiomyopathy, a heart condition which is reversible only in its early stages.

Lungs. The lower resistance of the problem drinker is thought to lead to greater incidences of tuberculosis, pneumonia, and emphysema.

Liver. An acute enlargement of the liver, which is reversible, as well as the irreversible alcoholic's liver (cirrhosis).

Spleen. Hypersplenism, which is reversible.

Stomach. Gastritis and ulcers, which are reversible only in their early stages.

Pancreas. Acute and chronic pancreatitis.

Rectum. Hemorrhoids.

Testes. Atropy of the testes, which is not reversible.

Long Nerves. Polyneuritis, a generally reversible condition, which is characterized by loss of sensation, as well as reverse sharp pains.

Muscles. Alcoholic myopathy, a reversible condition resulting in painful muscle contractions.

Blood and Bone Marrow. Coagulation defects and anemia, which are reversible.

Fig. 2-5   Some consequences of alcoholism

The initial stages of withdrawal are similar to those arising from barbiturate withdrawal, both drugs being closely related pharmacologically, with cross tolerance being possible. The person in withdrawal experiences tremors, nausea, weakness, and anxiety. He may begin to perspire, vomit, and have cramps. He may begin to see things, with his eyes closed or open. At this stage, his insight may not be affected yet. As the withdrawal process continues, insight is lost, and the person becomes confused, disoriented in time and space; delirium begins, and he may become agitated and have convulsions. His delusions and hallucinations may appear to be so real to him that even after recovery he may question their unreality. Recovery, known more colloquially as "drying out," usually takes four to seven days. As with many other drugs, death during withdrawal may be due to a serious depression of respiration.

It is indeed both ironic and tragic that our present reaction to the use and misuse of other drugs has taken our energies and attention away from alcohol misuse. A nation that must, in one way or another, care for 9,000,000 alcoholics can ill afford to do this. To fall into the trap of considering alcohol the drug of the adult population, who are then assumed somehow to be able to solve their own problems, and other drugs as being youth problems, to which the nation must respond, can only result in even more problems for everyone.

Teen-agers continue to drink and to get into difficulties thereby. Impaired cognitive efficiency and psychomotor coordination aren't limited to the over-30 generation; they are dose related. The alcohol-related abusive behavior may be even less tolerated by the young than by their elders. Teen-age drinking and excessive drinking are no better and in many ways may be a lot worse than the use or misuse of other drugs.

The passive acceptance of alcohol-related problems, when considered against the rather assertive, if not aggressive, attempt to minimize other drug-related problems, is but another part of the confusion that characterizes our approach to drugs and drug taking.

A serious issue that we must confront ourselves with is why we can continue to be upset about the use of various drugs and their consequences, while generally doing little about a drug that is associated with 25,000 vehicular deaths a year, 50 percent of accidents and absenteeism that cost industry approximately $4 billion annually, and is the major reason for approximately 50 percent of our prison population.

When we begin to grapple effectively with this kind of bizarreness, we shall be able to put the use and misuse of various substances into a more correct and manageable perspective and get on with the pleasures and problems inherent in being alive.

SOME EFFECTS DURING DRUG USE AND OVERDOSE

	Physiological	*Psychological*
Minor tranquilizers	Depression of nervous and muscular activity Drowsiness Ataxia Skin rashes Nausea Menstrual and ovulatory irregularities Increased sensitivity to alcohol Respiratory depression Coma Pain masking Slurred speech Tachycardia Double vision	Loss of inhibition Feeling of well-being Disorientation Confusion Memory impairment Trancelike episodes Personality alterations Rage reactions
Amphetamines	Increased blood pressure, pulse rate Tachycardia Increased blood sugar Dilation and constriction of blood vessels Dilated pupils Increased respiration rate Depression of appetite Relaxation of smooth muscles—ataxia Pain masking Skin rash Cramps Nausea Chest pains Abdominal pain Fainting Fever Headache	Increased wakefulness—insomnia—drowsiness Alertness, vigilance, increased initiative and energy Improved ability to concentrate—inability to concentrate Greater responsiveness to environmental stimuli Decreased fatigue and boredom—fatigue Mood elevation—mild euphoria—depression Feeling of sociability Increased verbal and other activity Restlessness—irritation—agitation Confused disorganized thinking—paranoia—psychosis Compulsive repetition of meaningless acts Self-consciousness Aggressive behavior Panic Pain masking
LSD	Dilated pupils Increased heart rate and blood pressure Sweating Increased body temperature Chills Increased blood sugar level Increased urination Headaches Decreased appetite Tremors Reduced coordination Pain masking	Synesthesia Space and time distortions Changes in body images Changes in rate and content of thought Inability to concentrate Lucid thinking Intellectual task performance Impairment Alertness Disorientation Hallucinations Agitation Aggressive behavior Panic/paranoia Psychosis

Drug	Physical effects	Psychological effects
Marijuana	Increase in heart rate Swelling of minor conjunctival blood vessels Slight drying of eyes and nasal passages Dryness of mouth Throat irritation Increased urination Increased appetite Incoordination—dizziness Ataxia Headaches Nausea	Euphoria—dysphoria Increased conviviality Enhanced rapport Increased sensitivity to environment Enhanced visual imagery Altered time sense Altered spatial relationships Lessening of inhibitions—loss of control Increased-decreased behavioral activity Difficulty in concentrating Fear—anxiety—panic Disorientation—delusions—paranoia Depression Irritability Confusion Lethargy Sense of heaviness, weakness, drowsiness
Opiates	Reduction in respiratory and cardiovascular activity Depression of cough reflex Constriction of pupil Minor reduction in visual acuity Itching Dilation of cutaneous blood vessels Warming of skin Constipation—diarrhea Nausea Vomiting Coma Pain masking Slurred speech Lacrimation Jaundice Gooseflesh Tachycardia Ataxia Cramps	Euphoria—dysphoria Drowsiness Dizziness Inability to concentrate Apathy—lethargy Agitation
Barbiturates	Slowing down of respiratory and cardiovascular system Kidney failure Impaired liver (jaundice) Skin allergies Impaired physical coordination Sleep Coma Convulsions Ataxia Pain masking Slurred speech Gooseflesh Cramps	Drug autism Euphoria—depression Hallucinations Agitation Aggressive behavior Paranoia/panic Psychosis Disorientation

Aspirin

History

Aspirin, the conventional name for *acetylsalicylic acid*, was developed in 1893 by Felix Hoffman, a chemist employed by the Bayer Company in Germany. Hoffman's father suffered from rheumatoid arthritis and was the first patient to be treated with this new drug which became known as aspirin, a contraction of the German name *acetylspirsaure*. It is interesting to note that at about the same time, heroin was also being synthesized by the Bayer Company. What is of interest is that one drug, heroin, is widely misused and is the focus of community concern and intervention, and the other, aspirin, is also widely misused with little community reaction or intervention. Aspirin tablets were introduced in the United States in 1915.

Therapeutic Uses

The principal uses of aspirin are the alleviation of pain, fever, and inflammations occurring in many types of diseases. It is nonaddicting. Aspirin is taken by mouth and is rapidly absorbed from the stomach and the small intestine. It is rapidly distributed throughout all body tissues, the highest concentrations occurring in the kidney, liver, heart, and lungs.

Aspirin is most effective in the treatment of low-intensity pains which are focused in muscles, bone, and other supporting structures of the body, and not too effective for the alleviation of pain arising from major body organs. Narcotics continue to be most effective in the treatment of severe pain.

Aspirin's second major therapeutic use derives from its ability to lower body temperature. It affects the body's "thermostat," which is probably located in the hypothalamus, and does so when a person has a fever, not when the body temperature is normal.

Lastly, its only other major effect is on inflamed tissues, in conditions such as rheumatism, arthritis, and rheumatic fever. People with rheumatic fever may be given doses of aspirin that are equivalent to 18 to 30 tablets per day.

It is estimated that more than 20 million pounds of aspirin are consumed in the United States every year. This means that about 44 million tablets are consumed every 24 hours, making aspirin the most widely used drug in the world.

Notwithstanding its extensive use, we still don't know how it works.

Consequences of Aspirin Use

There are individuals who are peculiarly sensitive to this central nervous system analgesic-depressant. One or two aspirins may result in hives, runny nose, asthma, and at times death has occurred.

The toxic results of the use and misuse of aspirin are fairly well known and well documented. Childhood poisoning is fairly common being due to the easy availability of aspirin and their ingestion in toxic doses when parents are either absent from home or too involved in other activities to observe the child's use of the drug. In 1966, more than one-third (92) of the 255 fatalities due to aspirin intoxication occurred in children under age 5. The usual fatal dose is 60 to 90 adult-size aspirin tablets; death results from the effect that aspirin has upon the metabolism of certain tissues.

There are individuals who ingest aspirin to get high. We even have a name for the signs and symptoms of this kind of intoxication: *salicylism.* The use of 15 to 20 adult tablets daily over a time may result in dizziness, ringing in the ears, diminished hearing, headache, and mental confusion. A more severe form of salicylism is called *toxic encephalopathy.* This results in mental confusion, restlessness, incoherent speech, vertigo, tremor, delirium, hallucinations, convulsions, and sometimes even coma. The psychological behavior may appear to be like alcohol intoxication and, indeed, has been called a "salicylate jag."

It appears strange that a drug whose misuse can "cause" the very psychological symptoms that concern us in other drugs is so readily accepted by our communities.

The stomach is a major focal point for reactions to aspirin. People often experience heartburn, nausea, vomiting, and general abdominal discomfort. They may develop erosions and ulcerations of the mucous membrane lining of the stomach and begin to hemorrhage from these as well. Aspirin induces an increased rate of bleeding from the gastrointestinal tract. A significant association between peptic ulcers and the use of aspirin-containing medication for tension has been noted many times.

Excessive aspirin ingestion may affect normal blood clotting and is associated with iron-deficiency anemia. It affects the kidney and can cause renal failure. When this occurs, the patient is treated with the use of an artificial kidney with the hope that the damaged kidney will eventually resume normal functioning. One form of nephritis (chronic interstitial nephritis) has been associated with the excessive use of aspirin, particularly those mixtures that contain phenacetin, which has been a major ingredient of headache preparations. A major United States manufacturer no longer advertises that its product, Anacin, contains three major ingredients, but only two—phenacetin has been dropped. The difficult thing to understand is that American manufacturers have known about other nations dropping phenacetin from their preparations for many years and have only changed their products and advertising recently. At the present time, only aspirin and caffeine are found in most American headache tablets and powders.

It is fairly obvious that aspirin causes, or is associated with, a variety of serious medical and psychiatric problems. The term *analgesic abuse* applies to the consumption of large quantities of aspirin or other analgesics without a doctor's prescription. Abusers often complain of tremors, irritability, insomnia, and other symptoms generally classified as neurotic.

Perhaps headache was the original symptom for which aspirin and other analgesic tablets were taken, but this is no longer the case. Perhaps it continues to be taken for so many conditions because it is conceived of as being innocuous and not really a drug, given its ready availability. Yet society tolerates its use to induce "relaxation," which it cannot do. In addition, the use of aspirin to prevent symptoms of the common cold is illogical. Aspirin has no effect on viruses or bacteria. Gargling with aspirin to treat a sore throat is also pharmacologically nonsensical.

Obviously, many people who use aspirin for various conditions which aspirin can't really help are feeling that they are getting the needed relief and help. This brings us back to the notion of a self-fulfilling prophecy.

What the use and misuse of aspirin point out to us is that a drug, which is being abused by many people, young and old, and which has dangerous consequences, is not considered in this light and, indeed, may never be considered this way. It becomes quite clear then that "the drug problem" is only somewhat related to what a drug does or doesn't do and a bit more related to the kinds of people using the given drug. What is perhaps of most significance is how we interpret the drug and the act of taking the drug and how we categorize the drug user. Logically, an "A-head" could be an aspirin head and not an acid head or an amphetamine head.

Caffeine

Caffeine   Coffee, caffeine
            Tea, caffeine, and theophylline
            Cocoa, caffeine, and theobromine
            Maté
            Cola drinks

When Juan Valdez gives his son coffee to drink and later comes down from the mountains of Columbia, when his distant relative *el execente* approves or disapproves of this year's coffee crop, when "high tea" is part of daily life in Great Britain, when hot cocoa is served to young children, and when the "now" generation is seduced into drinking more and more cola drinks, we don't get upset. We don't feel that the sale of these beverages is being done by drug pushers who are destroying our youth. We also don't assume that if someone becomes involved with a beverage stimulant, he will surely progress to the ingestion, injection, and sniffing of other types of stimulants. We don't feel any of these things because caffeine-based beverages have been accepted as social beverages, which are basic ingredients of our contemporary conventional rituals. That we perceive them in this manner in no way changes the fact that caffeine is a central nervous system stimulant, which is used therapeutically and which has various associated toxic effects.

History

The various caffeine-based beverages that have been in use for centuries, are classified as *xanthines,* and are chemically and structurally related to uric acid. Coffee is derived from the seeds of the *Coffea arabica,* tea from the leaves of the *Thea sinensis,* cocoa from the seeds of the *Theobroma cacao,* and cola soft beverages from the nuts of the *Cola acuminota* tree.

It is difficult to pinpoint man's first use of these substances. We do know that they were a trade commodity by the fifth century and that by the sixth century tea was part of the Buddhist-Shinto religious tea ritual in Japan. By 1559, tea had reached Europe and led to the development of the East India Company. Tea was introduced into America by 1665 through the Dutch.

Coffee was thought to have originated in Ethiopia or Abyssinia, although this is yet to be verified. Various myths have developed about its origin. One of them claims that coffee was discovered by a prior in an Arabian monastery. This story alleges that the prior became aware that goats that had eaten berries from the coffee plant were active all night instead of sleeping. This legendary prior, wanting to assure himself of remaining awake during the many hours of night, asked the shepherds to supply him with the berries in order to make an antisleep beverage.

By the eleventh century, coffee was noted in an Arabian medical text and began to be used by both Catholic monks and Moslems to keep them from dozing during religious activities.

The first known coffee house originated in Constantinople in 1554, and this soon gave rise to coffee houses in northern Europe; they reached

England during the seventeenth century. Coffee became more widely used when people learned to mix it with sugar.

The reaction to coffee was no different from the reaction to any substance that man ingests: Some were for it, and some were against it. There were many attempts to close down coffee houses and to condemn both coffee and its increasing number of drinkers. These attempts were so common that Bach was able to derive his *Coffee Cantata* from them. In this musical satire, parents were much concerned about their daughters' drinking coffee and attempted in various ways to get them to stop. They failed.

Despite the various attempts to limit the use of coffee, the use of this beverage-drug spread in an epidemiclike fashion. In the United States more than 2 billion pounds are consumed annually; more than 20 pounds for every single child and adult. In a sense, when one includes the other xanthines as well, these drugs become the most widely used mind-altering substances.

Therapeutic Uses

Caffeine, as a medication, continues to be used to treat various cardiac conditions such as acute congestive heart failure, in limiting the frequency and severity of angina pectoris, and for immediate intervention of coronary thrombosis. The therapeutic use of caffeine for these conditions has been questioned by numerous researchers and practitioners so that its contemporary medical use is often based on a strange bit of logic: The drug "may do the patient no good; it can do him no harm."

The xanthines are also used in the treatment of bronchial asthma by relaxing the smooth muscle of the bronchi, as a diuretic by increasing the production of urine, to relieve pain associated with acute biliary colic, and in the treatment of headaches including migraine. Caffeine is also used in treating cases of poisoning by central depressants such as morphine.

Caffeine is a very potent central nervous system stimulant; theophylline (from tea) is less strong; and theobromine (from cocoa) is least potent of all. Caffeine stimulates all portions of the cortex. Its effects result in rapid thinking which flows clearly, a sustained intellectual effort with an enhanced association of ideas, decreased drowsiness and fatigue with a keener appreciation of sensory stimuli and a faster reaction to them, and increased motor activity.

Tolerance is produced by the use of the xanthines, and there is no cross tolerance between the various substances in this drug family. There is no set of predictable withdrawal symptoms associated with them, although excitation of the central nervous system by large amounts of caffeine is most often followed by depression. Since large amounts of caffeine are needed for this effect, we are not sure if this occurs from the amounts of caffeine found in the average cup of coffee or tea.

Consequences of Caffeine Use

Toxic reactions can and do occur as a result of the excessive use of caffeine for most people, and even with small doses in individuals who are "allergic" to it. In animals, high doses of caffeine can result in convulsions and death due to respiratory failure. Caffeine-induced fatalities in man are highly unlikely; a person would have to drink approximately 65 cups of coffee, or 10 grams, to be fatally affected. The toxic effects that do occur are generally a result of caffeine's effect on the central nervous system and circulatory system. These toxic conditions include the following: insomnia, restlessness, excitement, mild delirium, sensory disturbances such as ringing in the ears and experiencing flashes of light, muscular tenseness and tremors, changes in heart rate, and increased respiratory and diuretic action.

The excessive use of theophylline, one of tea's basic ingredients, proves to be even more toxic than coffee (caffeine by itself). Death has been associated with its use, as have headaches, palpitations, dizziness, nausea, and fall in blood pressure.

These xanthine-induced toxic effects can occur irrespective of the way the substance gets into the body, that is, through oral, rectal, or intravenous routes of administration.

The last toxic result to be noted, chromosomal breakage, has caused much concern when related to LSD, but little concern when related to the xanthines.

It may be that this is so because all the data for LSD aren't in yet, whereas we do know that "the drinking of tea or coffee does not increase the mutation rate much above the small natural rate and so does not seem to present any significant toxic hazard in many."

One thing for sure, the label on that can of coffee, on the box of tea bags, on the tin of cocoa, or on the bottle of cola beverage never even alludes to any of this; neither does the advertising for any of these substances. One would not expect such information to be necessarily forthcoming for substances that are so widely used and accepted as part of man's social adaptation. Another interesting facet of the substance-use dilemma is that whereas most people are unaware of experiencing any stimulation from these beverages, they probably drink them in part of the stimulation. The average cup of coffee or tea contains a therapeutic dose of caffeine. Part of this unawareness may be attributed to the effect of not experiencing xanthines as drugs, and part to the variations in response to these beverages among people and for the same person at different times.

Whatever the chemical, social, psychological, and physical factors operating in relation to this family of drugs, one has to consider them as being yet another dramatic example of man's irrational behavior concerning our use and misuse of drugs.

PROJECTS

1. One can consider our relationship to the world we live in in a very structured manner. We have to learn to adapt to an external world of time, space, movement, and various degrees of structure or solidity as well as to an internal world of social, psychological, sexual, and physiological needs. Devise a chart which lists each of these areas we must adapt in and then list the various drugs you may have taken for medical or nonmedical reasons. Have these drugs enhanced your adaptation?

External adaptation	Narcotics	Sedatives	Tranquilizers	Stimulants	Psychedelics
Time					
Space					
Movement					
Structure					

Internal adaptation					
Social					
Psychological					
Sexual					
Physiological					

2. Consider whether any drugs you have ever used for medical or nonmedical reasons affect your *ability* to adapt.

3. When the nonmedical user of drugs purchases his favorite drugs, more often than not he will not really know what he is getting. This is a legitimate source of concern for our health officials. Remember back to the last few times your physician prescribed medications for you. Do you know what they were and more or less what they do? If you don't know, consider whether it would be difficult for you to ask your physician for this information. If it would, note the factors that would make it difficult to do this. Do you think that you need a drug to help you with these difficulties?

4. Act quite differently than you usually do in a small social gathering. After a while casually mention you are taking a new medication or drug, but continue acting in the same way. Consider the following issues:
   (a) How is your behavior responded to before and after your mentioning that you are taking a new medication or drug?
   (b) How many people suggest you should change the dose or stop taking the drug?
   (c) Does anyone suggest that you should see your doctor again and report the changes in behavior?

BIBLIOGRAPHY

Auerbach, R., and Rugowski, J. A., "Lysergic Acid Diethylamide: Effect on Embryos," *Science*, vol. 157, p. 1325, 1967.

Barrett, P. V. D., and Boyle, J. D., "Hippie Hepatitis: The Possible Role of Methamphetamines in Chronic Active Hepatitis," *Gastroenterology*, vol. 54, p. 1219, 1968.

Blum, R., and associates, *The Utopiates*. New York: Atherton, 1964.

——, *Society and Drugs*, vol. I. San Francisco: Jossey-Bass, 1969.

Borgatta, E. F., and Evans, R. R., eds., *Smoking, Health and Behavior*. Chicago: Aldine, 1968.

Brecher, E. M., *Licit and Illicit Drugs*. Boston: Little, Brown, 1972.

Cherubin, C., "Investigations of Tetanus in Narcotic Addicts in New York City," *International Journal of the Addictions*, vol. 2, no. 2, pp. 253–259, 1967.

——, "A Review of the Medical Complications of Narcotic Addiction," *International Journal of the Addictions*, vol. 3, no. 1, pp. 163–175, 1968.

Chopra, G. S., "Marijuana and Man," *International Journal of the Addictions*, vol. 4, no. 2, pp. 215–245, 1969.

Cohen, M., *et al.*, "Chromosomal Damage to Human Leukocytes Induced by Lysergic Acid Diethylamide," *Science*, vol. 155, p. 1417, 1967.

Coles, R., *et al.*, *Drugs and Youth*. New York: Liveright, 1970.

De Ropp, R. S., *Drugs and the Mind*. New York: Grove, 1961.

Diehl, H. S., *Tobacco and Your Health*. New York: McGraw-Hill, 1969.

Dishotsky, N. I., *et al.*, "LSD and Genetic Damage," *Science*, vol. 172, pp. 431–440, 1971.

Eddy, N. B., *et al.*, "Drug Dependence," in A. Wikler, ed., *Opiate Addiction: Psychological and Neurophysical Aspects in Relation to Clinical Problems*. Springfield, Ill.: C. C. Thomas, 1953.

Eddy, N. B., Halsbach, H., Isbell, H., and Seevers, M. H., "Drug Dependence: Its Significance and Characteristics," *Bulletin of the World Health Organization*, vol. 32, pp. 721–733, 1965.

Emboden, W., *Narcotic Plants*. New York: Macmillan, 1972.

Falek, *et al.*, "Human Chromosomes and Opiates," *Arch. Gen. Psychiatry*, vol. 27, p. 511, 1972.

Fink, P. J., Goldman, M. J., and Lyons, I., "Morning Glory Seed Psychosis," *International Journal of the Addictions*, vol. 2, no. 2, pp. 143–151, 1967.

Goodman, L. S., and Gilman, A., eds., *The Pharmacological Basis of Therapeutics*, 3rd ed. New York: Macmillan, 1965.

Griffenhagen, G. B., "A History of Drug Abuse," *Journal of the American Pharmaceutical Association*, vol. NS8, no. 1, pp. 16–28, 1968.

Guggenheim, W. Z., "Heroin: History and Pharmacology," *International Journal of the Addictions*, vol. 2, no. 2, pp. 328–330, 1967.

Helpern, M., and Rho, Y., "Deaths from Narcotism in New York City," *International Journal of the Addictions*, vol. 2, no. 1, pp. 53–84, 1967.

Hollister, L. E., *Chemical Psychosis*. Springfield, Ill.: C. C. Thomas, 1968.

Isbell, H., *et al.*, "Effects of $(-)\Delta$ 9-*Trans*-Tetrahydrocannabinol in Man," *Psychopharmacologia*, vol. 11, pp. 184–188, 1967.

Kluver, H., *Mescal and Mechanisms of Hallucinations*. Chicago: University of Chicago Press, 1968.

Leary, T., *et al.*, *The Psychedelic Experience*. New York: University Books, 1964.

Lerner, A. M., and Oerther, F. J., "Characteristics and Sequela of Paregoric Abuse," *International Journal of the Addictions*, vol. 2, no. 2, pp. 312–328, 1967.

Long, R. E., and Penna, R. P., "Drugs of Abuse," *Journal of the American Pharmaceutical Association*, vol. NS8, no. 1, pp. 12–16, 1968.

Louria, D. B., "Medical Problems Associated with Heroin Use," *International Journal of the Addictions*, vol. 2, no. 2, pp. 241–252, 1967.

Marin, P., and Cohen, A. Y., *Understanding Drug Use.* New York: Harper and Row, 1971.

Masters, R. E. L., and Houston, J., *The Varieties of Psychedelic Experience.* New York: Holt, Rinehart & Winston, 1966.

Mechoulam, R., and Gaoni, Y., "A Total Synthesis of dl-Δ'-Tetrahydrocannabinol, the Active Constituent of Hashish," *Journal of the American Chemical Society*, vol. 87, pp. 3273–3275, 1965.

Mikuriya, T. H., "Physical, Mental and Moral Effects of Marihuana: The Indian Hemp Drugs Commission Report," *International Journal of the Addictions*, vol. 3, no. 2, pp. 253–270, 1968.

Nelson, A. S., "Medical Problems Associated with Addiction to Opoid Drugs," *International Journal of the Addictions*, vol. 1, no. 1, pp. 50–61, 1966.

Nowlis, H. H., *Drugs on the College Campus: A Guide for College Administrators.* Detroit: National Association of Student Personnel Administrators, 1967.

Shearer, R. J., ed., *Manual on Alcoholism.* Chicago: American Medical Association, 1967.

Siler, J. F., *et al.*, "Marihuana Smoking in Panama," *Military Surgeon*, vol. 73, no. 5, pp. 269–280, 1933.

Soloman, D., ed., *The Marihuana Papers.* New York: Bobbs-Merrill, 1966.

Taylor, N., *Nature's Dangerous Gifts.* New York: Dell, 1963.

Weil, A. T., Zinberg, N. E., and Nelsen, J., "Clinical and Psychological Effects of Marijuana in Man," *Science*, vol. 162, pp. 1234–1242, Dec. 13, 1968.

Weyer, E. M., *Alcohol and Food in Health and Disease.* New York: Academy of Sciences, 1966.

Wolstenholme, C. E. W., and Knight, J., eds., *Hashish: Its Chemistry and Pharmacology.* Boston: Little, Brown, 1965.

CHAPTER 3

Drug Users: Who Are They?

the desire to take medicine is perhaps the greatest feature which distinguishes man from other animals. . .

Sir William Osler

Who are the drug addicts, dope fiends, drug abusers, recreational drug users, or whatever other term we use to describe the kind of people who use drugs in a way that concerns and disturbs us?

It is important to come to terms with the guidelines we use to decide that someone is an actual or potential drug-problem person. Is he generally young? Does he only use certain drugs? Does his overt behavior dramatize his drug use? Does he have long hair and wear dirty clothes? Is he passive or aggressive? Is he a family man or a social loner? These questions come to mind when we consider who a drug user is.

Table 3-1 will help us take a close look at our own stereotypes regarding the drug user. One can take any two drugs, one being legal and the other illegal, or one being used for legitimately approved reasons and the other for reasons generally considered to be illegitimate. Knowledge gained from any of the media, the grapevine, or any other source should then be used to complete this stereotype test. The major goal is to determine if the terms we use to describe various drug users have a human counterpart, or whether they are terms describing nonexisting people, which may indeed be potentially destructive.

One could, for example, use cigarettes and marijuana in this task—two easily available drugs which have both adherents and attackers. Using the various categories of characteristics that are listed, we could proceed to note the specific information that we "know" about each type of drug user.

91

BACKGROUND CHARACTERISTICS

1. *Age:*   Note the age range, from the youngest to the oldest user that you know about.
2. *Sex:*   Note whether there are more male or female users, or whether the sex of the user is of no consequence.
3. *Race:*   Note whether there are more white or nonwhite users, or whether the race of the user is irrelevant.
4. *Religion:*   Note whether the user has a particular religious involvement or not, or whether this appears unrelated to specific drug use.
5. *Intelligence:*   Note whether the user generally falls within your notion of the average IQ range, is above or below it, or whether IQ appears unrelated to specific drug use.
6. *Socioeconomic Class:*   Note whether the drug user is most often from the middle class, above or below it, or whether it doesn't seem to matter.

ADAPTATIONAL CHARACTERISTICS

7. *Physical Health:*   Note whether the user's physical health seems to be impaired or not, not concerning yourself for the moment whether the person's health status is directly related to drug use or not. Is the specific drug user healthy or not?
8. *Mental Health:*   Note whether the user's mental health is normal or abnormal, using your own definition of normality.
9. *Marital Status:*   If the specific drug user is married, note whether the marriage is stable or unstable (using your own definition of stability); if the specific type of drug user is single, divorced, or widowed, or whether marital status is not relevant (NR) to specific drug taking.
10. *Educational Status:*   Note the range of formal schooling—no formal schooling or lowest grade achieved to highest graduate level that you know about.
11. *Vocational Status:*   Note whether the drug user is employed or not employed, considering homemaking a full-time job.
12. *Legal Status:*   Note whether the drug user has come to the attention of law enforcement agencies or not, regardless of the reasons for this.
13. *Sexual Status:*   Note whether the drug user manifests normal or abnormal sexual interests and behavior, using your own criteria for normal.
14. *Leisure-Time Status:*   Note whether the drug user is involved or

uninvolved in leisure-time activities. Does he have hobbies, activities, interests or does he experience much empty time?

15. *Community-Participation Status:* Note whether the drug user is involved or uninvolved in community activities. Can his energies and skills be mobilized for and by his community or not?

DRUG ORIENTATION

16. *Drug-Use Pattern:* Note whether the drug user is a single-substance user (a drug gourmet) or whether he is a multiple-drug user.
17. *Meaning of Drug Use:* Note two things—whether the drug user knows why he is using his specific drug and whether it is essentially for pleasure or escapism.
18. *Manner of Drug Use:* Note whether the drug user appears to be committed to only one way of using his drug or whether he uses various techniques.

Table 3-1 Characteristics of drug users.

Background Characteristics	Cigarettes	Marijuana
Age		
Sex		
Race		
Religion		
Intelligence		
Socioeconomic class		
Adaptational Characteristics		
Physical health		
Mental health		
Marital status		
Educational status		
Vocational status		
Legal status		
Sexual status		
Leisure-time status		
Community-participation status		
Drug Orientation		
Drug-use pattern		
Meaning of drug use		
Manner of drug use		

Now that you have done a research project with a sample of one, yourself, can you distinguish in any meaningful way between one type of drug user and another? Most likely you won't be able to. If this is so, we have to question whether the little energy, time, and money available to effectively cope with drug misuse isn't being diminished by the labeling and sign-and-symptom syndrome. If you feel that you can clearly distinguish between types of drug users, can you communicate this effectively to others so that they can do the same? This is highly doubtful.

It would appear that the image of the drug addict and the signs and symptoms by which we spot him are clearer in the various media than in real life.

On September 20, 1970, the *Boston Herald* published an article, "Is There a Drug Addict in Your Home?" The article asked: "Is your son or daughter on drugs? The symptoms outlined here may help you tell." With dramatic drawings, the following drug-use signs were listed:

From clear, talkative, expressive . . . . To silent, confined, withdrawn
From vital, healthy, energetic . . . . To nervous, uptight, restless
From open, friendly, trusting . . . . To suspicious, antagonistic, alienated
From cheerful, optimistic, pleasant . . . . To cynical, pessimistic, moody
From poised, confident, self-assured . . . . To oppressed, tormented, persecuted
From helpful, attentive, dependable . . . . To vague, forgetful, disinterested
From eager, active, enthusiastic . . . . To passive, apathetic, hopeless

If we limit these terms to the teen-ager, the "negative" terms are simply part and parcel of adolescent adaptation. Whatever the reasons for mood swings—whether they are sexually rooted, identity crisis based, or what have you—adolescence is a period of physical, psychological, and social turbulence. Going beyond this one may also note an apparent greater incidence of the "negative" behaviors, rather than the positive ones, in the adult population as well. Regardless of political, social, and economic viewpoint, the last few years have given most people a lot to be confused, nervous, suspicious, pessimistic, passive, and antagonistic about.

The major issue is not what the signs and symptoms of drug abuse are. Rather, when a person's behavior changes either dramatically or even slowly over time, with no apparent reason for the change, one should attempt to assess both the reasons for the change and the meaning of the change. Drug use may or may not be associated with the new behavior.

One of the problems of labeling someone's behavior as being drug related is that this process tends to limit the options that seem to be available. For example, take the statements:

"My son is unhappy."
"My son is unhappy and using drugs."

The first sentence implies the possibility of further evaluation to determine what is wrong that can be righted, what is wrong that can't be righted now or ever, and who is to do what. The second sentence tends to explain the unhappiness in terms of drug use. If nothing else, this tends to block further evaluation as well as define and often limit who can and should be doing whatever it is that should be done around a particular set of events.

The only sensible answer to the question "Who is a drug addict or drug misuser?" is "Potentially and actually anyone." This statement is made because we have no substantiative evidence that can be used to categorize the drug user as a type who is quite distinct from his nondrug-using peer.

On a practical level, this means that if someone is involved with drug use as a life style, it will be little help to that person or those wanting to help him to categorize him as a drug user. In fact, it might be a hindrance because some resources and services may not be available to someone with a drug label.

Categories are generally developed by noting similarities among members of a given category and dissimilarities among the categories. The field of drug misuse has its fair share of categories. The term *addict* is one such category. This term is rarely used in an accurate sense by either professional or lay people. Even if its use was limited to excessive use over time of opiates and barbiturates, we still would generally leave alcohol out, and perhaps of more importance, the term would tell us little about the individual. From the community's point of view, the *type of drug taken* is generally not a significant discriminating criterion.

Drug users, on the other hand, often appear to be using types of drugs as discriminators. *Cokie, A-head, acid head, pot head,* and *junkie* are categories based on the type of drug used. Whatever common-sense validity these terms may have had in the past, the fact that more and more people are using more than one type of drug, simultaneously or sequentially, substantially limits the present value of such terms. Again, we must raise the issue—do all or most pot heads behave the same way?

Frequency of drug use does not appear to be an important basis for categorizing drug users for the nondrug-using public. Society generally tags people as drug "addicts" if the drug use is self-prescribed and taken for relief of other than physical pain, not how often a specific drug is taken. Users do utilize this factor for labeling. *Tasting* describes trying a drug once or twice out of curiosity or peer group pressure. *Situational user* describes the person who uses a drug when the occasion arises, but won't actively seek out the drug or the circumstance. *Greezy addict* is someone who takes anything available whenever it's available. Another frequency-based term is *chippying*, which usually refers to less-than-daily use.

Knowing the *amount of a drug* taken by a person within a given time period may help in the development of specific treatment plus knowing when particular medicines are to be used or not used, or it may help theoretically to distinguish between physical and psychological dependency, but it is useless as a classifier. To the general community, it is again the fact that a person is using drugs, not how much he is using that counts. On the other hand, in the drug-using community, minor use of drugs has an almost negative connotation. The street term *coke habit* is an example of this. It relates to the phenomena of drug users, most often heroin users, who imbibe a lot of soft drinks daily. The implication is that the person is drinking more coca cola or other beverages than he is taking drugs, while he may pass himself off as a very active drug user. The amount of drugs taken often comes up when the drug user either wants to minimize his behavior as a face-saving mechanism to the professional or when he exaggerates his actual drug use in order to attempt to receive higher doses of medication.

Many intriguing assumptions have been made about the meaning of the *age of initial drug use.* Again, it is interesting to note that not too much attention is paid to the initial age of the drug user's involvement with tobacco products, alcoholic beverages, excessive consumption of food, or to the use of medicines when perhaps they were not needed. The term *primary addict* has been suggested to describe the type of drug user who begins his use during his adolescence or even earlier. The assumption underlying this category is that since he has not had the necessary opportunity to develop the techniques necessary to adapt to life, which in a sense adolescence is all about, the likelihood of his giving up drugs or a drug-oriented life style is limited. Not having the tools to cope with social, psychological, and educational-vocational problems, and an insufficient reservoir of success experiences to fall back upon, he enters the world of drug-related answers to life's tests and traumas more and more. His adult relative is called the *secondary addict.* It is assumed that for this type of drug user, initiation into the drug scene was either due to self-medication or through a physician in response to an acute and stressful situation. A loved one died or was severely injured or left; a particular goal or style of life was interrupted, if not ended, and the person sought temporary relief.

It is assumed that since such an individual has had sufficient experience to develop the skills needed to adequately cope with life, he can be helped to effectively utilize them again or develop new and appropriate ones. The general goal with such an individual is to remind him that he has amply demonstrated in the past his ability to adapt effectively, that the present crisis is a temporary one, and that he can and indeed must return to nondrug alternatives to the problems of living. In a sense, the differentiating factor between the primary and secondary addict may not simply be their age of initial drug use or the presence or absence of adaptational skills, but rather the meaning that each of these theoretical types attributes to the drug being used.

The *length of time of drug use*, which very often is related to age of initial use, has been considered by one sociologist as being the key factor that may lead to terminating drug use. A statistical study of known or visible narcotic addicts who have been treated in public institutions or incarcerated has tended to point up very few records of such individuals who are beyond their mid-thirties. The notion of *burning out* assumes that the street addict tires of the full-time occupation of being an addict and retires by maturing out of it. The efforts and possible pleasures become more than outweighed by the many inherent difficulties. Whatever merit this notion may have for any of us, it must be remembered that this theory at best holds for the visible narcotic addict. Many young and older American drug misusers have been able to adapt to their drug-oriented life. When money is easily available, when certain drugs may be shared, when medical and psychological needs are taken care of confidentially in the office of the private practitioner, and when status barriers protect the person from the law, there may be little impetus to mature out. The physician or nurse who is addicted to Demerol, the executive who is addicted to barbiturates or dependent upon amphetamines for that daily lift, the artist, writer, actor, or musician who is smoking marijuana or using other hallucinogens—all lead lives that generally are so different from the stereotyped junkie that they simply don't have to burn out.

The manner of supporting one's drug use is often suggested as being another classifier of types of drug misusers. Although the community at large may continue to perceive "the addict" as being engaged in solely criminal activities to support his habit, it is obvious that this greatly depends upon the type and amount of drugs being used. The locale for this criterion also makes a great difference. When we move from the slum or inner city to the suburb or university, we may begin to call the person "hippie," "college user," or "drug abuser," even though the source of support is the same. If, however, the person sells drugs, almost irrespective of locale or social status, he gets put into the pile tagged "pushers." It may turn out, when the research data are in, that being a pusher is related to very specific characteristics, although at the present time not enough is known about this.

This raises another interesting classifier: The actual *source of categorization* which is often overlooked in this entire labeling process.

As we observe someone's behavior, we may at times describe it as being a problem or at other times as being a phase. The behavior is the same, but the meaning attributed to it significantly changes.

From the community's point of view, the use of various substances needs only two categories to include all its members, active and ex or recovered. One of the continuing destructive myths in our culture is "once an addict or alcoholic, always an addict or alcoholic."

This belief has indeed become part of the creed of a number of self-help groups. Drug misusers who identify with and are part of such programs as Alcoholics' Anonymous, Narcotics' Anonymous, Synanon and its various spin-off groups (Daytop Lodge, Phoenix House) actively use the notion if not the phrase "I am a ..." as an integral part of their rehabilitation. It may be that this label permits someone some sense of identity if he was confused about who he is. Certainly this is not a new phenomenon. Many of us during our maturation have been overwhelmed by conditions of ambiguity and may sell ourselves short by settling for any solution, any role, any answer, rather than putting forth the effort needed to achieve an appropriate solution. It may also be that substance misusers have latched on to the myth of "once ... then always ..." because they know that society at large is still unwilling to believe that they can change in any intrinsic manner.

Other categories that are in use are based upon the effects of a specific drug, the actual manner of drug taking, and the drug orientation of the person.

The *pain-prone addict* is a type of individual who becomes addicted as a consequence of trying to alleviate severely experienced pain, the physical source of which can't be determined. These people use drugs, not for the high, not for recreation, not because of peer group pressure, but to relieve pain. They are most often treated by physicians and often undergo surgery which upon completion has had little effect in minimizing their pain. It remains difficult to assess whether their pain is physiological or psychic, but since they are perceived and treated as patients and, not as junkies, they are often prescribed pain killers which are addicting. Although they are often concerned about becoming addicted, many achieve this status because of their use of addicting drugs over time.

The term *speed freak* is an attempt to describe another individual who is affected in certain ways by a specific drug. Similarly, individuals combating fatigue by drug use may be yet another such category.

It would appear that most drug users partake of or are committed to drug use because of actual or assumed psychological benefits. Dr. Joel Fort has, in this sense, created a most appropriate label—MADS—mood-altering drugs. Intensifying or diminishing a particular mood, lessening worries or keeping them at a distance, inducing sleep or preventing it, venting dreams and/or hallucinations or neutralizing them are often primary factors for both initial and continued use of drugs.

These *mood alterers* may be further divided into other categories. One group will consist of individuals who use drugs regularly, but who rarely, if ever, develop tolerance or withdrawal symptoms. They are generally the recreational users. They use drugs for relaxation and for the kick they claim to get. Generally they prevent themselves from getting addicted or too dependent upon a given drug by imposing rigorous controls on their drug use. More often than not, this group was made up of medical and paramedical people in the past. Newer members of this group now include individuals from many other walks of life. A related category consists of individuals who, although seeking psychological relief and pleasure, do not appear to be concerned about addiction; they may experience tolerance and withdrawal symptoms.

The manner of drug use has been a traditional differentiator of drug users. In Chapter 1, we were able to see how smoking opium became instrumental in labeling drug use generally as being deviant.

The term *needle addict* is another dramatic example. It has been suggested that some drug users get their kicks from injecting themselves. What is in the hypodermic appears to be almost irrelevant to the act. Such a category might help explain the recent injecting of peanut butter or mayonnaise. For this group of drug users, the needle experience may be more an orgasmic sexual one than a drug experience. As with many other theories which on the surface appear to be logical, there is little hard data to sustain this one.

The *source of the drug* is another important ingredient in the drug scene. For many, an emotional involvement, often called "transference," is built up with the drug dispenser, rather than the drug or the paraphernalia used. There are, for example, many instances in the drug culture where a person is afraid to inject himself and depends upon a specific person to inject him. Similarly, some drug users have others buy or "cop" drugs for them. The issue of a relationship is not new in drug use. Patients often get better even when the medicine is a *placebo* prescribed by a doctor they trust. Indeed, relationship-based drug use may be a useful handle or opening through which to initiate relationship-based nondrug alternatives.

In an era in which it becomes increasingly difficult for someone, particularly a younger person, to publicly acknowledge he hasn't at least tried one of "those" drugs, it should not surprise us that there are nonusing drug addicts. They may label themselves because they are part of a group or want to become part of a group for whom drug taking has high-status value. In a sense they are hooked on the principle of drug taking, even though they may never really use various drugs in the way that they describe. Such feigned drug use may also permit them to feel more in control of their life situation because the conventional world may make few conventional demands upon them.

Almost anyone can create a typology of drug users, but to date none is really helpful as a guideline for community planning or for the family experiencing their drug problem. It should be increasingly difficult for us to view the drug-using individual as a homogeneous entity—"the addict."

This group has become the symbol of addiction, for both the lay and professional population. In my own arbitrary categorization, I choose to tag this type of drug user as a *visible or street user.*

This individual is less hidden from the public than other groups are. His source of support is most often criminal, and he uses drugs for psychological rather than physiological reasons. His status is such that few conventional citizens will cover up either his general or drug-related behavior. The probability of arrests and incarcerations is high for him. His treatment is likely to occur in public facilities and not behind the confidentiality of the private practitioner's doors. Although his psychological and intellectual functioning may differ little from the other kinds of drug users, he may differ quite a bit socially, educationally, vocationally, financially, as well as in legal status. Since he is so available, most research uses him as a subject, but then somehow forgets that data derived from this group are not easily extrapolated to other groups.

In practical terms, this means that the plans suggested for intervening in the life of an addict or drug misuser as described by TV, radio, newspapers, the sheriff, district attorney, or other professional who is not tuned in to the heterogeneity of today's drug users may be inappropriate for the needs of those we are most concerned about.

CHARACTERISTICS AND BEHAVIOR OF DRUG USERS

Trying to make sense out of the stereotypes we hold and the many "types" of drug users we are warned about is no easy task. Making things even less clear is the professional and lay literature that tends to provide profiles of the average addict—whoever he is.

Profile	*Problems Posed by Profile*
1. Adolescents and young adults make up much of the addict population.	1. Who then are the barbiturate and alcohol misusers?
2. There are six to seven times as many male addicts as there are female addicts.	2. Is there a propensity for one sex to turn to drug-related alternatives for living and not the other sex? Is there a sex preference for types of drugs? Are females more likely to be part of the invisible drug-using population?
3. Addiction is a more significant problem among nonwhites than among whites.	3. Although drug use is apparently associated with an ethnic and social group, are its various consequences for the individual, his group, and society at large more serious for certain groups than other groups?
4. Addiction is a more significant problem among Christians than among non-Christians.	4. Does a particular religion hold out less adaptive maneuvers to present-day living or does it offer greater potential for an invisible drug-using status?
5. Addiction is less likely to result in stable marriages or marriages at all.	5. Does the contemporary institution of marriage, to the same person for many years because of increased longevity of life, serve as a meaningful alternative to drug misuse for a given person? Can the couple who stay together use drugs together or not?
6. Addicts are more likely to be members of lower socioeconomic classes.	6. Does sustaining this myth in anyway change the pattern of drug misuse in the nation and does it offer solace or any other reasonable help to individuals of other socioeconomic classes, as they face up to drug misuse in their own homes and communities?
7. The addict's IQ is likely to be within the average range, particularly when the level of schooling is considered.	7. Can a person's ability to intellectually and intelligently understand his drug behavior be sufficient to get him to consider as well as to attempt a life style which is not based upon a drug orientation, or only a minimal one?

8. The lack of intact families is the norm, with a stable significant male often missing from a household, which is dominated by a seductive mother implicitly reinforcing drug use by unconsciously manipulating her child to act out her own needs.

8. With less and less people able to develop the much needed tolerance for close, intimate family life, what changes are needed in family life to effectively compete with the less intimate demands of drug-induced and drug-related living?

This profile has the immediate consequence of leading many of us to believe that the addict or drug misuser is someone alien to us, that the drug problem is someone else's. Is this really so?

A few years ago, many of us might have truly felt that there was much information about drugs and drug users that we were ignorant of, and, thus, we might have settled for the stereotypes. Now, towns of only a few hundred have their drug users. Now, whether we like to admit it or not, we know that the picture of the addict, based upon the observable "visible" addict, is only a small part of the story and may offer only partial insights to our own drug misusers.

In the American classic on drug use, Terry and Pellens (1971) indicate that at the beginning of this century, with half of our present population, approximately one million of our citizens, many of them women, middle class and upper class, were either addicted or were using addicting drugs. Since there wasn't any great concern about drug use then, the personality characteristics of the users weren't written about. One can only assume that these drug users were often family people living conventional lives.

Given the apparent reoccurrence of drug use in the white middle class these last few years both among the young and their adult models, it is important to note that the profile has not changed from the post World War II stereotype. We find it hard to call our own "junkies" and to treat them in the traditional public institutions which house America's junkies. While many of us can understand, appreciate, and perhaps even continue to condone the invisible drug user, his invisibility makes it unnecessarily difficult to intervene effectively with him and for him. That such an individual is generally protected from the consequences of the law and treated privately by practitioners who are often untrained to meet the needs of the person has serious consequences for everyone concerned. Perhaps the most serious consequence for the invisible user is that he never really has the opportunity to adapt to one of the rules or guidelines of reality: If you play, you must be prepared to pay.

The status of being a visible drug user has a similar consequence. This type of user is generally unable to support his drug use through conven-

tional means and often resorts to criminal behavior which most often results in removing him from the mainstream of life through enforced rehabilitation or incarceration. Having been removed from the active conventional norms of society may mean greater difficulty in learning how to
integrate oneself to them. Secondly, this person, while experiencing
"playing and paying," often feels he's paying for a lot of other people as
well, resents this, and continues to behave in the same antisocial way in
what can be described as an impotent rage. He doesn't learn that he can't
get away with his behavior because once he's been tagged as a visible
user, he's as marked as Cain was. Someone has to pay for drug use if
society condemns it, and he's the most likely candidate.

It is the visible addict's behavior that generally serves as the rationale
for tagging him. His average achieved educational level is the eighth
grade. His work history is poor if existent at all, and the skills he brings to
the marketplace are minimal. He is thought to have no close friends, relating superficially at best, and involving himself primarily with other drug
users. Most of his time is spent in drug-related activities, and whatever
free time he does have is filled with action-oriented rather than intellectual or cognitive activities. The hobbies and interests that many of us
pride ourselves in are thought not to be his cup of tea. In a society which
utilizes the present to plan for the future, he is seen as being stuck to the
present, not having learned from the past or planning in any positive sense
for his or his community's future. The addict's life is noted as being antisocial prior to drug use, with an acceleration of such behavior subsequent to drug use. Drug use for this person results in a variety of medical
ailments as well as other related conditions which necessitate intervention
by many agencies and institutions. It's as if he created a mess which conventional society feels it is left to pick up. Lastly, although we acknowledge that the visible addict can have any kind of personality structure, he
is generally noted as suffering from personality disturbances, particularly
of the passive-aggressive type.

This type of profile results in an unfortunate consequence for literally
everyone. It pushes us into believing that the drug user must fit in
somewhere along a criminal-sick gradient. To accept this notion seriously
prevents us from considering the interaction that exists among the drug
user, his drugs of choice, and his own community aside from society at
large. This profile serves to reinforce our existing predisposition to assume that the user is both the center of the contemporary drug problem as
well as the source of solution for it. Lastly, it can only serve to confuse us
if we somehow don't perceive the ones we are concerned about as being

criminals or sick. What do we do then—wait until the first criminal acts occur or until obvious sick behavior stares us in the face? Profiles are for reading about—perhaps studying. People are for caring about, loving, enjoying, and helping when help is needed.

A series of questions, which each of us must somehow begin to answer, is raised by this kind of profile as well:

1. As a person grows, what are the processes and interactions that affect his behavior? In what way? And how and when can concerned people step in?
2. What factors in a person's specific community, as well as his more total society, tend to reinforce and/or inhibit turning to drugs rather than to people?
3. Which of the physical, psychological, and social dysfunctions that have been related to drug use are actually a function of the drug's effects, the manner in which the drug is used, and the style of life of the drug user? And who is best suited to effectively intervene with each of these factors?
4. What are the costs of maintaining a drug user's invisibility for the user, his "people," and his community?

It is obvious by now that the use of terms like "addict," "dope fiend," or other such denigrating terms has more to do with moral positions than with descriptions of people that can guide our own plans and decisions. Most of the drug-misuser categories from the literature offered in this chapter are slanted toward the "sickness" rationale. They tend to overlook the complexities inherent in being a drug misuser and the handles, the nondrug options, that are available for society to rechannel life styles.

The following descriptions of two visible or street heroin addicts are offered to reinforce this book's position that the drug user as a specific type of person doesn't exist in the real world. Rather, we have different people using the same or different drugs in various ways even during their own drug-oriented life style.

The drug addicts whose lives are presented in this section were either being medically detoxified or had completed detoxification at the time of their interviews. The interviews took from one day to five days to complete. The patients were asked to participate in the interview as part of a research project, which was to be used to train professionals and others working in the area of drug addiction. It was clearly spelled out to them that their participation would in no way directly aid them in their present stay in a New York City drug-addict program.

The interviews were open-ended, focusing upon conventional and illegal behavior as well as involvement with addicts and the drug culture. Phases in the person's life were pinpointed in terms of changes relating to nonmedical drug use (beginning of drug use, changes in types or patterns of drug use, attempts at detoxification or other treatments, drug-related arrests, periods of abstinence from drugs, etc.).

The major reason that street addicts are being presented rather than other types is that they have traditionally been the most stereotyped. If we can begin to see the variations in life styles for this group, then surely we shall be better able to react appropriately to the drug user we are concerned about rather than to his stereotype.

Each narcotic addict's life is presented initially in an outline followed by a narrative and then a summary. As one reads them, the thought may come to mind that what is or isn't emphasized is due to arbitrariness. Indeed, that is probably so. What is important, however, is that given any different and arbitrary focus would still result in an antistereotype.

JOE

Characteristics:

Joe is a 33-year-old black single male. He is the only child from a divorced family and was raised as a Protestant. He completed one year of high school and received an honorable discharge from the army.

Joe's family background is such that one could easily assume that the drug-addict stereotype fits. His parents, both of whom had difficulties with alcohol, were separated when he was a child. His father died when Joe was 12 years old, and his mother remarried one year later. He was really raised by his grandmother, and he traditionally turns to her when he needs help. It is his grandmother, not his mother, who always bails him out of jail.

Joe's mother is only 13 years older than he is and since the age of 29 has attempted suicide numerous times. Joe is much upset by this as well as his mother's continuing promiscuity. His major source of conscious family conflict relates to his mother. He continues to feel that his mother doesn't care about him. He can't remember any conflicts with his father and acknowledges that his stepfather does appear to be concerned about him. Joe has been arrested 28 times.

If we were to stop at this point, we might easily conclude that all the ingredients for drug abuse are present. There is an unstable family, living in Harlem, using a drug, alcohol, as an adaptation to life. Prior to drug use,

Joe was a member and then vice president of a street gang. One of Joe's cousins is a visible heroin addict.

Phases of Substance Use:

Phase I (to age 20): No narcotic drug was used during this period.

Phase II (age 20–23): Joe began smoking marijuana occasionally. He sniffed heroin for two months and then began mainlining it. Arrested for possession of narcotics twice, he kicked cold turkey in jail and returned to drug use the first day he was back in the community. During this phase, Joe began his bootlegging activities.

Phase III (age 23–25): Joe continued to mainline heroin and smoke marijuana occasionally. His 15 arrests were for bootlegging activities. Four of these times he kicked cold turkey in jail, always returning to heroin on his first day out of jail.

Phase IV (age 25–28): In addition to mainlining heroin and continued occasional use of marijuana, Joe began to drink wine daily. He was arrested three times for possession of narcotics, selling narcotics, and bootlegging.

Phase V (age 28–33): Daily wine drinking and occasional marijuana smoking continued. Joe began skinpopping. He felt he did not have veins left for mainlining. His three arrests were identical to the three in the previous phase.

Phase VI (age 33–   ): Joe continued to skinpop heroin and occasionally smoke marijuana. He began to use Seconal and continued to drink heavily. During this phase he was arrested twice for attempted burglary and once for violating the Sullivan Act.

Narrative:

Phase I (to age 20)

Family: During this phase Joe lived with his mother, father, or stepfather in Harlem. He remembers his mother and father having a poor relationship, although he got along fine with his father. He never remembers having a good relationship with his mother, and he rarely listened to her. He was eight years old when his parents separated. One result of this separation was his being left alone very often. He began to turn more and more to his grandmother whom he claims he always listened to. When he was 13, his mother remarried. His stepfather attempted to get close to him. He helped Joe join the YMCA and taught him to swim. His mother began heavy drinking as well as a series of suicide attempts during his adolescence.

School: Prior to his becoming a gang member at age 13, Joe was an honor student in school, math and history being his major interests. School did not continue to hold his interest. There were a number of reasons for this: It was not a challenge to his native ability; the school was in a sense the "turf" of a rival gang so that he was afraid of getting hurt there; there was glamour in street life and little of it in the Harlem school he attended; there were insufficient academic reinforcements coming from home. Joe began truanting at 14 and quit school at age 16.

Work: Joe took his first job at age 14, as an evening elevator relief operator. This lasted for one year. At 17 he enlisted in the U.S. Army and was honorably discharged three years later as a corporal in the Quartermaster Commissary. Joe has often regretted not making the army his career.

Friends: During this predrug phase, Joe always remembered having friends. Prior to his gang membership, age 13, he described them as "squares," afterward as "slicksters."

Girls didn't play a role in Joe's life until age 14, and this finally occurred only because they were part of gang life. Joe never went steady during this phase.

Leisure-Time Activities: During this phase Joe was involved in two main kinds of leisure activities: athletics and antisocial behavior. Prior to age 16, he swam at the YMCA and swam and boxed for the NYC Park Department. After age 16, he no longer responded to the 9 p.m. curfew and spent most of his time with his gang. A year later he joined the army.

Use of Community Resources: The YMCA, the NYC Park Department, and his church were the community resources he turned to.

Illegal Activities: The two sources for illegal activities during this phase were truanting, age 14, and membership in a street gang. Joe remembers that: "I felt more important when I joined the gang; I got more recognition."

Addict Involvement: Although Joe wasn't using drugs during this phase, some of his fellow gang members were, and they were an important part of his life space. He felt friendly toward them and often gave them money when he was on furlough from the army.

Support of Substance Use: Joe had no habit to support during this phase.

Life-Style Summary: Joe's style of life for his first 20 years would be assessed as being moderate to high in conventional behavior, low to moderate in illegal behavior, and low in drug-oriented behavior. Joe was still part of the square world—although he surely was testing it as well as being tested by it.

Phase II (age 20–23)

Family: Joe returned to live with his mother in a "lousy" part of Harlem after being discharged from the army. Their relationship was as bad as ever. Drinking as heavily as before, she often blamed her suicide attempts on him. Joe resumed his close relationship with his grandmother, visiting her as often as he could. His mother was suspicious about his behavior and began accusing him of drug use. He denied this, and apparently both made believe that drug use wasn't a problem.

School: Joe commenced being trained in TV repair work under the GI Bill, but quit after six months. He was using drugs: "All I did was nod all day in school."

Work: Using drugs, Joe worked at two jobs for one week each during this period: as a carpenter's helper and in an automobile parts department.

Friends: During this phase Joe's motto was: "When you got money, you got friends." He felt he had many acquaintances, but no friends. His acquaintances were drug users, some worked legitimately, and some were involved in policy numbers. Joe was still girl shy. He had two minor involvements with female addicts which ended with a narcotic sale arrest for one and a hospitalized detoxification for the other. Joe was looking for a "square girl" to stabilize his life. "I was lonely. I felt shy with girls. I didn't know what to do with them." During this phase he had nothing to do with nondrug-using females.

Leisure-Time Activities: Narcotic-centered activities as well as criminal activities took up most of Joe's time. Socializing was generally described as "partying" with other drug users.

Use of Community Resources: The only resource Joe used was his GI Bill sponsored TV repair course. He did not return to the YMCA.

Illegal Activities: His major activity was bootlegging in Harlem. The tone of his other activities was illegal, however, in that all of his relationships, male and female, were with narcotic addicts or marijuana users. He was arrested twice for possession of drugs and served 60 days for each charge in jail.

Support of Substance Use: With heroin use playing a major role and marijuana use a minor role, Joe supported his drug appetites through his bootlegging activities. For the two weeks he worked, his salary also went to support his drug use.

Life-Style Summary: During this three-year period, Joe's conventional behavior was low-moderate to low; his illegal behavior was moderate to high-moderate; and his drug-oriented behavior was low-moderate. Joe had entered the drug scene. From a common-sense perception, he was beginning to live the life of a junkie. From an equally "as you well know" perception "once an addict always an addict," his life should vary only in terms of deeper involvement as a junkie.

Phase III (age 23–25):

Joe still lived with his mother in the same slum in Harlem. He no longer denied his drug use to her, and according to Joe she "gave him the business" daily about his drug behavior. In a sense, drug use tied them together, since he experienced her arguments as concern and attention— the first she had ever shown him. His relationship with his grandmother remained close. Whenever he ran short of money, grandmother, knowing of Joe's drug habit, would give him money.

School: Joe didn't attend any type of school during this phase.

Work: Joe didn't have any legitimate jobs during this phase.

Friends: Joe began to isolate himself from his peers more and more. Not only did he continue to feel that he had no friends, he also dropped almost all of his acquaintances. Getting high and supporting his drug habit was on almost full-time occupation. During this phase he had two significant heterosexual relationships. The first one Joe described as a "square," who was similar to his mother. Elaine knew of his drug use, argued with him constantly about it, while she herself began getting seriously involved with drinking. Joe left Elaine after one year. Soon after, he met Mary, who he described as an occasional user: She "dipped and dabbled" in drugs and the drug world. Mary's casual drug use changed after Joe began seeing her. "Soon after we met, I got her hooked." The relationship was terminated quite abruptly by Joe at the end of this phase. Joe was arrested on a possession of narcotics charge. Thinking she was helping him, Mary claimed that the drugs were hers. In return for his, Mary asked Joe to pick her up at the House of Detention. "I didn't, so we broke up" is Joe's terse description of how he ended a relationship with a female who, in her own way, showed concern about him.

Leisure-Time Activities: Drug use and drug-oriented behavior and the games he played with his mother, Elaine, and Mary left almost no time for any sustained leisure-time behavior.

Use of Community Resources: Joe did not turn to any community agencies or representatives during this phase.

Illegal Activities: During these three years, Joe continued to be actively engaged in bootlegging. He was arrested 15 times for this, being fined 11 times and jailed 4 times. He was occasionally a runner for policy numbers, having been given a 30-day suspended sentence during this phase.

Addict Involvement: The only people Joe knew at this time were addicts. He spent as little time as he had to with them, although his life necessitated his being with them daily.

Support of Substance Use: Joe supported his daily heroin use and occasional marijuana use by bootlegging and with money given him by his grandmother.

Life-Style Summary: Joe's life declined in conventionality to a low level of conventional behavior, increased to being high in illegal behavior, and his drug-oriented behavior was low. In a sense, if he wasn't using heroin, he would be indistinguishable from the many Americans who are involved in small-time crime and who are and feel fairly isolated from both deviant and conventional patterns of life. Joe's life for this three-year period was that of being pretty much a loner who used drugs.

Phase IV (Age 25–28)

Family: At age 25 Joe moved out of his mother's apartment. He went to live with his grandmother a few blocks away. Joe claimed his mother was "bugging me too much." He consciously resented her hypocrisy. "She was going on binges every two weeks and was on my back because of my drug habit." Grandmother remained his sole tie with the conventional world. She continued to help him support his drug habit.

School: Joe did not attend school during this period of time.

Work: Joe continued not to work at any legitimate jobs during this phase.

Friends: Joe increased his interpersonal isolation. He reinforced this by being completely uninvolved with friends.

Leisure-Time Activities: Joe's reaction to drug life, being a loner, resulted in no leisure-time activities.

Use of Community Resources: Having begun to drink wine quite heavily, Joe was hospitalized at age 26 for D.T.'s. He did not turn to any other community agencies or representatives, nor did he follow through on posthospital treatment for his newly acquired drinking problem.

Illegal Activities: Joe continued with his bootlegging and now began to sell narcotics as well. He was arrested once for selling drugs. The charges were dismissed after he spent two months in jail.

Addict Involvement: Joe's description of this is terse and to the point. Aside from selling drugs to addicts, "I spent just enough time to get high when I wasn't pushing drugs."

Support of Substance Use: In addition to the support of a daily mainline heroin habit and occasional marijuana use, Joe now needed a little more money to support his half gallon to a gallon of daily wine consumption. His illegal activities sufficed him, and when he ran short, there was always grandmother.

Life-Style Summary: Joe's life essentially remained the same as it had been during the last phase. His conventional life style was low; his illegal behavior was high; and his drug-oriented behavior was low. Joe was more involved in criminal behavior, had broadened his drug appetites while remaining at a distance from other drug users, and turned less and less to the world of people to meet both his legitimate and illegitimate needs.

Phase V (Age 28–33)

Family: Continuing to live with his grandmother, he now resumed seeing his mother more often. Joe began to feel that his mother was beginning both to understand and accept him as a person. Although arguements over his drug use continued, they were far less frequent than before.

School: Joe continued to remain uninvolved from anything resembling school.

Work: Legitimate work was still for "squares."

Friends: Interpersonal isolation continued. As for girls: "I didn't go with any girls. The ones I wanted I couldn't get, and I had a low opinion of other girls."

Leisure-Time Activities: There were none.

Use of Community Resources: There were none.

Illegal Behavior: More time and energy were put into this area. Joe stopped bootlegging, but continued selling drugs, and added robberies to his life style. He served 30 days in jail for bootlegging and was given 3 years' probation for possession of narcotics, contingent upon his being treated at the U.S. Public Health Service Hospital in Lexington, Kentucky.

Addict Involvement: Although Joe continued to feel distant from addicts, he spent more time with them. When he was not selling drugs to them or getting high with them, they were his partners in robberies.

Support of Substance Use: Joe's drug appetites were entirely supported by his criminal activities. "My grandmother no longer gave me money because she didn't have any to give." His drinking had intensified and at age 29 was skinpopping heroin. "I had no veins left for mainlining." Marijuana use remained an occasional habit.

Life-Style Summary: Joe's life remained low in its conventional aspects, became increasingly more criminally oriented, and his drug-oriented behavior was now low to moderate.

Phase VI (Age 33–)

Family: Joe's relationship with his mother deteriorated. He saw her less and less and felt more convinced than ever that the only person he could count on was his grandmother, with whom he continued to live.

School: Joe didn't go.

Work: Legitimate work continued to be out of Joe's life style.

Friends: Joe was as isolated as ever.

Leisure-Time Activities: There were none.

Use of Community Resources: Joe continued not to turn to any agency or institutional representative for help.

Illegal Activities: Pushing drugs and robberies remained Joe's two illegal pursuits. He was arrested once for carrying a knife in his pocket. The charge was dismissed. He was also arrested twice for attempted robbery, but the charges were dismissed when the "victims" didn't appear in court.

Addict Involvement: Joe began to isolate himself from addicts again.

Support of Substance Use: Joe continued to support his daily skin-popping, daily wine drinking, and occasional marijuana use by his own illegal behavior. His drug appetite now included Seconals, which he used as a "booster" to extend his heroin high.

Life-Style Summary: Joe's behavior continued to be low in the conventional areas, high in illegal manifestations, and reverted to being low in drug orientation.

Summation: Joe's life went through a number of phases. It decreased from predrug moderate-to-high conventionality to an almost constant level of low conventional behavior subsequent to drug use. His low-to-moderate involvement in illegal or antisocial behavior prior to drug use became one of increasingly greater involvement subsequent to drug use. His involvement with addicts remained essentially minimal both prior to and subsequent to his drug use.

Joe has been diagnosed as being psychotic. He is also a multiple-substance user. He has been detoxified 19 times for his heroin habit: 13 times medically and 6 times in jail without medication. Seven of his hospitalizations were ordered by the courts. Arrested 28 times, but incarcerated 6 times, he has always returned to his various drugs the first day out. In a sense drugs were the least of Joe's problems.

Aside from his relationship with his grandmother, all his relationships with females were conflict ridden, and those with men were transitory. He remained at a distance from people, generally relating to them as objects. After losing interest in school and dropping out after one year of high school, he was never again to return. He was only involved in work prior to his drug use; afterward he just dabbled at it for two weeks. Even prior to his drug use, conventional leisure-time activities were not an important part of Joe's life. Joe's antisocial behavior, initiated as an adolescent gang member, became increasingly more criminal with time.

Both as a youngster and for a three-year period in the U.S. Army, Joe indicated a desire and willingness to be part of the conventional world of adaptation. The conventional world with its various representatives appeared to wait for Joe to reaffirm his commitment to them and for him to reach out. In the process of testing Joe, the community lost whatever energy and talent Joe could have contributed and, in a sense, reinforced his initial psychological needs for keeping at a distance.

TONY

Characteristics:

Tony is a 28-year-old white Italian single male. He is the youngest of three children from an intact family and was raised as a Protestant. He completed one and one-half years of high school.

Tony's family would not, at first glance, be considered a breeding ground for a drug addict. He remembers getting along well with Sam, his older brother, and Mary, his older sister. They were six and three years older than he. He remembers little about his father, a hard-working truck driver who died of a heart attack when Tony was six years old. Like Joe, Tony felt that his mother was not too sensitive to his needs, and thus he spent a good deal of time in the streets of Greenwich Village—his immediate community. Tony was the only substance user in his family.

Tony has been arrested eight times. Prior to drug use, he was a member of a semistructured neighborhood street group.

Phases of Substance Use:

Phase I (to age 15): No narcotic drug was used during this period.

Phase II (age 15–18): Tony began weekend smoking of marijuana at age 15. A year later he began sniffing heroin. He continued sniffing it for nine months and then skinpopped for one year. Tony was neither arrested nor detoxified during this period, and he became actively involved in criminality.

Phase III (age 18–23): Tony began mainlining heroin. He experienced all of his eight arrests during this phase, kicking cold turkey in jail seven times. He always returned to heroin the first day back in the community.

Phase IV (age 23–26): Tony continued mainlining heroin and began to use Doriden. He was arrested twice for violation of parole. On one charge he was reinstated on parole; for the other one he served one and one-half years in prison. The latter resulted in his kicking cold turkey in jail once.

Phase V (age 26–   ): Tony's pattern of drug use changed markedly. He switched to Doriden, using heroin to counteract the sleepy effect, and then began using Dilaudid. Tony was detoxified nine times during this period: six times medically and three times cold turkey. Each time he returned to drugs as soon as he was in the community. He was arrested three times for violation of parole, twice going to jail, and once being sent for treatment to the Federal Hospital at Lexington, Kentucky.

Narrative:

Phase I (to age 15)

Family: During this predrug phase, Tony lived with his mother, father, brother, and sister in a four-room apartment in Greenwich Village. His father died when Tony was six years old, and he remembers very little about him. During this entire period, as he remembers it, he got along well with his siblings, but poorly with his mother. Part of the problem which he was unable to clearly comprehend, even as an adult, was that his mother spent most of her time and energy with her own seven siblings, and Tony felt left out. He described it as: "There was a lot going on at home, and I was sort of the maverick of the family." His reaction to his feeling of rejection was to spend little time at home. Whether it was the cause or the effect, Tony had little family supervision or guidance.

School: Tony remembers always being a poor student. He defends this by suggesting that school was unable to catch his interests or motivate him. At age 14 he began truanting. Little was done about this. A few months later, he got the school to react. He started a fire in a classroom wastepaper basket. He was immediately sent for psychiatric observation to Bellevue Hospital, where he remained for one month. He returned to school—but was not followed up for any psychiatric intervention.

Work: Tony had not begun to work yet.

Friends: Tony had a very active social life with male friends whom he saw daily. He shyed away from girls, feeling that he "couldn't compete with other fellows for girls."

Leisure-Time Activities: For most of this phase, Tony's leisure time was taken up "by hanging around with the guys." He was not part of any kind of formal group, neighborhood, athletic, church, or after school. From age 14 on, when he joined a loosely structured street gang, part of his leisure included "breaking into stores for the fun of it."

Use of Community Resources: Tony's only involvement with a community agency was with a psychiatric hospital for one month of observation.

Illegal Behavior: In a sense, during this phase, Tony's behavior is best described as delinquent, not illegal or criminal. Truanting, meaningless burglarizing of stores, and infrequent "minor wars with guys around the corner" set the tone for Tony's testing of conventional society.

Addict Involvement: Tony neither had any addict friends, nor did he know any addict peers.

Support of Substance Use: Tony had no drug habit to support during this phase.

Life-Style Summary: Tony's style of life for his first 15 years can be categorized as low to moderate in conventional behavior, low in illegal behavior, with no involvement in drug-oriented behavior.

Tony's ties were to the street. There was evidently not only safety and security in the street, but also ongoing interest and concern by his peers there. Conventional society responded to Tony only when he dramatically pushed it to do so, and then he was sent to be psychiatrically labeled with no one following up on this. We must keep in mind, however, that the street and the school of hard knocks have traditionally educated many of conventional society's leaders. The point is that the first 15 years of Tony's life give us no clues to whether he would turn to drugs and if so, why.

Phase II (age 15–18)

Family: Family life began to be experienced as being more of a pressure for Tony. There was steady tension in the household. He still managed to get along with his siblings, but he now felt that his mother didn't understand him at all. "She felt that all I had to do was to get a job, and everything would be okay." Tony spent even less time at home.

School: From Tony's perspective, society did its first good deed—having reached age 16, he was allowed to drop out of school.

Work: Tony went through the motions of trying work. Using heroin, he held five jobs as an unskilled laborer, none for more than two weeks.

Friends: His previous neighborhood friends had turned to drugs. He maintained his friendship with them, and they were his only friends. It was as if the slogan "friends that turn on together, stay together" was being acted out. His relationships and his activities with these old friends had as a focal point drug use.

Leisure-Time Activities: There was no leisure time for Tony and certainly no conventional kind of social life. Time was spent by Tony supporting his drug use through illegal activities and just "rapping" with his addict friends.

Use of Community Resources: Tony didn't reach out for any kind of help to any person or group, and no one reached out to him.

Illegal Behavior: In his predrug adaptation, Tony's antisocial activities were primarily done for kicks—what many parents euphemistically call going through "a phase," or "boys will be boys." After his initiation into the drug scene, Tony became increasingly involved in criminal behavior to support his drug use. He began shoplifting, breaking into cars, stealing, and, toward the end of the phase, selling narcotics. He managed to avoid being arrested.

Addict Involvement: Tony spent all of his time with addicts, who were really his old-time neighborhood friends. He described feeling close to them and felt that their friendship was important to him.

Support of Substance Use: When Tony began smoking marijuana on weekends at age 15, he only needed about one dollar a week. This he got from his family. A year later when he began using heroin, he supported its use basically through his criminal activities. When he ran short of money, he initiated a collusary relationship with his mother. "When I screamed enough, my mother gave money; I imagine she knew what it was for."

Life-Style Summary: Tony's life subsequent to his use of drugs changed markedly. His conventional adaptation decreased to a low status, involvement in his illegal behavior and drug-oriented behavior became high.

Many of us may feel that Tony had entered the drug scene because of two factors: the wrong crowd and poor parental supervision. His behavior fit the traditional stereotyping—moving away from conventional modes of living to drug-centered, criminal ones. From a stereotyped perspective, Tony's life should continue to worsen.

Phase III (age 18–23)

Family: Tony continued to live at home. His sister became the main support of the family since his brother married. What overt tension there was generally consisted of arguments at home with his mother. Tony attributes this to his family beginning to give him up "for hopeless." He no longer cared about maintaining any kind of a relationship with his sister or brother. Tony took on the role of being a boarder—he only slept at home.

School: Tony did not return to any kind of schooling or training.

Work: Tony did not work at any legitimate job during this phase.

Friends: Tony began to isolate himself from his friends more and more. His rationale was: "You know how junkie friends are—they beat their friends, and I'd beat them." For the first time he began dating girls, but in a rather limited way. He would only date when he had enough drugs available for his needs and enough extra money "to buy clothes and go out."

Leisure-Time Activities: Infrequent dating and occasional "rap sessions" with other addicts were his only leisure-time activities. Oddly enough, Tony didn't feel that these should be included as leisure activities. One possible interpretation of this is that he felt so isolated from others that even when he was with others he felt alone.

Use of Community Resources: Tony remained at a distance from available community agencies and representatives.

Illegal Behavior: During this phase Tony continued to sell drugs. He also began to serve as an intermediary between other addicts and other drug pushers. He was arrested eight times, seven times for possession of drugs and once for breaking and entering a car. As a result of these arrests, he served five 60-day and one 4-month sentence in jail and spent 2 years in prison of a one and one-half to 5-year sentence. More than half of this five-year phase was spent in jail or prison. His family's giving up on him was, in great part, a result of his many arrests.

Addict Involvement: Although Tony spent time primarily with addicts, he was less involved with them than before. In the past they had been his friends. Now he didn't consider any of them as friends and trusted none of them.

Support of Substance Use: Tony began mainlining heroin, a habit he generally supported through his criminal activities. Those times he ran short of money he would cajole his mother and, at times, his sister to help him support his drug use.

Life-Style Summary: During this phase Tony's mode of living can best be described as continuing to be low in conventional adaptations, decreasing to being low in nondrug-oriented illegal behavior, and high in drug-oriented behavior. The major focus of his life during this period was drugs: using drugs, selling drugs, and getting drugs for other addicts. In a sense, had Tony not been using drugs, he might still have been a social casuality for the community, but he would not have affected us through criminal behavior. This is quite different from Joe's life style, which was primarily a criminal one.

The difference is not a minor one. Joe would come to society's attention because of his nondrug criminal behavior (bootlegging, burglary, policy numbers), but during this phase of his life, Tony would come to our attention because he had taken on the role of being a street junkie whose life revolved around drugs in a variety of ways.

Phase IV (age 23–26)

Family: Tony continued to be a boarder at home. His relationship with his entire family deteriorated even further. His married brother had as little to do with him as was possible. Tony felt that his drug behavior seriously interfered with his sister's social life. He felt that the major reason she had gotten married toward the end of this phase, when he was 25, and not earlier, was because "she stayed home to support the family." There was little doubt in Tony's mind that his "family had given me up for hopeless." His mother's single tie with him remained that of nagging him to get a job with the hope that full-time legitimate work would remove him from the drug scene.

School: Tony continued to stay away from developing any academic or vocational skills.

Work: During a short period of abstinence, Tony worked at an unskilled factory job. He quit this job as soon as he returned to drug use.

Friends: His peer relationships became even more isolated than before. Tony describes this in very succinct terms: "Guys moved away from the neighborhood; guys took overdoses, and because of the many debts I owed." Tony also stopped the dating pattern he had initiated in his previous phase. He met one girl, Nan, whom he fell in love with. He knew that Nan was a bisexual and a nondrug user. Tony also learned that he was the first man she ever permitted herself to care about. Tony felt that they were both very similar and, thus, could lean upon each other and help each other out. "We both had vices which we were trying to stop." He made Nan pregnant and planned to marry her. The plans never came to fruition. One night Tony saw Nan in a Lesbian bar. He felt betrayed. "I lost my head and beat her up. She was the first person I ever cared for." A few days later Nan left Tony. "She told me she had lost the kid because of the beating."

Leisure-Time Activities: For the length of their relationship, being with Nan and a few other people was Tony's major leisure-time involvement during this phase. He would not go to parties or dances. Tony tended to keep his socializing at a distance from others.

Use of Community Resources: For the first time in his life, Tony felt impelled to seek out help. He went to two New York City drug-addict rehabilitation programs, the Village Aid Society and Greenwich House, both of which were in the area he lived in. Protecting himself from anticipated rejection, he describes his reaching out in the following way: "I didn't ask for help. I went to kill time, but hoped I'd get help. I was just going there. I didn't feel like a member."

Illegal Behavior: Tony's illegal behavior changed radically to being less drug oriented and more criminal. He stopped selling drugs and making connections for other addicts. He shoplifted occasionally and took on the role of being a fence for stolen merchandise. He was arrested twice for violation of parole. Once he got away with it in a sense that his sentence was being reinstated on parole. The second time he was sent back to prison for one and one-half years. Thus, half of this phase was spent incarcerated.

Addict Involvement: Working on the assumption that addicts "are the only people you could spend time with when you're using drugs," Tony's social life included Nan and addicts.

Support of Substance Use: Tony decreased his mainlining of heroin and began to use Doriden. He began to use both drugs in sequence. "I took heroin only to take the sleepiness away from me." Lowering his heroin use meant that less money was needed to support his habit. His occasional shoplifting and fencing, plus infrequent funds supplied by his mother and sister, were sufficient to take care of his drug appetites.

Life-Style Summary: Tony's life style remained low in conventional adaptation, increased to moderate in illegal behavior, and decreased to moderate to high in drug-oriented behavior. While remaining at a distance from the conventional mainstream of life, he became increasingly more involved in criminal life and less so in the drug scene.

Phase V (age 26–   )

Family: Tony continued living at home with his mother. His married brother and sister saw little of him. An aunt and uncle showed interest in him to the extent that they often gave him money for drugs. Tony's relationship with his mother remained poor and inconsistent. He described his family's response to him in the following way: "They feel hopeless about me. They pray for me but nothing else."

School: Tony didn't return to any kind of schooling and had no plans to do so.

Work: Tony didn't work at any legitimate job.

Friends: He felt more isolated than ever before even though he claimed he now had one addict friend. "Addicts won't accept me" was the way Tony described his peer status. His heterosexual relationships had worsened significantly. Not only did he not go with a particular girl during this phase, but his experience with Nan had apparently resulted in his staying at a greater distance from girls. The only girls in his life at this time were addicts.

Leisure-Time Activities: Tony did not participate in any kind of leisure-time activities, nor was he involved in any particular interests or hobbies. Aside from his drug-oriented behavior, he filled his time with "rapping." Tony felt that one of the effects of Doriden was that it made it easier for him to talk to others.

Use of Community Resources: Tony did not reach out to anyone or any group during this phase.

Illegal Behavior: Although Tony continued shoplifting and fencing, he noted that during this period of time he was less involved in criminal behavior than at any time before since he became actively involved in the drug scene. During this period he was again picked up for violation of parole three times. He was returned to prison twice for short periods of time. When incarceration apparently had little effect on changing either his illegal or drug pattern of behavior, Tony's parole officer finally insisted that he volunteer to go to the U.S. Public Health Service Hospital at Lexington, Kentucky. Tony went through the motions of following through on this strong suggestion. He signed out after eight days and returned to New York and drugs again.

Addict Involvement: Tony continued seeing other addicts daily and spoke of one addict being a friend of his. The other addicts whom he knew and saw he did not consider being friends or even acquaintances of his.

Support of Substance Use: Tony's use of heroin was now minimal. Most often when he did use heroin, it was along with Doriden, to counteract its sleepy effects. Tony now used 12 Doridens a day. At times he also used Dilaudid. He had become a barbiturate addict. One of the immediate results of switching his drug-using status was that he needed less money to support his drug habit. As a consequence, Tony found that he didn't have to engage too much in illegal activities. Another seemingly ironic consequence of his change in drug appetites was Tony's ability to expand his collusary relationships with his family. "Most of my habit was supported by money coming from my mother and my aunt and uncle. They knew what the money was for."

Life-Style Summary: Tony's adaptation during this phase was low in conventional and illegal behavior and low-moderate in drug-oriented behavior.

Summation: Tony's adaptation to life has gone through a number of changes in style. His predrug use, low-moderate conventional adaptation decreased to a constant low level. His delinquent and antisocial street behavior prior to drug use became translated into criminal-illegal behavior for his first two years of drug use and has decreased ever since. This is particularly so since his drug of choice has become Doriden, for which he needs approximately $3 a day. Tony's involvement with addicts and the addict subculture has likewise changed. When his drug of choice was heroin, he used it with other addicts, stayed with them, rapped with them and considered them as friends. As he began to use heroin less and switched over to a barbiturate habit, he has felt more and more isolated from addicts and their ways even though he has essentially spent the same amount of time with them.

At no time prior to or subsequent to his drug use has Tony had any major illness. He has been diagnosed as a sociopath, an antisocial individual. He was detoxified 17 times—7 times medically, 9 times cold turkey in jail, and once cold turkey in a hospital. The kinds of medical detoxifications are interesting to note. Once he was administratively discharged after 4 hours because in his own words "I caused a disturbance." He never returned to that hospital, which was the largest program in New York City. "I was blackballed; I couldn't get in no more." Five times he signed out against medical advice, and only once did he fully complete an institution's detoxification program. For Tony it made little difference if his detoxifications were made more comfortable or less comfortable—he always returned to drugs on his first day in the community. His eight arrests similarly appeared to have little rehabilitative effect on him, since he was picked up for violation of parole five times. Nevertheless, and this is the really important issue, Tony's life was not uniform, and his adaptations were not homogeneous.

Notwithstanding the conflicts that were present in his family relationships, he always saw to it that there was some family member he could turn to. Whatever personal meaning it had for him, he also saw to it that the four-room apartment in Greenwich Village remained home base for him. When he dropped out of school, he never returned again. His work history, however, differed. Although it was a poor one in that he never stayed at a job more than a few weeks, during two of his phases he did attempt to work at legitimate jobs. Although conventional leisure-time activities were never an integral part of his life, being with others and rapping with them were. His "loner" style of living, unfortunately, continued to make him feel that he was isolated from others—even when he was with them.

We can only assume that his first and only predrug involvement with a community agency, when he was sent to a psychiatric hospital at age 14, did little to reinforce his desire to turn to others for help. Nevertheless, after eight years of drug use, he reached out voluntarily to two treatment centers in his community. His patterns of illegal behavior, drug use, involvement with addicts, and support of his drug use significantly changed over time. Oddly enough, changes were better for society and worse for him personally. As a barbiturate addict, he attacked society less, but put himself in greater physical jeopardy.

Joe and Tony, their families and friends, their choice of drugs and patterns of drug use, and the ways in which they tested society are but two examples of the various kinds of people who enter the drug scene and reside there in their own particular ways.

Case histories could have been given of suburban "hidden addicts," and the same conclusions would have been drawn. Whether the drug user is white or any shade of off-white, young or old, hidden or visible, a governor's son, a publisher's nephew, a psychiatrist's daughter, or an unskilled laborer's child or spouse, their styles of life are not a particular kind, nor are they necessarily either the result of or the cause of drug use.

Each of the known, as well as the many unknown, factors that are related to the use of drugs relate to one another in a kaleidoscopic manner. This means that we cannot accurately predict what will happen to the drug user when we intervene or choose not to intervene in his life. Monday morning quarterbacking has no predictive planning value for all concerned. The one thing we can be more certain of is that the extent to which we dehumanize the drug user by sterile labeling and stereotyped responses to his needs and demands, the less likely it is for the necessary and possible changes to come about.

The reason for this is really quite obvious. When both the perceiver and the perceived, we the socially approved drug users and they the socially disapproved drug users, attempt to adapt to the stereotypes we hold of each other, rather than to who and what we are, there is less room for maneuverability. With less maneuverability and flexibility available, one shouldn't expect too many meaningful results in changed behavior.

THEORIES EXPLAINING THE USE AND MISUSE OF DRUGS

Knowing what drugs do, learning the so-called signs and symptoms of drug use and the behavior and characteristics of specific types of drug users still leave us at a loss as to why so many people turn to drugs as a temporary or full-time way of living. There is the prevalent notion in many areas of human functioning that if we only understand why someone does something, it will be easier to either reinforce or inhibit or prevent that behavior. This kind of common-sense logic is questionable as we shall see from a review of the theories that have been offered to explain drug use.

There are three major types of theories which are used to explain both drug use as well as the particular attempts to diminish it. They are based on: (1) genetic or physiological causes, (2) psychological or learning causes, and (3) environmental or social causes.

Genetic-Physiological-Biochemical Theories

These theories, often associated with biochemical factors as well, assume that the person has been born with some kind of deficiency. Once he initiates drug use, for whatever immediate reason, the process of drug dependency is most likely to continue unless concerted daily efforts are made to counter this inevitable process.

One is more likely to hear this kind of theory in the world of alcoholism than in the other drug arenas. The analogy often used by the person who is in trouble with alcohol is that his condition is similar to that of the diabetic. His system reacts to alcohol differently than that of the social drinker or the abstainer. Unfortunately, there is little real evidence to support this kind of statement. That we may discover the needed evidence in the future is of little help to him or the theory now. What this person is really saying, in his own way, is that he knows that having been stigmatized as an alcoholic, it will be very difficult to make and hold on to positive changes in his life. In a sense, society will continue to test him and not trust his new behavior. "Once an alcoholic, always an alcoholic" is an example of this. Turning to a genetic-physiological biochemical-deficit theory permits the drug user to say in an unthreatening way to society: "Get off my back; drug use is neither my fault nor your fault. If I was born with a club foot, or a cleft palate, or rheumatic fever you would be either sympathetic or, at the very least, nonpunitive toward me."

In a sense, this is probably so. The parent who gives birth to a child with a physical deformity may be very upset, but rarely feels guilt ridden. On the other hand, if psychological or other antisocial behaviors develop, the parent very often feels "where did I go wrong" internally, but reacts to the child as if the behavior is entirely the child's own fault.

In a dynamic sense, the genetic-physiological theories permit a truce to develop for all the parties concerned.

From the community's perspective, this theory does not help us understand why most people who begin using or experimenting with drugs don't continue to do so. Obviously, if we chose to, we could pervert the theory and logic by asserting that those who continue to use drugs are the ones for whom the theory works. A more important criticism of this theory is that it in no way helps explain why some drug users stop their drug habits permanently or for long periods of time. Lastly, since most contemporary drug use is of the multiple-drug variety rather than the single-drug type, this theory is of little help in explaining this phenomenon, especially when the drugs used are often pharmacologically unrelated.

A serious consequence of this theory is that solutions to problems based on genetic-physiological deficiencies or observations are more likely to be chemically based than people oriented. We give insulin to the diabetic, not verbal therapy. Likewise, many people advocating methadone treatment for the addict assume it will correct his chemical difficulties which are a major source of his drug problem.

Returning to the two case studies, we notice that it would be useless to rely on this theory to explain Joe's use of heroin, marijuana, and wine (whereas his parents stuck to alcohol), or Tony's being the only drug user in his family with his preference switching from heroin to Doriden.

Psychological-Learning Theories

Psychological and learning-based theories of drug misuse assume that the person has learned to adapt to life by depending upon drugs rather than people. The personality-development theories assume the existence of an "addict personality." The model of this type of theory is based on Freudian notions of psychosexual development. Retrospectively, one discovers in "the addict" that early in his life he has been psychologically hurt or traumatized so that he either never chances moving beyond the oral level of development or he regresses to it. From then on his needs are essentially oral ones. Many professionals often interchange the terms addict personality and oral personality.

Again there is inadequate evidence to substantiate this theory. A major difficulty with this theory is that it can't stand on its own assumptions. Freudian notions of personality development assume that each level of psychosexual development has associated with it particular psychiatric diagnoses. Yet if the same psychiatric examination is administered to a group of drug users, who even use the same drug in the same way, we shall discover that psychiatrically they encompass the entire spectrum of known diagnoses.

It may very well be that the essence of diagnosing a person as an "addict personality" does not lie in the science of classifying, but rather in the moral interpretations of available behavior at a given point in time. When Freud and his colleagues met in gay Vienna and sought to understand and systematize human behavior, their perceptions of the drug user may have been colored by the kinds of people that they treated and observed as well as the drugs available at that time. Barbiturates were relatively new; amphetamines had yet to be discovered; the hallucinogenic alphabet was alien to them; and tranquilizers were still many decades away. Opiates and cocaine were available, but they were not being injected for recreation. They were ingested. Alcohol was, in all likelihood, the prime drug that was being used and misused. It was imbibed moderately and immoderately. Thus, the theory of the addict and oral-dependent personality was based on interpreting the behavior of people using a variety of substances in all conceivable, and sometimes inconceivable, ways.

One serious consequence of relying on a specific personality theory to explain drug use in general or a particular person's drug use is that one is forced to assume that psychopathology is at the root of it and that the person should be in some type of verbal therapy to correct his personality. Chemotherapy is generally offered to such a person most often, because he has not gotten better in his previous word-therapy or because he is felt to be too sick to benefit from it at the time. Treatment will be fully discussed in Chapter 8, but it is important to once again note that not everyone who uses drugs is sick, not everyone who is healthy is abstinent, not everyone who is sick turns to drugs, not everyone who uses drugs is effectively helped by the available treatments, and that psychological sickness and health are basically a function of cultural norms.

The most often used learning theory for explaining drug use is based on the concept of conditioning. It is a notion that many of us have learned or heard about. If we do something long enough, that behavior will become part of our daily adaptation because we tend to reinforce it by doing it and strengthen it even more when there are no forces present to inhibit or weaken it. Conditioning theories of drug abuse assume that the person becomes a drug user and maintains this role by becoming conditioned to both internal and external stimuli that are related to this kind of behavior.

Professionals working with the drug user have many anecdotal tales to support this theory. The most often used one is that of the narcotic addict who has left his home for treatment at the Federal Hospital in Lexington, Kentucky. He remains there for six months and attends his individual and group therapy sessions. He studies so as to receive his high school equivalency diploma and even begins to learn a trade. He appears to be motivated and sincere and proves this in part by not partaking of any of the drugs that are illicitly available at the hospital, as they are in any institution. His day for discharge arrives, and he says his good-byes. This time he is not returning. He feels this; the staff feels this; and his fellow addict patients feel this. He gets on the train and makes mental notes of what he plans to do in order to straighten out his life. Everything appears to be fine until he senses he is almost home. He gets off the train or bus still convinced he will change and make it this time—and takes his first shot of heroin.

What we have to remember is that just as the map is not the territory, the anecdote is not the theory nor an explanation of behavior.

There is insufficient empirical evidence to understand how internal and external stimuli affect a pattern of drug use which may vary in terms of the types of drug used, the manner of their use, the meanings attributed to their use, and the patterns of abstinence and readdiction. Given that we really don't understand the process of drug use or drug action, nor the variations of drug users, it would appear to be of little advantage to seriously commit ourselves to a conditioning or any other learning theory to explain a person's drug use. For example, what do we make of the fact that most individuals who first use heroin feel nauseous or even vomit, and yet many go on to use it again and again? What stimuli are present to reinforce this negatively experienced event? What stimuli are present for the new marijuana user who still hasn't learned to experience those pleasant feelings his friends have told him about, but nevertheless he continues to smoke marijuana.

Although we may continue to believe that drug use is learned and, therefore, can be unlearned, it is not the same thing as committing ourselves to a particular learning theory. The learning theories have to stand on their own with hard data or be sufficiently modified to be manageable and useful.

At the present time, conditioning theories are the theoretical foundations for the use of specific drugs called narcotic antagonists. These will be discussed in the chapter focusing on treatment. At this point, it is sufficient to know that narcotic antagonists prevent a person from experiencing a euphoric feeling or a "high" when using the narcotic of his choice. The assumption is that if such a person continues to use narcotics while being treated this way and experiences no "high," his habit will be inhibited more and more until it ceases completely, because there is no reinforcement present to strengthen it.

In theory this makes sense. However, since people often do things that give them little or no pleasure or satisfaction, the theory doesn't work out as well in practice.

Social-Environmental Theories

These theories are, in a sense, the newest ones being offered. They suggest that a certain environment or something about a particular environment is more conducive to drug use than another locale would be.

"Retreatism" is one variety of these theories. It assumes, in a sense, that long before Head Start and Sesame Street developed the cognitive abilities of what was once called the ghetto child, he recognized that his ability to leave his oppressive environment was almost nil. As a result of an internal monologue, he turned to drugs. "I live in and on a drug heap. I can only move from one such heap to another—never away from them. The only movement available to me is horizontal—not vertical or diagonal and out. Therefore, I am going to move inward and away, and neutralize the impact of my immediate surroundings on me by turning to drugs. I will escape and retreat through chemistry—because people don't care about me." Such an orientation can also be termed as *anomic* or rootless. The person has either never developed roots to his environment and other significant ones in it, or has severed his roots. He wants out, and the theoreticians suggest that drugs are his way out.

The evidence for this kind of theory is once again anecdotal. When the theory was developed, many families had drug-using members. It is important to remember, however, that it was the rare family in which all of its members were drug users. The "fact" that the environment was experienced as being oppressive by a family didn't result in all of them turning to drugs. This can't be emphasized enough. When enough exceptions are made to a theory, the result is an intellectual goulash and not a usable tool. The next obvious difficulty for this theory is its inability to explain both contemporary middle-class white suburban drug use and traditional middle- and upper-class urban drug use.

One obvious consequence of leaning toward environmental or *anomic* theories of drug use is that society would have to change radically so that the sources of anomie could be alleviated. If this were the case, verbal and chemotherapeutic techniques, hospital beds and outpatient facilities, and changes in drug laws, whatever their nature, would have low priority. Rather, social or community organization and social action would be the modalities of choice. From the perspective of social change, the bulldozer would be of more help than therapy.

The reality is that we have no evidence that drug use or a commitment to a drug-oriented life is associated with particular surroundings or that it is socially contagious. Drug users continue to be part of every segment of society in the United States as well as throughout the world.

In all likelihood, environmental theory is our euphemistic way of holding on to the dangerous belief that the drug use is a problem for someone other than ourselves or the people we choose to concern ourselves with. History doesn't substantiate this myopic view. The hallucinogens of Haight-Ashbury, the heroin of Hong Kong, the amphetamine epidemics of Tokyo and Stockholm are recent examples of mankind's drug use. The contagion, if that is the correct term, is not related to a drug and its action or to a person selling or sharing his drugs, but, rather, to a society's permitting and reinforcing drug solutions to people's problems. In that sense any given environment or society may be considered to be one huge drug pusher.

A person's external environment is a significant factor in his decision to enter into or remain in the drug scene to the extent that it offers him a variety of behavioral options or alternatives to engage in, both internally or externally. In this sense we may assume that when drugs are readily available, when they are presented as panaceas rather than tools with given limitations, and when nondrug options to living are not experienced as being available, attainable, or functional, many more people will try drugs.

One can look at this in another light. When ongoing community traditions or individual traditional roles are seriously challenged or changed, and (1) the community or person is unprepared for the change; (2) new traditions and roles have not been fully developed; (3) new traditions and roles have not taken root; (4) various drugs, some acceptable and others not, are readily available, then drug use is turned to as one option to counter the unsettling ambiguity of the moment.

The tradition of a low incidence of alcoholism among the Jews and Chinese has changed in the United States. More and more members of both of these groups, having left the security of their own traditions and not fully replaced them with equally satisfying ones, have identified with the tradition of American drinking and have gone beyond it.

The American Indian, separated more and more from his traditions, relegated to the status of second-rate citizen, and not having created new, meaningful, and viable traditions for himself, has increasingly turned to alcohol.

The recreational user of LSD in Haight-Ashbury, expressing love, criticizing the hypocrisy of the establishment and its traditions, but unable to develop meaningful traditions for himself, dropped out of society and turned to the needle, amphetamines, and heroin.

Many more examples could be given. The point is that drug use as a tradition can and does continue when other traditions aren't a sufficient challenge to it or fulfilling of the person's many needs.

Using drugs or not using them is a complicated decision that individuals ultimately make themselves against a background of many personal and social factors. We still don't understand how the person and why the person decides never to use drugs or to use them. We are beginning to understand how we can help a person decide to stop his drug use and stay off drugs. We enable him to substitute nondrug behavior for drug behavior that has meaning for him.

After many stereotypes, theories, and two case histories, it is frustrating to have to conclude that there is no such person as a drug addict or that we really don't know why someone starts, stops, or never turns to drugs. Actually, when we view drug use as part of life, the fact that we don't fully understand it may not be so frustrating. There is much about life that we don't understand—and that doesn't stop us from living it. That the theories aren't answers or don't supply sufficient guidelines for action in this area should not be viewed with alarm. It's what we do or don't do because of the theories that should be our focus. Theories are useful when they enlighten. While the research is going on, we still have to respond and react to others in our own human fumbling fashion.

Intervening in drug use doesn't mean saving a drug addict. It does mean relating to a particular person we are concerned about, love, or are required to help, and challenging his drug orientation with nondrug alternatives that are acceptable and meaningful to him and achievable by him. It means helping a person develop, discover, or redevelop and rediscover the skills and abilities to make decisions that are unaffected by the action of drugs. It means enabling him to make decisions while experiencing the multitude of feelings which often are uncomfortable, which may have overwhelmed him in the past, but which are a necessary ingredient of being alive. Obviously, no single book, no matter how long and erudite it is, can supply the alternatives that will work for every person or group of people.

What we need to know is not who the drug addict is, but who the person is and how he plans and makes decisions. In the American tradition of fairness, we also ought to know who we are, how we make our decisions, and on what they are based, if we ever hope to help him. With these pieces of knowledge and some sense of hope, something meaningful ought to result. If it doesn't, we try again until we succeed in some way or decide to give up. It's the meaningfulness of the effort and the constant evaluation of the effort and not how we try it that is important.

PROJECTS

1. Notwithstanding what you have read up to this point, list those characteristics of behavior that you use as your rule of thumb for categorizing a person as being a drug user. Separate them into major and minor characteristics. Then analyze and list the difficulties you feel you may have in attempting to see these characteristics in a nondrug-related way (your attitudes) as well as the difficulties in changing your overt behavior toward a "drug user."

The Drug User	Attitudes to Overcome	Overt Behavior to Overcome
Major characteristics		
Minor characteristics		

2. Given Model's definition of drugs, each of us is a drug user. Each of us has also decided who the drug misusers or abusers are. Keeping one of them in mind, whom we know, note whether you have reached out to help them. If you haven't, note why you haven't. If you have, consiser whether you feel it was a rewarding or unrewarding experience and why this is so for you.

BIBLIOGRAPHY

Ausubel, D., *Drug Addiction: Physiological, Psychological and Sociological Aspects.* New York: Random House, 1958.

Becker, H. S., *Outsiders: Studies in the Sociology of Deviancy.* Glencoe, Ill.: Free Press, 1963.

Bejerot, N., *Addiction and Society.* Springfield, Ill.: C. C. Thomas, 1970.

Birdwood, G., *The Willing Victim.* London: Secker and Warburg, 1969.

Blachly, P. H., *Seduction.* Springfield, Ill.: C. C. Thomas, 1970.

Blum, R., and associates, *Students and Drugs.* San Francisco: Jossey-Bass, 1969.

Brecher, E. M., *Licit and Illicit Drugs.* Boston: Little, Brown, 1972.

Brotman, R., and Freedman, A., ed., *A Community Mental Health Approach to Drug Addiction.* Washington, D.C.: U.S. Dept. of Health, Education and Welfare, 1968.

Chein, I., *et al., The Road to H.* New York: Basic Books, 1964.

Cocteau, J., *Opium.* New York: Grove, 1958.

Cohen, S., *The Drug Dilemma.* New York: McGraw-Hill, 1969.

Coles, R., *The Grass Pipe.* Boston: Little, Brown, 1969.

Cork, M. R., *The Forgotten Children.* Toronto: Addiction Research Foundation, 1969.

Crowly, R., "Psychoanalytic Literature on Drug Addiction and Alcoholism," *Psychoanalytic Review*, Vol. 26, pp. 38–54, 1939.

Glaser, F. B., "Narcotics Addiction in the Pain Prone Female: A Comparison with Addict Controls," *International Journal of the Addictions*, vol. 1, no. 2, pp. 47–60, 1966.

Goldstein, R., *One in Seven: Drugs on Campus.* New York: Walker, 1966.

Harms, E., ed., *Drug Addiction in Youth.* Oxford: Pergamon, 1965.

Jellinek, E. M., *The Disease Concept of Alcoholism.* New Haven: College and University Press, 1960.

Kron, Y. J., and Brown, E. M., *Mainline to Nowhere.* New York: Pantheon, 1965.

Krystal, H., and Raskin, H., *Drug Dependence.* Detroit: Wayne State University Press, 1970.

Landis, C., "Theories of the Alcoholic Personality," in *Alcohol, Science and Society.* New Haven: College and University Press, 1945.

Larner, J., and Teffertelles, R., *The Addict in the Street*. New York: Grove, 1964.

Laskowitz, D., "The Adolescent Drug Addict: An Adlerian View," *Journal of Individual Psychology*, vol. 17, pp. 68–79, 1961.

———, "A Comparison of the Intellectual Performance of the Juvenile Addict with Standardization Norms," *Journal of Corrective Education*, vol. 14, pp. 31–32, 1962.

Louria, D. B., *The Drug Scene*. New York: McGraw-Hill, 1968.

Lucia, S. P., ed., *Alcohol and Civilization*. New York: McGraw-Hill, 1963.

Maickel, R., ed., *Bio-Chemical Factors in Alcoholism*. Oxford: Pergamon, 1967.

Malcolm, A. I., *The Pursuit of Intoxication*. Toronto: Addiction Research Foundation, 1971.

Maurer, D. W., and Vogel, V. H., *Narcotics and Narcotics Addiction*, 3rd ed. Springfield, Ill.: C. C. Thomas, 1967.

Nowlis, H. H., *Drugs on the College Campus: A Guide for College Administrators*. Detroit: National Association of Student Personnel Administrators, 1967.

Nyswander, M., *The Drug Addict as a Patient*. New York: Grune and Stratton, 1956.

O'Donnell, J. A, et al., "Marital History of Narcotic Addicts," *International Journal of the Addictions*, vol. 2, no. 1, pp. 21–39, 1967.

Preble, E., and Casey, J. J., Jr., "Taking Care of Business—the Heroin User's Life on the Street," *International Journal of the Addictions*, vol. 4, no. 1, pp. 1–24, 1969.

Robins, L. N., and Murphy, G. E., "Drug Use in a Normal Population of Young Negro Men," *American Journal of Public Health*, vol. 57, p. 1580, 1967.

Russell, E., *The Last Fix*. New York: Harcourt, Brace, Jovanovich, 1971.

Shearer, R. J., *Manual on Alcoholism*. Chicago: American Medical Association, 1967.

Smith, D., and Gay, G., *It's So Good Don't Even Try It*. Englewood Cliffs, N.J.: Prentice-Hall, 1972.

Snyder, C. S., *Alcohol and the Jews*. Glencoe, Ill.: Free Press, 1958.

Tart, C. T., *On Being Stoned*. Palo Alto, Calif.: Science and Behavior Books, 1971.

Terry, C. E., and Pellens, N., *The Opium Problem*. Montclair, N.J.: Patterson and Smith, 1971.

Travers, M., *Each Other's Victims*. New York: Scribners, 1970.

Wakefield, D., ed., *The Addict*. Stanford, Conn.: Fawcett Pub., 1963.

Winick, C., "Maturing out of Narcotic Addiction," *United Nations Bulletin on Narcotics*, vol. 14, no. 1, 1962.

Zinberg, H. E., and Lewis, D. C., "Narcotics Usage," *New England Journal of Medicine*, vol. 270, pp. 989–993, May 4, 1964.

CHAPTER 4

Grim Fairy Tales

One of the most clear-cut regularities of social behavior is the scapegoat principle: When things don't go well, people blame the difficulty on individuals or groups who are innocent but defenseless. Through this moral exchange, the scapegoat becomes guilty and the scapegoater innocent.

Thomas S. Szasz

There was a time when fables were used to teach morality and to control children's behavior through fear. We question some of the contemporary myths that serve to color and confuse our understanding of today's drug scene. A collection of the fairy tales and fables about drug use might be called "Groovy Grass, by the Grimms Brothers." The contents:

1. "Cocaine Cindy," the story of a rejected girl who seduced her man through the aphrodisiac powers of cocaine;
2. "Snow White and the Seven Nodding Dwarfs," the story of how a rejected daughter challenges her unstable mother by using heroin;
3. "Red Writhing Hood," the story of an adolescent amphetamine user whose perceptual distortions prove to be almost fatal;
4. "Tom Numb," the story of an inadequate teen-age boy who masks his unresolved oedipal conflicts by getting high on drugs;
5. "Hairy and Grotesque," the story of the horrors of an LSD trip that takes place in the woods of California.

Each of these fairy tales would contain an element of truth, but overall they would confuse rather than illuminate.

In any community, there will be a series of inaccurate beliefs about drug use that are widely circulated and accepted. They continue to be believed because of a nonsensical human notion that if many people believe something, it must be true. This kind of thinking in the Western

135

world could be described as *majority-common-sense conceptions*. When we find it in primitive societies, we call it magical thinking. Here are a number of such beliefs:

1. *Once an addict, always an addict (or alcoholic).*

There is no empirical evidence to support this belief. Drug use describes what a person is doing, not what he is. This myth puts the onus of drug use on the individual, forgetting that he lives in a social framework that surely affects his "drug" decisions.

For some people who use drugs, their behavior may best be explained by the possibility that they have identified with the popular opinion of them. If a parent associates long hair, "bizarre" clothes, loud music, and a lack of reverence for adult values with drug use, the child may ultimately comply by acting out the parent's fantasy. If the person, particularly the adolescent, is unsure of his identity and is feeling excessively anxious because of this, he may be willing to settle for any kind of identity, including that of drug addict, to quell the internal conflict. Surely, the fact that many drug users do cease their drug behavior suggests that addicts need not remain addicts.

2. *Addiction is a disease.*

Someday technology may discover the virus, bacteria, organ deficiency, or those predisposing factors that doom a person to the status of "addict personality." Until that day arrives, there is no solid evidence that addiction or its relative, drug abuse, is a disease in the medical sense of that term or that it is a particular psychiatric entity. At the present time, addiction and drug abuse are more appropriately considered particular kinds of *life-style* adaptations which may be associated with physical, psychiatric, social, academic, vocational, and legal consequences.

3. *Addiction is contagious.*

Medically, contagion is that process by which a person who is not naturally immune or medically immunized will acquire particular diseases to which he is exposed. If one accepts that addiction is not a disease, then obviously it can't be contagious. One consequence of "decontaging" addiction is that solutions to the problem may be sought in the social arena.

Given our present state of knowledge, it becomes clear that no single person or group and no specific situation is the carrier of addiction. In fact, addiction or drug abuse is not passively achieved. Rather, it is personally acquired through great effort and reinforced through time. Were addiction contagious, the majority of individuals living in high-drug-use areas would have acquired the disease when, in fact, they have not.

From the community's perspective, the "contagion" theory can serve as a built-in cop-out. It tends to put the onus for drug use on the individual. The addict's community can sit by passively waiting for personal insight, incarceration, accidents, or death to remove the drug problem from their midst. However, if a community really wants to remove the drug problem, it will have to actively intervene with meaningful effort, not empty rhetoric or fragmented reactions.

4. *Addicts have specific personality defects.*

There are no hard data to support this contention. Addicts and drug abusers are members of a heterogeneous group called mankind who use different drugs in different ways for all sorts of reasons. Psychiatrically, their diagnoses run the gamut of psychiatric classifications. The notion of the existence of specific personality defects, which somehow explain the person's entrance into the drug scene, probably arises from the assumption that something must be wrong with a person who uses drugs in a particular way. Fortunately, if we are engaged in the use of socially accepted drugs, this theory does not apply to us. Aside from this incredible luck that many of us have, it is difficult to understand how many people with the addict-prone personality defect have managed to feel inadequate, anxious, depressed, inwardly angry, and sexually hung up without turning to drugs. It is, of course, possible that they have been saved because they are somehow immune; they are so sick that they can't sustain the daily pressures of being a street addict or they are given a different and more devastating social or psychiatric tag.

Once again, we must be aware that a "personality-defect" myth gets society off the hook by making drug use an individual problem.

5. *The process of addiction is predictable: It goes from soft drugs (marijuana) to hard drugs (opiates).*

There are no data to support this. Although most people would agree that ordinary people differ, we are loath to acknowledge that addicts and drug abusers also differ. Rather, starting with the underlying moral assumption that an addict is weak-willed or sick, it seems logical that once he begins taking a particular drug, he somehow must move on to more detrimental drugs. He should also become increasingly more involved in drug use. The public—us—does not equally assume that the cigarette smoker constantly increases his number of cigarettes or that the smoking pattern must include chewing tobacco, cigars, and pipes. Nor do we assume that beer in the kitchen will lead to "Sneaky Pete" on skid row.

The irony is that hard data are currently available which strongly suggests that among youth, cigarette smoking is associated with both the experimental and ongoing use of marijuana and other drugs; whereas noncigarette-smoking adolescents are less likely to enter the drug scene. Perhaps the formula should read: carcinogenic drugs—soft drugs—hard drugs. One could build a case for this formulation, but who would believe it and what would they do about it?

The soft-drug, hard-drug approach again seduces us into thinking that our present increasingly drug-oriented life style is simply the result of certain people using certain drugs. The simplistic solution in this simplistic approach would be selected euthanasia for populations at risk and destruction of all soft drugs. This would leave us with a smaller population who might not turn to the remaining opiates.

6. *Drugs lead to progressive physical deterioration.*

People deteriorate when they don't take care of themselves, when they take any substance to excess, and when they take any drug under other than sterile conditions. All drugs are toxic, and all drugs are lethal. The same things can be said about people. Most of the time it is not how the drug or the person acts that is the crucial issue. Rather, it is how the drug is administered, what it is mixed with, what other drugs it is combined with, the state of the drug user's health—physical and mental—and the state of his surroundings that are the critical factors.

The same analysis holds true in determining the state of health of a community. How it is administered, the people that it is mixed with, the institutional and ritual structures, the state of the community's social and environmental health, as well as that of its surroundings, are the critical factors. The analogy might appear to be farfetched at first glance. The point is that neither a person's nor a community's health or sickness is simply the result of a single factor, but may result from various interacting factors and forces. Drugs are at most only one factor.

7. *Drugs lead to addiction.*

Addiction is an arbitrary end-result definition of a process. When addicting drugs (opiates, barbiturates, alcohol) are taken in sufficient quantity by a particular person over a long enough period of time, then cellular tolerance and withdrawal symptoms can develop. This process is variable among people and differs for the same person from time to time. The social reality is that we are not concerned about the process of addiction, but rather we are afraid of the overt behavior of the addict.

8. *Alcohol is less dangerous than other drugs.*

Empirical evidence continues to indicate that the drug effects of alcohol still make it the most dangerous drug known to man when used to excess.

The number of seriously affected drinkers far exceeds the number of other types of seriously affected drug abusers. Likewise, the number of social drinkers exceeds the number of recreational drug users. More deaths, accidents, absenteeism from work, and incarcerations are due to drunkenness than to the effects of other drugs. Alcoholism is one of America's most prevalent public health problems (together with cancer, mental illness, and heart disease). All of this obviously holds true only when we consider alcohol a drug. As a social beverage do we compare it with Coca Cola, Dr. Pepper, 7-Up, or what? Obviously, as long as we consider alcohol as being a social beverage, and not a drug, we won't consider it as a dangerous drug. After all, would we knowingly imbibe a dangerous drug? Would you?

9. *Drugs, particularly marijuana, when used by drug users, are aphrodisiacs.*

There is no empirical evidence to substantiate this. A drug user may experience less anxiety and inhibition when high and may become more easily aroused or even perform better sexually. Sexual behavior in man, unlike other creatures, is not an innate biochemical reflex. Man's psyche is the crucial factor. Many street addicts apparently have little desire or time for lovemaking, but they do report several encounters. They are not too different from their nondrug-using peers who also have little time for love, but find the time for sex. Perhaps the pharmaceutical industry will someday synthesize a pill for lovemaking. We could call it LOVE ACT for the married, SEX ACT for the single adult swingers, and TEASE for the younger set. Excessive use of each could result in the following categories: L-heads, S-heads, and T-heads. Absurd? Not any more so than the myths about sex and drugs.

10. *Drug addicts commit violent crimes.*

A drug user, addict or not, who doesn't have money to support his drug habit is quite likely to engage in deviant or criminal behavior. To date, crimes to support drug habits have generally been committed against property and not against people. Given the changes in the patterns of drug use from single- to multiple-drug use, from opiates to pills, etc., less money is often needed to support drug use. In addition, the recreational use of a number of drugs within a social framework where they are shared has tended to decrease the huge sums needed to support daily heroin habits.

One factor that must be considered when associating types of crimes with drug use is the type of drug being used. Stimulants may lead to assaultive behavior and violence, whereas sedatives and opiates are not likely to. Alcohol may result in physical aggressiveness and verbal abusiveness in a person with such tendencies. Hallucinogens, which are experienced as overwhelming by a person, may lead to aggressive behavior. It would be theoretically helpful if one could know beforehand that certain drugs are more likely to be associated with violent behavior, other drugs with passive behavior, and some drugs with a sense of well-being. Drug action, as we presently know it, is unpredictable, and recent events in America have shown us that violence is a basic pattern of life, even without drugs.

11. *Pushers are responsible for the spread of addiction.*

Although there is no evidence to substantiate this, many people continue to believe it. Addiction specifically and drug misuse generally are big business, involving both drug users and nonusers, illegal chemical factories, and quite legal pharmaceutical houses. The nonaddict pusher is a businessman, often a pillar of his community, supporter of the community chest and other social, religious, and political causes; he sells wholesale. The street pusher is a drug user supporting his own drug habit.

The drug wholesaler or street pusher does not wait in parks, playgrounds, or school yards. The drug user waits for him. Drug use, on other than a casual experimental level, results from a person's active participation. The drug user must either find and wait for his local pusher or find a "script doctor" and a pharmacy to fill his prescription. He must then find a place in which to take his drug, experience whatever he experiences, and then start the cycle again. The pusher is no more responsible for the spread of addiction than the barkeeper or liquor store owner is responsible for the spread of alcoholism or the food store for obesity.

A major advantage of this myth is that it again permits us to falsely believe that we have nothing to do with today's pattern of drug use. If we got rid of the pusher, the only thing that would be predictable is: not *less* drug use, but that other pushers would take their place. We apparently do not lack in numbers of criminals, even though we continue to arrest many of them.

12. *Other nations are responsible for America's drug problem.*

Communist nations may grow and easily make available various drugs to America, but that doesn't explain why Americans use and misuse drugs. When United States servicemen, adolescents, and young adults use drugs in Vietnam, it isn't simply because the Viet Cong have purposely left them in bunkers. Drugs are readily available in South Vietnam as they are in most parts of the world. Mexico, France, and Turkey are singled out by our government for protests as well as for special interventions such as Operation Intercept. We tend to forget that between our own legitimate pharmaceutical industry and the illegal chemical laboratories, we could easily expect many "dangerous drugs" and drug problems. After all, isn't "progress through chemistry" essentially an American creation? The crucial issue is not which nation caused what, but how existing nations can effectively mobilize for a better kind of living than we all presently experience.

13. *The psychedelic experience is a religious experience.*

Religious experiences of any kind, whether or not they are part of a formal religion or religious ritual, result from a person working out his relationship with his deity. During this process, drugs, at best, can serve only as catalysts. Experience with alcohol has tended to show that it is the meaning attributed to the alcohol and not what it actually is or its drug action that is significant. History confirms for us that it is the ritual that is important in religious experiences and not the various objects associated with the ritual. From a drug perspective, the ritual and the associated religious experience could utilize placebo as well.

14. *Marijuana and other psychedelics are religious drugs.*

What we lack in evidence we can surely make up in faith. Substances in and of themselves are not religious. The context within which a substance is used determines its meaning. How a person integrates that meaning is a very personal matter and is not a function of the drug's action. Unlike people and their societies, drugs are neither religious nor sacrilegious.

15. *Drug use and misuse are immoral.*

Substances as well as people are not moral, immoral, or amoral. Society determines how a certain drug, person, or philosophy is to be categorized. Once tagged, it becomes difficult to get untagged. Viewing a drug as being less than wholesome permits the drug user and his nonusing community to focus on what to do with the drug, and not on what each might do for each other.

16. *Drugs can result in increased creativity.*

Obviously, drugs can affect a person's state of anxiety and depressions, his energy level, and his drive for doing creative work. By reinforcing or inhibiting anxiety, drive states, and other human qualities, a person's creative orientation and work may be affected. It is important to understand, however, that anxiety, drive states, and energy levels are not sufficient to result in creative efforts.

17. *Drugs show a person the real reality.*

Reality is what a person experiences. For the psychotic, hallucinations are quite real, and they are his reality at that time. For the amputee, sensing a limb when none is there is also real. Although literature, philosophy, and religion may have the luxury of speculating about reality, for the person reality is what he is constantly attempting to adapt to, and some people never learn to do this adequately in their life time. Drugs don't *show* people anything.

18. *The generation gap is reinforced by permitting alcohol to be legally available while marijuana is outlawed.*

Obviously, this kind of behavior is hypocritical, irrational, and illogical. However, to be alive and mere mortal is, among other things, to be hypocritical, irrational, and illogical. Not only have generation gaps always been with us, they probably also will continue. The real difficulty is that it is often hard to acknowledge that we have greater difficulty in understanding and accepting our peers, talking to them, and wanting to be with them than is true for other generations that we know. If marijuana wasn't the intergeneration irritant, surely we would come up with an equally potent "substantive" issue.

19. *Drug use should be permitted to be a personal choice as long as it doesn't affect anyone else.*

It is difficult to understand how this assumption could work in a country like the United States of America. Obviously, whatever we do affects not only people we know and care about, but also those we don't know. The pragmatic issue is not whether a particular appetite is justifiable, but rather when it is engaged in, is that person ready and able to handle the consequences whatever they are?

20. *Drug use is caused and reinforced by the present state of literature and music.*

The underlying dynamic of this myth is really if we don't know what causes drug misuse and we don't like certain aspects of the contemporary cultural scene, we can blame one on the other. Surely, there are songs and literature that indirectly and directly focus on drugs and drug use. The key question is whether they are a bandwagon phenomenon that has commercialized an already existing condition or are they instrumental in creating the existing drug phenomenon? While people may polarize on this issue, the fact remains that the use and misuse of drugs have been with us for thousands of years. The reality is that the complexities of drug misuse can't be "caused" by any single factor. Second, and perhaps of more importance, is that much of the increased sensory stimulation may be impinging on us, but it is questionable whether it is getting through. It often appears that we have so adapted to being violated by our surroundings that we turn on minimally and tune out maximally. We don't smell the pollution; we don't have to hear the increasing noise, nor see what people we are most concerned about are doing, nor feel others reaching out or retreating, nor sense our own internal competing feelings, nor taste the blandness of our foods.

Songs and literature, whatever their message, must be somehow integrated before we can blame certain behavior on their impact. One could easily use the recent phenomenon of rock festivals as an example of drug use being associated with certain music. Photographs of spaced-out youth, living and sleeping under less than adequate accommodations, could be interpreted as proof positive of the myth under discussion.

There is, however, at least an equally valid interpretation that can be made of this phenomenon. Many youth representing all of us may be telling us that the formal institutions of society, family, school, houses of worship, and the marketplace are no longer offering them meaningful social rituals which are necessary for contemporary living. Indeed, the family is no longer an extended one, and this deprives the growing child of a variety of adult models. The school is increasingly concerned with cognitive development at the cost of emotional growth—in order to prepare the student for more school and not for living. Houses of worship are in a crisis as they argue whether God is dead, what new games and techniques they should introduce in order to attract members (somehow forgetting that they could offer unpackaged hope and solace), and how to raise money for their new building when the old structure would be more than ample for their deity. The marketplace continues to offer little sense of pride or satisfaction to its constituents as it preaches a philosophy of commitment to technology and not to people, making it possible for more people to have more leisure time which they don't know what to do with.

The triad of songs, drugs, and meadows is not an inevitable package. Perhaps, if the youth and the adults of America could refocus their attention to implementing those social rituals that might negate many of the devastating pressures affecting us, the songs would just be experienced as songs, which may or may not suit one's personal tastes, but which wouldn't be heard as threats.

There are, no doubt, many more myths—perhaps as many myths as there are people. As a framework for appropriate drug-abuse intervention, they are toxic and perhaps even lethal. We are daily confronted by real people and not fictional characters in the field of drug abuse. We should respond to them as real people and not as mythologized entities. Whereas fairy tales generally end well with their main characters having had little to do with the outcome, drug abuse won't simply go away on its own. It didn't come to us on its own.

The choice of what we do, how we do it, and when we do it is obviously ours to make. The decision to intervene is not an easy one, and there are no tried and true guidelines to follow. But this is the normal process of life: doing, evaluating, redoing, and reevaluating. If we choose to do nothing about drug abuse, waiting for someone else to act for us, the myths will surely increase in number and in their terrible consequences. The people that we are most concerned about, as well as we ourselves, are not mythological characters. We can ill afford to permit drug myths to grow and influence our behavior when the challenge facing all of us is how to limit our many real problems.

PROJECTS

1. Starting with a well-known fact about drugs, drug use, or drug users, explore the evidence that substantiates its being a scientific fact.
2. Make up a drug-related fact and try and pass it off to a family member, friend, etc. Note whether the person accepts this new fact, and then question him regarding the factors that went into such acceptance.
3. Consider whether there are any drug-related facts or myths that are interfering with relationships you have or would like to have. Analyze what you can do to change the fact or myth and what you can do about the relationship.

BIBLIOGRAPHY

Anslinger, H. L., and Cooper, C. R., "Marijuana: Assassin of Youth," *American Magazine*, vol. 124, pp. 19–20, 150–153, 1937.
Barber, T. X., *LSD, Marijuana, Yoga and Hypnosis.* Chicago: Aldine, 1970.
Bejerot, H., *Addiction and Society.* Springfield, Ill.: C. C. Thomas, 1970.
Blum, R., and associates, *Society and Drugs.* San Francisco: Jossey-Bass, 1969.
Brecher, E. M., *Licit and Illicit Drugs.* Boston: Little, Brown, 1972.
Brown, C. C., and Savage, C., eds., *The Drug Abuse Controversy.* Baltimore: National Educational Consultants, 1971.
Burroughs, W., *Junkie.* New York: Ace, 1953.
Burroughs, W., and Ginsburg, A., *Yage Letters.* Calif.: City Lights, 1963.
Carstairs, G. M., "Daru and Bhang: Cultural Factors in the Choice of Intoxicants," *Quarterly Journal of Student Alcohol*, vol. 15, pp. 220–237, 1954.

Cocteau, J., *Opium*. New York: Grove, 1958.

Cohen, C., "Multiple Drug Use Considered in the Light of the Stepping-Stone Hypothesis," *International Journal of the Addictions*, vol. 7, no. 1, pp. 27–56, 1972.

Cohen, S., *The Drug Dilemma*. New York: McGraw-Hill, 1969.

Coles, R., *et al.*, *Drugs and Youth*. New York: Liveright, 1970.

Crowly, R., "Psychoanalytic Literature on Drug Addiction and Alcoholism," *Psychoanalytic Review*, vol. 26, pp. 39–54, 1939.

DeRopp, R. S., *Drugs and the Mind*. New York: Grove, 1961.

Ebin, D., ed., *The Drug Experience*. New York: Orion Press, 1961.

Emboden, W., *Narcotic Plants*. New York: Macmillan, 1972.

Ginsburg, A., "The Great Marijuana Hoax: First Manifesto to End the Bringdown," *Atlantic Monthly*, vol. 104, pp. 107–112, November 1966.

Goldstein, R., *One in Seven: Drugs on Campus*. New York: Walker, 1966.

Griffenhagen, G. B., "A History of Drug Abuse," *Journal of the American Pharmaceutical Association*, vol. NS 8, no. 1, pp. 16–28, 1968.

Grinspoon, L., *Marijuana Reconsidered*. Boston: Harvard University Press, 1971.

Hoffman, N. Von, *We Are the People Our Parents Warned Us Against*. New York: Fawcett World, 1969.

Huxley, A., *Doors of Perception: Heaven and Hell*. New York: Harper and Row, 1954.

Keniston, K., "Heads and Seekers: Drugs on Campus, Counter Culture and American Society," *The American Scholar*, vol. 38, pp. 97–112, 1968, 1969.

Kramer, J., "Controlling Narcotics in America, Part I & II," *Drug Forum*, vol. 1, no. 1, pp. 51–70, 1971; vol. 1, no. 2, pp. 153–168, 1972.

Kron, Y. J., and Brown, E. M., *Mainline to Nowhere*. New York: Pantheon, 1965.

Krystal, H., and Raskin, H., *Drug Dependence*. Detroit: Wayne State University Press, 1970.

LaBarre, W., *Peyote Cult*. New York: Schocken, 1971.

Larner, J., and Tefferteller, R., *The Addict in the Street*. New York: Grove, 1964.

Leary, T., *et al.*, *The Psychedelic Experience*. New York: University Books, 1964.

Lolli, G., *Social Drinking*. New York: Collier, 1961.

Mandel, J., "Hashish, Assassins and the Love of God," *Issues in Criminology*, vol. 2, pp. 149–156, 1966.

Marin, P., and Cohen, A. Y., *Understanding Drug Use*. New York: Harper & Row, 1971.

Masters, R. E. L., and Houston, J., *The Varieties of Psychedelic Experience*. New York: Holt, Rinehart & Winston, 1966.

Metzner, R., *The Ecstatic Adventure*. New York: Macmillan, 1968.

Michener, J. A., *The Drifters*. New York: Random House, 1971.

Mikuriya, T. H., "Physical, Mental and Moral Effects of Marijuana: The Indian Hemp Drugs Commission Report," *International Journal of the Addictions*, vol. 3, no. 2, pp. 253–270, 1968.

Oursler, W., *Marijuana: The Facts, The Truth*. New York: Paul S. Eriksson, 1968.

Playboy Panel, "The Drug Revolution," *Playboy*, pp. 53–74, 200–201, February 1970.

Polsky, N., *Hustlers, Beats and Others*. New York: Doubleday, 1969.

Robins, L. N., and Murphy, G. E., "Drug Use in a Normal Population of Young Negro Men," *American Journal of Public Health*, vol. 57, p. 1580, 1967.

Roszak, T., *Making of a Counter Culture*. New York: Doubleday, 1969.

Solomon, D., ed., *The Marijuana Papers*. New York: Bobbs-Merrill, 1966.

Taylor, N., *Nature's Dangerous Gifts*. New York: Dell, 1963.

Thomas, P., *Down These Mean Streets*. New York: New American Library, 1967.

Travers, M., *Each Others Victims.* New York: Scribners, 1970.

Trocchi, A., *Cain's Book.* New York: Grove, 1969.

Watts, A. W., *Joyous Cosmology.* New York: Random House, 1970.

Winick, C., "The Use of Drugs by Jazz Musicians," *Social Problems*, vol. 7, pp. 240–253, 1960.

Zinberg, N. E., and Weil, A. T., "A Comparison of Marijuana Users and Non-Users," *Nature*, vol. 226, pp. 119–123, 1970.

CHAPTER 5

The Contemporary Drug Culture: Sights and Sounds

Reformers who begin with determination to stamp out sin usually end by stamping out sinners . . .

Richard Hofstadter

Blaming behavior, particularly behavior that's considered to be a problem on external forces, is not new to man. Scapegoating is the essence of this. The *ins* have always tended to blame the *outs* as being the cause of whatever it is that has upset, frightened, confused, and very often challenged the status quo.

Most recently the increase in drug use has been placed at the door of a youth culture that supposedly celebrates life through drug songs and drug literature.

The logic of this assumption is quite simple: If you sing about drugs and read about drugs in literature considered to be less than orthodox, you soon will be using drugs. The second step in this assumption is that once you begin using drugs, you will involve yourself more and more in the sight and sound of drugs, making it all the more difficult to break away and return to a drug-free mainstream of life status.

On the surface there appears to be enough evidence to substantiate this view. The "generation gap" seems to stem from a "youth culture" whose appetites and manner of satiating these appetites are quite different from those of the over-thirty generation. Politically, the appetites of the young seem to veer toward violence and radicalism; sexually, their appetites appear to many adults to be almost insatiable, perverse, and transitory; musically, their tastes seem to have exchanged harmony and melody for volume, strange lighting effects, and a commitment to drugs.

147

The adult population has begun to turn to contemporary music to point out the evidence that the young are wild, reckless, and committed to destroying the foundations of American society.

It is quite easy to be seduced into thinking and believing that the written and the sung word is a major factor in the changing patterns of American life. Most of us have been brought up on the notion that "the pen is mightier than the sword." But is it still?

It is easy to understand why many Americans are concerned and up-tight about contemporary lyrics. An issue is whether their concern is focused in on the key factors associated with what reinforces and/or inhibits contemporary drug misuse, or whether energies are being meaninglessly spent on the smoke and not the fire.

In October of 1970, Vice-President Spiro Agnew implied that music may indeed be a major cause of people turning to drugs. He asked his audience to "consider the influence of the drug culture in the field of music. [In] too many of the lyrics the message of the drug culture is purveyed."

Indeed, many contemporary lyrics directly or indirectly are about drugs, drug effects, and a drug-oriented life. What we have to ask ourselves is whether these songs are causing the drug problem, mirroring the drug problem, or whether they have any effect at all on contemporary human behavior.

Before we can hope to turn to these questions, we should have more than a fleeting awareness of the lyrics that concern many of our citizens. And the best way to do this is to listen to the songs, not simply to study or read the lyrics.

MARIJUANA

Along Comes Mary

The most obvious interpretation to be made is that marijuana (Mary) sets people free and permits them to experience the real reality. At the same time, the lyrics are replete with warnings about some of the dangers to be encountered when one is seduced by marijuana.

Have a Marijuana

Given that drug use has become a political issue in various federal, state, and local elections, it should not be surprising that political songs exposing marijuana have been written. Indeed, candidates running on a platform of "freak power" and "pot power" have won local elections.

Table 5-1 Drugs in music.

Song	Artist	Album	Label
A Day in the Life	The Beatles	Sgt. Pepper's Lonely Hearts Club Band	Capitol
Along Comes Mary	The Associations	Greatest Hits	Warner Bros.
Amphetamine Annie	Canned Heat	Canned Heat Cook Book	Liberty
Ball of Confusion	The Temptations	Greatest Hits	Gardy
Billy D	Chris Kristofferson	The Silver Tongued Devil and I	Monument
Black Crow Blues	Bob Dylan	Another Side of Bob Dylan	Columbia
Bottle of Wine	Tom Paxton	Morning Again	Elektra
Cindy's Crying	Tom Paxton	The Complete Tom Paxton	Vanguard
Cocaine Blues	Dave Van Ronk	Folksinger	Prestige-Folkways
Codeine	Buffie Saint-Marie	It's My Way	Vanguard
Coming into Los Angeles	Arlo Guthrie	Runnin Down the Road	Reprise
Cloud Nine	Temptations	Cloud Nine	Gardy
Crystal Blues	Country Joe and the Fish	The Best of Country Joe and the Fish	Vanguard
Crystal Ship	The Doors	13	Elektra
Day Tripper	The Beatles	The Beatles	Capitol
Eight Miles High	The Byrds	The Beatles	Columbia
Everybody's Got Something to Hide Except for Me and My Monkey	The Beatles	The Beatles	Apple
Fixing a Hole	The Beatles	Sgt. Pepper's Lonely Hearts Club Band	Capitol
Flower Lady	Phil Ochs	Pleasures of the Harbour	Elektra

Table 5-1 Continued.

Song	Artist	Album	Label
Freddie's Dead	Curtis Mayfield	Super Fly	Custom
Greasy Heart	Jefferson Airplane	Crown of Creation	RCA
Half a Century High	Phil Ochs	Tape from California	A & M Records
Happiness Is a Warm Gun	The Beatles	The Beatles	Apple
Have a Marijuana	David Peel	Have a Marijuana	Elektra
Heroin	Lou Reed (Andy Warhol)	Transformer	RCA
Hey Jude	The Beatles	Hey Jude	Apple
Higher	Sly and the Family Stone	Dance to the Music	Epic
Just Like a Woman	Bob Dylan	Blonde on Blond	Columbia
If You Feel	Jefferson Airplane	Crown of Creation	RCA
I Happen to Like Whiskey-Sir	Tom Paxton	Morning Again	Elektra
I'm So Tired	The Beatles	The Beatles	Apple
In Your Own Backyard	Dion Dimucci	Goodies	Warner Bros.
Junk	Paul McCartney	McCartney	Apple
King Heroin	James Brown	There It Is	Polydor
La Cucaracha			
Lady Jane	Rolling Stones	Flowers	London
Let's Go Get Stoned	Ray Charles	A Man and His Soul	ABC
Little Child Running Wild	Curtis Mayfield	Super Fly	Custom
Lucy in the Sky with Diamonds	The Beatles	Sgt. Pepper's Lonely Hearts Club Band	Capitol
Mellow Yellow	Donovan	Mellow Yellow	Epic
Memphis Blues Again	Bob Dylan	Blonde on Blond	Columbia
Mother's Little Helper	Rolling Stones	Through the Past Darkly (Big Hits Volume 2)	London
Mr. Tambourine Man	Bob Dylan	Bringing It All Back Home	Columbia

Song	Artist	Album	Label
Nothing on Me	Curtis Mayfield	Super Fly	Custom
Outside a Small Circle of Friends	Phil Ochs	Pleasures of the Harbor	A & M Records
Psychedelic Shack	The Temptations	Psychedelic Shack	Gardy
Pusher Man	Curtis Mayfield	Super Fly	Custom
Rainy Day Woman Nos. 12 & 35	Bob Dylan	Blonde on Blond	Columbia
Sad Eyed Lady of the Lowlands	Bob Dylan	Blonde on Blond	Columbia
See What You Done, Done	Delia Gartrell	Single	Right on Records
Sexy Sadie	The Beatles	The Beatles	Apple
Spinning Wheel	Blood Sweat and Tears	Spinning Wheel	Columbia
Subterranean Homesick Blues	Bob Dylan	Bringing It All Back Home	Columbia
Sunshine Superman	Donovan	Sunshine Superman	Epic
Super Fly	Curtis Mayfield	Super Fly	Custom
Talking Vietnam Pot Luck Blues	Tom Paxton	Morning Again	Elektra
Tape from California	Phil Ochs	Tape from California	A & M Records
The Pusher	Steppenwolf	Steppenwolf Gold the Greatest Hits	Dunhill
The Truth Shall Make You Free	King Hannibal	Single	Aware
Timothy Leary's Dead	Moody Blues	In Search of the Lost Chord	London
Tommy	The Who	Tommy the Who	Decca
We're Not Gonna Take It From Tommy	The Who		
White Rabbit	Jefferson Airplane	Surrealistic Pillow	RCA
With a Little Help from My Friends	The Beatles	Sgt. Pepper's Lonely Hearts Club Band	Capitol
Yer Blues	The Beatles	The Beatles	Apple
Yellow Submarine	The Beatles	The Beatles Yellow Submarine	Capitol

PILLS

White Rabbit

At the very least, there is a double message in this song: Pills affect the way we experience ourselves, and mother is part of the pill generation. Both statements are true, and neither one necessarily idolizes drug use.

Yellow Submarine

The message seems clear: "a life of ease" among one's friends based on the notion of the contagious spread of pill use (Seconal) in which all of our needs are taken care of. Escaping or retreating from the world of reality is obviously an issue for all of us to be concerned with. The underlying issue is, however, of greater significance: Why must one retreat? Are there no options other than drug-related ones available?

Spinning Wheel

Once again there is at least a double message: You can temporarily avoid the problems of living by experiencing a different reality, but you will have to experience them sooner or later.

HEROIN

Heroin

Mainlining heroin is exciting, but one has to contend with the potential experience of feeling like someone else, which can be upsetting and anxiety provoking in and of itself.

COCAINE

Cocaine Blues

Cocaine results in both uncontrollable behavior and being removed from the mainstream of living. One's perceptions of who you are, what you are all about, and what you can and can't do become distorted.

HALLUCINOGENS

White Rabbit

Using Alice in Wonderland as an example, this song relates the confusion that results in perception and judgment from using hallucinogens. While it is most legitimate to be concerned about the glorification of hallucinogenic experiences, we must once again ask what is there about contemporary life that leads people to seek an altered inner life over which they have little, if any, control.

Lucy in the Sky With Diamonds

Notwithstanding the fact that John Lennon has explained that this song was really one about a picture his son had painted, the belief continues that this is really a paean to LSD. Even were we to assume that this is an LSD song, the world that is described is inhabited by strange objects and odd people. Our greater concern should be for those who want to visit this world, why they feel impelled to travel there, and what role all of us may have in this trip.

The Crystal Ship

The world of experience is juxtaposed of people who go through the motions of a relationship—never really touching base. Again we must ask whether this song describes the effects of drugs upon developing and maintaining relationships or whether people, particularly the young, are turning to drugs in part to help them with the normal discomforts associated with building relationships. If the latter is so, we are obligated to understand what more meaningful interpersonal options, other than drug use, are available, and how do we get people to take a chance with them.

SPREADING DRUG USE

Mr. Tambourine Man

This song is anything but a glorification of drug use. It acknowledges that someone, somewhere, can give us progress through chemistry, but only for a short time and at a substantial physical, psychological, and interpersonal cost. Again the significant issue is not that people are willing to reach for their favorite pusher or for their favorite chemical solace, which many of us are doing daily, nor why this is so. Rather, it is what can be offered to any person that is sufficiently meaningful and challenging to him so that he becomes willing to give up the world of drugs and phantom people for the world of relationships with real people.

With little effort one could build up a linkage between music, particularly rock music, and drugs. We might even be able to pinpoint the height of this association. During 1967, the trinity of Haight-Ashbury, Hippies, and Hallucinogens appeared to be spoken for by the Beatle's Sgt. Pepper record.

One writer describes the developing association of music and drugs in the following way:

> Frank Sinatra had sung of the heart, the Stones of the groin, but the new rock star sang to the head—the head's head. The Beatles had gone from wanting to hold your hand to wanting to turn you on.
>
> Dope, especially marijuana, seemed to be the key. Smoking up was an act of passive resistance to the world at large. Smoking up was also a reaffirmation that another community existed, one banded together by the revelations dope afforded and rock expressed.

But the connection between drugs and music, particularly with the evolution of the rock movement, has not been a clear and only one-sided one. Constancy and ambiguity have made up the association for some time now, and most recently what appears to be an antidrug music trend has developed.

For example, when Sly and The Family Stone sang at Woodstock: "I wanna take you higher!" the meaning could be both a drug high and a musical high. To the now generation, the "Yellow Submarine" no doubt meant Seconals, but to the *National Review*, it was "a beautiful children's song."

Once again we become aware how personal reality and perception are indeed so important, and why defending them both from overwhelming distortions is also so important. Not only is beauty in the eye of the beholder, but so are sin, evil, and problems.

It is quite doubtful that any of our contemporary song writers or singers are holding up the life of drug use as a status to be aspired to. There is little doubt that the drug-related deaths of Brian Jones (Rolling Stones), Al Wilson (Canned Heat), Janis Joplin, and Jimi Hendrix have been a source of concern for both music makers and music listeners. But, as we all know, concern in and of itself may not be enough to turn people off, particularly if we don't know what turned them on originally or what can mobilize their interests and energies now.

One should keep this in mind when we listen to another part of the contemporary music scene—the one that may be interpreted as describing our drug culture in anything but positive terms.

God Damn the Pusher

To blame a nation's commitment to progress through chemistry on the pusher is at the very least naive. To think that traditional forms of religion and violence will effectively root out the negative side effects of modern technology is dangerously deceptive. To suggest that changes in national life style are the prerogative, indeed a major responsibility, of a nation's leader is most appropriate. But life style changes need more impetus than nice sounding rhetoric such as the one voiced by former Vice-President Agnew: "[Dependence on hard drugs is] a depressing life style of conformity that has neither life nor style."

Amphetamine

The message is loud and clear—speed kills. And indeed methedrine use seems to have subsided during these last few years. But how do we get a nation of young and old to slow down and really experience their lives when we have become seduced into believing that speed is of the essence in life? Can this much needed deceleration only result with tranquilizers and barbiturates?

The constancy, ambiguity, and protest against and about drug use remain with us. The song "With a Little Help from My Friends" may be easily interpreted as pushing the drug experience. But what about the less than joyful lyrics in the same song?

Surely it points out that whatever pleasures can be derived from a drug experience, there are no chemicals that can immunize one from the pangs of anomie. This is not a new insight. We've known this for years, but somehow that knowledge has not led to appropriate and necessary personal and national life-style changes. But it is important to note that when people begin to relate drugs with music, there is music that is pinpointing some of the dangers associated with drug use.

There is even music that is crying out for help to intervene in the misuse of drugs by the parents of America.

Mother's Little Helper

This song points up an important role of music, both today and yesterday. Lyrics and music describe, and perhaps mimic and/or exaggerate, the feeling, tone and problems of a given era. Not only is Mother turning to drugs, but so are many other people who feel confused and overwhelmed.

The song "Ball of Confusion" is a musical attempt to describe the kind of world that many people feel they are presently living in.

Irrespective of the position that any of us takes on contemporary issues and problems, there is little doubt that there is a lot going on outside of us that may be causing or reinforcing the confusion that is growing inside of us.

In a sense, the dynamics of contemporary life and the so-called generation gap are succinctly expressed in "The Times They Are a-Changin." Notwithstanding the stark reality of the lyrics, they fail us all in one important way: They suggest that the causes and even the solutions for significant contemporary problems are to be laid at the feet of only one segment of the population. There is little comfort to be gained from this for anyone, except for the possible temporary experience of an ego trip. And after the ego trip is over, we still have to decide not who is at fault for what, but what role each of us can have in alleviating what's wrong.

COMMERCIALS AND ADVERTISEMENTS

Although it is quite understandable that the hard and loud sell of "drug" songs attracts our concern and attention, we must also be aware of the soft sell of today's spoken commercials and printed advertisements. These advertisements and commercials appear to be imitating and reinforcing the insidious contemporary trend of progress through chemistry.

Each of us has learned well the modern catechism of what to do about that special headache. And if Excedrin and Compoz are not sufficient for the pain which may be caused by the daily tensions of living at a more-than-human tempo, and with less than human satisfactions, a loving wife can "slip" her husband a Sleepeeze, when all he asked for was an aspirin. Somehow the media don't see that Mom's pushing drugs is as bad as anyone else's pushing drugs. And when your sinuses are clogged and you can't get to Arizona, there's always Dristan. Obviously, appropriate medication for uncomfortable conditions makes sense. But does it make sense to clear out one part of your body and then clog up your pores in order not to sweat, particularly when sweating is part of normal healthy functioning?

The mass media, particularly television, have taught us a lot. Most of us never knew we had a cough center until TV showed it to us. That which school didn't communicate, and educational TV didn't focus on, commercial TV pointed out. In the process of pointing out the cough center, they also showed both parent and child that drugs alone are sufficient for all the discomforts associated with coughing.

Remember the series of advertisements in which a young boy or girl wakes up coughing in his own middle-class room in the middle of the night? Mother rushes in and gives the child some medicine and immediately rushes out. Hopefully, the medication will relieve the cough, but who will supply the necessary TLC—tender loving care? Certainly not father—he never appears. In fact, the only time he ever appeared, father and mother got so hung up with the delightful taste of the medication that their coughing child got overlooked.

The viewer is reminded that this product is not a narcotic. And as we move down the body, both young and old are offered a variety of products which are meant to solve the internal discomforts caused by the excessive use of food, alcohol, etc. These products offer instant relief for conditions caused by instant excessiveness. One of the products—Bromo Seltzer— goes so far as to suggest: "If you don't have the time to feel badly, take a Bromo Seltzer." In this day and age, there is a lot to feel badly (and good!) about. In fact, if we don't feel badly perhaps almost daily, we must be dead. And if we are not actually dead, we are functionally dead to ourselves and our community when we refuse help from others by saying, "I'll do it myself" (remember those advertisements) and then choose a pill over a person.

Each of us could surely add our own anecdotes about advertisements, songs, stories, and articles which have served the dual function of raising progress through chemistry to a way of life to which we should aspire, and at the same time, that they have been part (but not necessarily the cause) of our increased awareness of drugs, drug use, and drug-related options for living. Surely, the absurdity of the youthful attack on alcohol and defense of marijuana and the opposite stance taken by most adults is somehow related to the media's encouragement of the use of various alcoholic beverages and their implicit promise of instant ease, instant sex, and instant success.

It is equally clear that drug use does not and cannot represent a particularly desirable way of life in which deeply experienced social values can be achieved, let alone experienced. And this is the crucial issue. It is not really what the songs are saying, what the advertisements are selling, what literature and films and magazines and newspapers are describing that are all that important. It is the values that they communicate or fail to communicate that are crucial, not only to our understanding of the contemporary drug scene, but to finding a personally meaningful role in life itself.

Many teen-agers have already begun to reject a drug-oriented life style. Many rock stars have given their time and energy to challenge drug life through the rock modality. But is this enough? Is this sufficient to stem the tide of drugs' easy answers to life's complicated and often unanswerable problems? While the rock stars sing out against drugs, and the federal government produces antidrug literature and films, who protects us from the new American dreams?

"Blow your mind." (FORD)
"Up, up and away." (TWA)

The sight and sound of drugs are indeed with us. Obviously, we cannot really measure the effects of the drug media upon any segment of a population. Equally obviously, we should make an effort to know both what the media's messages say and what they imply. But we should be as wary of finding solutions and the causes of drug use in these messages as the drug user should be of finding comprehension of life in chemical combinations. The drug's messages surely will continue to remain with us, because in part a free enterprise system guarantees the right to exploit man's appetites.

There are few songs that have as succinctly caught the drug sell of contemporary media as has "Paper Maché." Indeed, the reality of life is that however we advertise it, we all have to experience it in the best way we can learn how. This in no way absolves the responsibility that the media have for selling us a bill of goods. Obviously, this also in no way absolves all of us of the responsibility for permitting ourselves to be sold a bill of goods. The same system we all live under offers us the possibility to develop life styles which don't have as their foundations conditions that are likely to result in personal chemical orientations. Indeed, as we explore the ultimate effects of the sight and sound of drugs upon both young and old, we may tend to overlook two important issues. Firstly, although the written, spoken, and sung word has traditionally served to express ideas and experiences, it has been *committed people* who have turned personal ideas and experiences into viable and meaningful options for their neighbors. Secondly, the prime requisites for enabling healthy social change—and social change occurs whether we want it to or not—are hope and optimism and an adequate reservoir of energy. The analysis of the sight and sound of music may serve as an intellectual exercise, which seduces us away from confronting the more important tasks of implementing viable nondrug options for those who seek temporary relief from a world they did not make, and from which they cannot escape.

PROJECTS

1. Write a statement about a social issue that concerns you other than drugs. Attribute the statement to any well-known nondrug user. Ask some family members or friends to

indicate what they think the statement really means, then attribute the same statement to a known drug user and ask other family members and friends to interpret it. Are both of the interpretations similar or quite different?

2. Analyze drug-related media advertisements in terms of their latent and manifest messages to you. Then ask a group of children what they think the advertisements mean.

3. Write a letter to the FCC concerning a drug-related advertisement that most distrubs you. What kind of response do you get back?

4. List 10 songs that are your all-time favorites. If you can listen to them all, note what the song is asking the listener to do, feel, see, etc. When you listen to the song, are you following through on its message? If not, why?

BIBLIOGRAPHY

"An Intermission in Their Existence," *Rolling Stone*, p. 10, September 17, 1970.

Goddard, P., "Pop's Link with Drugs: Constant and Ambiguous," *Toronto Telegraph*, January 13, 1971.

"Growing Opposition to Rock Lyrics with Drug References," *Toronto Telegraph*, January 30, 1971.

Johnson, N., "Dear Vice-President . . .," *New York Times*, sect. 2, p. 1, October 11, 1970.

Lennard and associates, *Mystification and Drug Misuse*. San Francisco: Jossey-Bass, 1971.

"Mike Curb and Richard Nixon Battle Dopers," *Rolling Stone*, p. 71, November 26, 1970.

Staff, "An Analysis of 24 TV Dramas," *TV Guide*, March 13, 1971; March 20, 1971.

CHAPTER 6

What Do I Do? What Do I Say?

I don't know what your destiny will be, but one thing I know, the only ones among
you who will be really happy are those who have sought and found how to serve.

Albert Schweitzer

When the "drug" songs stop playing, and the drug myths and stereotypes
are exposed, we understand what drugs do and what they don't do, and we
finally pinpoint the "real" drug issues and life is just about livable, then
we discover that someone we care about is using drugs.

Suddenly, theories don't help. Suddenly, the world seems smaller—as if
it were closing in and exposing our frailties (or is it our mortal condition?)
to our neighbors and friends.

Drug abuse has hit my family, my neighborhood, my community, my
people—*What do I do? What do I say?*

This question is a real one for tens of thousands of youngsters and
adults. Many of us are discovering in a variety of ways that the contemporary drug problem is not simply something we read about or talk about.
This discovery can occur in the strangest of places and at quite unpredictable times.

A schoolteacher has just finished taking her class of 10-year-olds
through an exciting drug-abuse exhibit in a museum in New York City. As
the children are leaving the museum with her, a number of them ask her if
they can talk to someone about their use of drugs. She has been their
teacher for six months and has never considered the possibility that any
of her students was using drugs.

A community leader comes home one night and discovers a *set of works*
on the floor of his son's room.

A nine-year-old girl, involved in sibling rivalry with her older sister who
is living away at college, discovers a strange-looking cigarette in one of
her sister's drawers and shows it to her father. It is marijuana.

161

A working couple come home to discover that their honor student son is lying on his bed dead of an overdose.

A philanthropist-businessman is mystified about the strange gait of his chauffeur-valet. The man has been acting strangely lately, but there's no smell of alcohol. It turns out he's been using barbiturates to excess.

A governor is faced with the fact that his son has been arrested for possession of marijuana.

A mother goes up to the roof of the slum tenement she lives in to call her son for dinner. He has gone there to feed his pigeons. The pigeons have literally flown the coop. Her 11-year-old son has passed out, his head is still in a brown paper bag. He has been sniffing glue.

A Vietnam veteran, with one purple heart, is discharged from the United States Army. The parents' joy at seeing him is somewhat lessened when they discover he's using heroin, a habit he picked up in Vietnam.

Although the particular situations may vary when we are faced with having to react to drug use by someone we love, most of us shall feel unprepared. Because we have confused and ambivalent attitudes about drugs, drug use, and drug users, we shall generally have greater difficulty in arriving at meaningful responses to a "drug discovery" than for many other kinds of discoveries.

Drug use continues to be one behavior about which most people easily become angry and hysterical. Prostitution, homosexuality, juvenile delinquency, and crimes against children engender similar responses. These are the so-called deviant behaviors. We have to understand that what makes them deviant is that we tag them as deviant.

The person whom we label "drug addict," "junkie," "speed freak," or "alcoholic" we often experience as having challenged some of the values that we hold in high regard. Manifesting little respect for the property of others, he is considered to be dangerous. By permitting himself to be tagged as a deviant, he takes on the role of being a "loser," in a society which, at best, respects only "winners." Perhaps of greater importance, he is experienced as having *voluntarily chosen* to use substances in ways that society didn't intend them to be used. By and large, most of us continue to feel that the mythical drug addict is responsible for his behavior and the consequences of his behavior. When his drug behavior permits the experiencing of personal pleasure for which he has not worked, in a conventional sense, we may become enraged. The concept of responsibility and limiting personal pleasure is deeply embedded in American society and in our Protestant ethic.

The notion of the drug addict being the cause of his own present condition is, however, not sufficient to explain our usual hysterical, punitive, and guilt-provoking reactions to him. After all, the smoker surely knows he is responsible for diminishing his life span or causing himself illness or discomfort, yet we don't react negatively to him. The social drinker who, while drunk, is abusive or causes an accident is generally not the focus of our anxiety or concern. Why, then, is the drug abuser the focus of such concern?

A major factor is that we assume that he may not be able to control his behavior and that he may not be amenable to the social and legal controls that are built into his society. As a nation, we are much concerned about a person's ability to control himself or his willingness to be controlled by others. If a person uses a chemical substance that is prescribed by a physician, we assume that he will follow the prescription and that he is under the physician's care—under the control of self and of another. When the person uses drugs for other than medically or socially approved reasons, we may feel that controls are weak or totally lacking and that we may become the focus for drug effects that are uncontrollable. The images that we often have of the drug abuser tend to reinforce our fears. "Speed freak" does not connote passive, controllable behavior. Neither does "acid head," "pot head," or "dope fiend." The tag "alcoholic" most often connotes an abusive, sloppy, disheveled, loud, boisterous, and even aggressive person. By and large, we tend to react to the alcoholic and addict as if he has no control over his behavior. When we give this same person, as part of his rehabilitation, a legitimately prescribed medication (antabuse, methadone, tranquilizers, etc.), we feel safer because we assume that his behavior is controllable, and he is now more manageable.

Another important factor that affects our reaction to the drug addict is the conspicuousness of his drug-related behavior. Working under the assumption that if we don't see something it can't hurt us, we tend to react differently to the visible and the invisible addict. Indeed, learning to "play it cool" helps the drug addict to hold on to an invisible status and in many ways protects him from becoming the brunt of society's negative reactions. Many of us get caught up in this by attempting to cover the drug-related behavior of people we care most about. While we may be protecting their reputations, we also see to it that whatever available and meaningful help that could be offered to them will not be.

Table 6-1 schematizes three of the factors that significantly effect our response to drug misuse: the source of responsibility, the absence or presence of stigmatization, and whether we think positive change (good

Table 6-1   Types of deviant behavior by imputed responsibility, stigma, and prognosis.

Prognosis	Responsible		Not Responsible	
	No Stigma	Stigma	No Stigma	Stigma
Curable	Parking violation	Obesity	Pneumonia	Leprosy
Improvable but not curable	Tax violation	Burglary	Crippling condition	Manic-depression
Incurable and unimprovable	Professional mercenary	Drug misuse	Dwarfism	Schizophrenia

prognosis) is possible. Drug misuse is evaluated in this table with other situations viewed as deviant.

Many of us perceive the drug misuser as being clearly responsible for his behavior. In part, we stigmatize him because we think he's not like us. In the process of stigmatizing him, we reinforce the notion that he is unchangeable—incurable and unimprovable. Over time, we have seen that as attitudes and values change, we come to change our own definitions about what behaviors are problems and which ones aren't. For example, leprosy was once the target of the same attitudes now popularly held toward drug misuse.

One of the dilemmas that we face is that whereas we can hold someone else's drug-using child or spouse responsible for his drug behavior, we don't do it as easily with our own. Whereas we can perceive someone else's drug behavior as being violent and uncontrollable, we don't see it the same way in people we care about. Whereas we can stigmatize the behavior of others, we resent it when it is done to the ones whom we feel close to or responsible for.

By the time we discover that someone we care about is using drugs, that behavior is no longer new behavior. Most often the clues have been staring us in the face, and we have denied them—the major clue is usually some change in behavior. And most often we feel betrayed, angry, and hopeless. Very often we make believe that we are effectively dealing with our "discovery" by going through the guilt-provoking "where did I go wrong?" or "where did I fail you?" gambit. Pragmatically, the issue is not what was wrong or right in the past, but rather what is going on in the present and what can be realistically planned for in the future.

This chapter will not attempt to pinpoint the right and wrong reactions to drug use. There really aren't any. Whatever we do will result in certain consequences, some predictable and some not. What is important is to be sufficiently flexible with our reactions so that we help rather than harm others and ourselves.

Here are a number of examples of "drug" incidents which many of us face.

PROTECTING A CHILD FROM EXCESSIVE CONCERN ABOUT DRUGS

The scene is this: A nine-year-old daughter has returned home after spending a number of hours with a girl friend she has not seen in months. The girl friend has been away from the city and has just returned. The daughter is happy and excited.

"Pamela looks the same! She let me play with some beautiful French dolls, and I tried on some of her new clothes. We had a lot of fun."

"Did she have a nice time in France?"

"She had a good time, but it was hard at first because she didn't know French."

"Does she know it now?"

"I guess she does. The babysitter who was there does."

"What was the babysitter doing there?"

"Taking care of us. Pamela's mother wasn't home. The babysitter's boy-friend showed us a neat thing."

"What?"

"How to make roach holders."

After the silence:

"Do you know what roach holders are?"

"Now I do. He said that they are used to smoke marijuana—to hold it. You look angry, Daddy. What's wrong?"

"I am. I'm angry because I think that the babysitter and her boyfriend did something stupid. Do you know what marijuana is?"

"It's a drug that you smoke in a cigarette. We learned about it in school. Sometimes you talk about it."

"Were the babysitters smoking marijuana?"

"I think so. But they were fun to be with. They were laughing and nice. Are you going to report them? Please, don't get them into trouble."

"I don't know what I'm going to do about them right now. I'm too angry. I'm not angry at you. I'm angry at them for smoking marijuana when they were there to take care of you and your friend. And I'm angry at myself because I really don't know what I should do about telling your friend's mother."

"Please, don't tell her. They were nice to us."

"They may be lovely kids, but I don't expect them to do things that are silly when they should be responsible for you. It may sound confusing to you."

"What are you going to do?"

"I don't know. I'll have to think about it. One thing for sure—from now on you'll see Pamela in our house or when her mother is home!"

The conversation went on for quite a while. I've given an accurate rendition of it. I was the father, and the daughter is my eldest child, and the situation was quite an experience for me since I was confronted with a "drug problem" in my own home. Somehow, the theories didn't help. I'm not sure that I responded in the right way or the wrong way. But I did respond. And I responded in my usual way—expressing feelings, thoughts, and acknowledging that I wasn't quite sure what I was going to do about part of the event—the teen-agers.

The important issue for me was to get across my feelings and my thoughts to my child and for myself. This is the kind of relationship we have. One of the consequences to my insisting that my daughter only see her friend after school at our home or when her mother was home was that it seemingly lessened their bonds. Perhaps another parent would have attempted to see that this didn't occur. My concern was to try to see to it that my daughter's safety was not jeopardized. Her social life continues to be a full one. This in no way guarantees that she won't ever turn to drugs. But the important issue, if we are concerned about prevention, is to prepare our children and to reinforce in our adult peers the ability to adapt to the world of people and not the world of drugs.

In attempting to do this, we help others learn what are appropriate and inappropriate roles, what are the limitations and responsibilities of these roles, and what are the consequences of behavior. One of the ways we do this is just by *being*, by serving as a role model to be identified with, tested, or rejected. None of these can be accomplished if we behave in a phony way. And by "phony way," I mean acting markedly different from our usual ways.

If we are concerned that someone we care about and feel responsible for may be tempted to use or experiment with drugs, we should tell him so. But we should not act in a way that is quite different from our usual behavior. And if we don't want him to use drugs, we had best offer alternatives that are meaningful and achievable, rather than just reasons. Having done and said whatever we did and said, we ourselves have to acknowledge that there may be little else we can do then. Perhaps a friend or relative can be asked to intercede. But the next step is being able to wait and see what happens against a background of mutual trust. If the trust is missing, this indeed is a bigger problem than potential drug use.

At first glance, it would be nice if we calmly approached our child or spouse or friend and pointed out in a rational way why he should not involve himself in drug misuse. The unfortunate (or is it fortunate?) reality is that many of us aren't calm. Our feelings about drugs aren't rational, and we aren't the only people or forces that affect the decision making of those we feel close to. This is an important piece of knowledge to attain, not only for ourselves, but to be able to pass on to others. The best thing we can do or say about potential drug misuse directly relates to our recognizing ourselves as being mortals—with all limitations that such a condition connotes.

INTERVENING IN DRUG EXPERIMENTATION

Living in a world which has made it possible to explore the oceans and the planets in what, at one time, was a science fiction fantasy, we may also be confronted with the behavior of someone's exploring life via drugs. In fact, it's more likely that any one of us shall have to decide what to do or say about someone's drug experimentation than it is that we shall have to learn to adapt to life under water or on the moon. The strange thing is that whereas we would view adapting to the conditions on the moon or under the ocean as a task or series of tasks to be learned and integrated, many of us view adapting to someone else's drug experimentation as a burden that is to be agonized.

The scene is the Sunday breakfast table. The parents are continuing a discussion initiated at that week's PTA meeting, which discussed the signs and symptoms of drug use. They remember that tiredness, irritability, something about the eyes, being unkempt, staying out late, and a lack of appetite are some of the symptoms. The 17-year-old prodigal son comes to the table.

MOTHER: "What do you want for breakfast, David?"
SON: "Nothing."
MOTHER: "You have to have something. Aren't you hungry?"
SON: "No, I'm not hungry."
FATHER: "Is something wrong—you usually pack it away Sunday morning."
SON: "Nothing is wrong—stop bugging me! I'm going out."

FATHER: "Now, wait one minute. I want to talk to you. You seem irrit-
able. Lately you're walking around snapping at everyone—dressing
like a slob. Mother says you're tired most of the time, particularly
when it comes to household chores. Yet you find the energy to stay
out late with *that* group of boys!"

SON: "What do you mean by that 'group' of boys?"

FATHER: "Now, David, you know very well what I mean. Do I have to
spell it?"

SON: "Yes, please do! What are you getting at?"

MOTHER: "Let's not get excited. Let's talk about things calmly, David."

SON: "What things—what are you getting at?"

MOTHER: "Dad and I have been concerned about the change in your behavior for some time. We are worried. There are times when we just
don't recognize you. What's wrong?"

SON: "Nothing. What's bugging you? What are you accusing me of?"

FATHER: "No one is accusing you of anything. We just want to help you.
We are your parents. We love you. David are you . . ."

SON: "Am I what?"

FATHER: "You know what I mean. Well, are you?"

The conversation went on in the same vein for a while. Finally, David
acknowledged he was smoking marijuana, had used LSD a number of
times, and had a few times taken some pep pills.

The father forbade him to see that group of boys again. The mother
pointed the finger of guilt at herself. Both parents insisted that their son
see a psychiatrist. The result was that David continued to see his friends
on the sly; one person was blamed for behavior which had multiple roots,
and the behavioral problems of adolescence were formalized by seeking
treatment which wasn't really needed.

The real issues were overlooked. Was David having difficulty in school?
He wasn't. Was he helping out less around the house than usual? No, he
wasn't. Did he have friends? Quite a few. Was he dating? Yes, he was. He
wasn't going steady. Did he have many interests and hobbies? No. He
seemed to have lost interest in his old interests and hadn't replaced them
yet.

David was going through a normal adolescence, which at best is unstable and volatile. He was using drugs in a group setting. He really didn't
know why (but he would have denied this). He also would have denied
that he was doing it to be part of the group. He also would have denied he
was scared at times when he thought about the possibility of being

arrested. He also would have denied that he was embarrassed at times that he didn't seem to experience what his friends apparently experienced when they were high or stoned. He would not have denied the pleasure he experienced. He would not deny that he felt somewhat more grown up when high. He would not deny the excitement he felt when he came home somewhat high, and his educated parents didn't detect anything. Indeed, there were many things that he would have denied and many that he would have acknowledged, but no one really seemed to care what he felt. They only appeared to be concerned about what he did—and what he shouldn't do.

And for David, and there are many Davids, getting him to stop his drug use starts with an understanding of the role drug use plays in his life. To achieve that, we have to understand what he feels, what he thinks, and what meaning he gives to his feelings, thoughts, and actions—and not only the drug-related ones.

In the process of doing this, we have to be able, given our limitations, to get across to the Davids and Marys and Teds and whoever else what our concerns, feelings, and thoughts are. While feelings of guilt may creep in, they have no healthy functional role. We may relate not only our present feelings, but the ones from the past as well. After all, David isn't really experiencing something new with his drug behavior. While drugs may diminish or exaggerate behavior, the behavior has to be there originally to be diminished, exaggerated, or even distorted. And that basic behavior is part of our human condition.

Maybe we have to remind David of this. Maybe it will help him if he understands that both his drug and nondrug-related behavior are not so unique, that we've experienced some, if not most of it, and perhaps still do. After all, do we who drink and smoke really know why we continue to do so? Do we easily acknowledge that we are subject to group pressures or anxieties, fears and depressions? Do we easily confess to the embarrassments of living?

Will telling David all of this get him to stop his casual drug use? Will sending him for treatment accomplish this? We really don't know. At best, if talking to him is part of an ongoing relationship which has personal meaning for him and all the others involved, he may develop the necessary skills and the sense of trust and hope that are needed for taking a chance on turning to and depending upon people rather than drugs or other things. There is no tried and true way of developing trust and hope. There is no model relationship that can protect a youngster from trying drugs.

There are, however, a variety of relationships which, if they come to have meaning for the youngster, may outweigh the pleasures, excitement, and seductiveness of drugs. (See Table 6-2.)

We must also bear in mind that drugs, as they come to play a more central role in our daily lives, are just another part of the world that people have to adapt to. Some people adapt by active testing, others by passive assessing. While it is realistically and understandably difficult for a nondrug user to stand by and look on as a person they care about tests out his relationship to others and to drugs by using drugs, we must remind ourselves that testing goes on for a lifetime. It is perhaps miraculous that so many children survive without electrocuting themselves, burning themselves, seriously injuring themselves, or from other sources of potential danger.

The adult population must learn to communicate the idea that life is precious and worth living. (We often don't believe this ourselves.) All the lectures, family dramas, and treatment in the world may be neutralized by offering adult role models to the young that, instead of celebrating life, desecrate its values and its potentials.

How do we not fall into this trap? By not acknowledging and showing who we are. By focusing on people and not on drugs. By acknowledging the arbitrariness of many of our needs and the ways we satisfy them. By not mixing up pride and feeding our own egos with concern for the pleasures and problems of others.

In essence, we have to come to terms with taking a chance on living life and not playing at it. If we want to stop someone from experimenting with drugs, we have to struggle through at least two issues:

1. Why should he give up drugs? What's in it for him and what's in it for me?
2. After drugs, then what?

INTERVENING IN A DRUG-ORIENTED COMMITMENT

Maybe we can stop someone from using drugs by refocusing his interests, energies, and attention or by reinforcing his nondrug orientation. Maybe we can diminish or inhibit experimentation with drugs by understanding the meaning and role drugs play for someone who is testing himself, others, and the world in which he's growing up. But what about the person who apparently has passed from the stage of drug testing into that of drug commitment? Can he be reached? Should we bother? The immediate answer that comes to mind is: Dare we not!

If we have permitted ourselves to be brainwashed into believing "once an addict, always an addict" and that "addicts are special kinds of people," then we may give up before we start. Or if not that, we may enter into relationships in which we concentrate on the type of drug used, the amount and frequency of use, and as the types change and the amounts or frequencies increase, we may reassure ourselves that this person—whom we still claim to love, but toward whom we are less than caring—cannot be helped. He is too sick. He needs professional help.

The scene is America at noon. Father has been called home by mother. Their son, Jerry, was just suspended from school. His school work has been going downhill for the last year. He is no longer as interested in sports as he was. Lately, he's been talking about not going to college. He feels that there's no sense to it. And now he's been suspended for suspicion of drug use. A few days from now the suspicion will be verified. Jerry is snorting heroin. As far as his parents knew, he used to be smoking only marijuana occasionally.

FATHER: "What happened?"

SON: "Nothing."

MOTHER: "Tell Dad the truth."

SON: "He wouldn't believe me."

FATHER: "Try me out."

SON: "I've been tired, and I wasn't listening in class. I guess my eyes were closed. The teacher accused me of using drugs."

FATHER: "Were you?"

SON: "Dad, you know better than that. I smoke grass once in a while. We've been through that. I thought you trusted me."

FATHER: "I thought so, too. I didn't mind your smoking marijuana. I guess I didn't think it would harm you. It didn't seem to change you too much. Your work at school was okay, and you were your usual self at home. But you've changed a lot lately."

MOTHER: "Dad's right. Even your sister has noticed it. And I overheard our neighbors talking about how different you seem. You're not your usual self. What's wrong? How can we help you?"

SON: "Nothing's wrong. Just get off my back!"

FATHER: "Now hold on! No one's on your back. I may not know everything that's wrong, but I do know part of it is that you're on hard drugs."

SON: "Who says so? It's not true. You just don't trust me. You don't understand me. You never did, and you never will?"

FATHER: "Just hold on a minute! The school doctor called me. He said

Table 6-2 Alternatives to drugs.[1]

Level of Experience	Corresponding Motives (Examples)	Possible Alternatives (Examples)
Physical	Desire for physical satisfaction Physical relaxation Relief from sickness Desire for more energy Maintenance of physical dependency.	Athletics Dance Exercise Hiking Diet Health training Carpentry or outdoor work.
Sensory	Desire to stimulate sight, sound, touch, taste Need for sensual-sexual stimulation Desire to magnify sensorium.	Sensory awareness training Sky diving Experiencing sensory beauty of nature.
Emotional	Relief from psychological pain Attempt to solve personal perplexities Relief from bad mood Escape from anxiety Desire for emotional insight Liberation of feeling Emotional relaxation.	Competent individual counseling Well-run group therapy Instruction in psychology of personal development.
Interpersonal	To gain peer acceptance To break through interpersonal barriers To "communicate," especially nonverbally Defiance of authority figures Cement two-person relationships Relaxation of interpersonal inhibition Solve interpersonal hangups.	Expertly managed sensitivity and encounter groups Well-run group therapy Instruction in social customs Confidence training Social-interpersonal counseling Emphasis on assisting others in distress via education Marriage.
Social (including sociocultural & environmental)	To promote social change To find identifiable subculture To tune out intolerable environmental conditions, e.g., poverty Changing awareness of the "masses."	Social service Community action in positive social change Helping the poor, aged, infirm, young, tutoring handicapped Ecology action.
Political	To promote political change To identify with antiestablishment subgroup To change drug legislation Out of desperation with the social-political order To gain wealth or affluence or power.	Political service Political action Nonpartisan projects such as ecological lobbying Field work with politicians and public officials.

Category	Motives	Program
Intellectual	To escape mental boredom Out of intellectual curiosity To solve cognitive problems To gain new understanding in the world of ideas To study better To research one's own awareness For science.	Intellectual excitement through reading, through discussion Creative games and puzzles Self-hypnosis Training in concentration Synectics—training in intellectual breakthroughs— Memory training
Creative-aesthetic	To improve creativity in the arts To enhance enjoyment of art already produced, e.g., music To enjoy imaginative mental productions	Nongraded instruction in producing and/or appreciating art, music, drama, crafts, handiwork, cooking, sewing, gardening, writing, singing, etc.
Philosophical	To discover meaningful values To grasp the nature of the universe To find meaning in life To help establish personal identity To organize a belief structure.	Discussions, seminars, courses in the meaning of life Study of ethics, morality, the nature of reality Relevant philosophical literature Guided exploration of value systems.
Spiritual-mystical	To transcend orthodox religion To develop spiritual insights To reach higher levels of consciousness To have divine visions To communicate with God To augment yogic practices To get a spiritual shortcut To attain enlightenment To attain spiritual powers.	Exposure to nonchemical methods of spiritual development Study of world religions Introduction to applied mysticism, meditation Yogic techniques.
Miscellaneous	Adventure, risk drama, "kicks," unexpressed motives Pro-drug general attitudes, etc.	"Outward bound" survival training Combinations of alternatives above Pro-naturalness attitudes Brain-wave training Meaningful employment, etc.

¹From Cohen, A. Y., "The Journey Beyond Trips," *Journal of Psychedelic Drugs*, vol. 3, no. 2, Spring 1971 (with permission).

you were *nodding* in class. He says that the teachers have suspected your using heroin for some time."

MOTHER: "Is that true?"

FATHER: "Of course it's true. Just look at him! When did you start using heroin? How long ago?"

SON: "A while ago."

FATHER: "Don't get snotty with me! What's a while?"

SON: "About two months ago."

FATHER: "How often do you use it?"

SON: "Does it really make a difference?"

FATHER: "You bet your ass it does! How often?"

SON: "It depends."

FATHER: "On what?"

SON: "On money and how I'm feeling."

MOTHER: "What money do you use?"

SON: "Don't worry, Mom. I haven't stolen anything from you. I use my allowance and I do odd jobs."

FATHER: "How odd are the jobs?"

SON: "Very funny! Can I go now?"

FATHER: "Can you go! You're becoming a drug addict, and you're talking about going. You must be off your rocker! How much of that poison do you use?"

SON: "I don't know."

FATHER: "What do you mean, you don't know? Don't get smart-alecky with your mother and me!"

SON: "Okay, okay. I buy a few bags at a time, and I sniff them one at a time. Are you satisfied?"

FATHER: "I'm, satisfied enough to put you away in a hospital. Don't you care that you're killing your mother? Haven't you always gotten what you wanted? Is this how you repay us? What's wrong with you?"

SON: "I don't know, and your sermon isn't helping."

And in a way, he was right. He didn't really know if anything was wrong. He hadn't even ever taken the time to consider if things were right for him. Intuitively he knew that sermons or lectures weren't what was needed.

And in a way, the parents were right. They had done all that they felt they could and should do. They also had never taken the time to discuss and assess what they were doing in relation to each other and in relation to their son. Hard drugs would never happen to their son, and marijuana smoking was just a phase.

All three of them somehow got out of focus. Somewhere along the line this youngster involved himself more and more in the world of drug-related living and just acted as if he were engaged by the world of interpersonal relationships.

Guilt, recriminations, sarcasm, and threats may be good as a psychic enema, but they surely are not going to help us attract a person back to the world of people when many of his needs are met by the world of drugs.

What are the alternatives open to us?

1. *Ship him off to treatment.*

Treatment may work if he has problems that are treatable, by the kinds of treatment that are available, and if he is willing to be treated. And these are just three of the *ifs* that are important.

2. *Turn him in to the police.*

Incarceration may help a person by structuring his life if he needs it, but jail and prison at best teach a person how to adapt to jail and prison and not the general community. Although some parents "turn" their children in in order to protect them from dying, we must keep in mind that law enforcement institutions are meant to punish and isolate and not to save the lives of the inmates. The parent may also want to question whether his child needs the kind of education that prisons are infamous for. Contemporary education may be irrelevant for the challenges of today's patterns of life, but it is even more questionable whether the sadism, paranoia, homosexuality, and brutality taught in prisons are any more relevant.

3. *Deny he is using drugs.*

Psychological myopia eventually catches up with all of us. Sooner or later, usually later, we discover drugs are being used. Denial buys us time. But for what? If we are engaged in the process of denial because we think we don't know what to do, how will the passage of time serve to enlighten us?

4. *Acknowledge the drug use and plan with the drug user what can and can't be done.*

The greatest danger for the youngster who is committed to drug use is not what the drug may do to him physically or psychologically or even socially. The greatest danger is that, during the most crucial and exciting period of his life, drug use may result in his forfeiting learning what his strengths and weaknesses are and what he can do about them and with them.

The parent or peer must be able to point this out to the drug user. What we want to communicate is in a delicate balance. We want to express that we are hopeful and that we do care and are concerned and will remain so. We also want to communicate a sense of respect and trust, which we can best do by not coming across with all the answers. In the first place, there are not "the answers." Secondly, even if there were, it is doubtful that one mortal would have them. Finally, the vaudeville act of "with my answers and your efforts, life will be beautiful" is no more than a hypocritical gambit. Our efforts should not be to save or even to salvage. They should be to help, with both the helper and the helped learning what his role, responsibilities, and limitations are.

So how do we get the so-called committed drug user to give up his drugs? By learning who he is and by helping him to learn. He may not know. By learning what he can do and what he can't do. By learning what his concerns and aspirations are and how drug use fits into them or negatively affects them. By expressing our fears and concerns about the drug user's way of life and his values, at the same time that we permit him a chance to discuss them with us. By reacting to him as a person and not as a stereotype. And by acknowledging the point at which we feel we have had it with him. Self-righteous continuation of an activity may lead to martyrdom after death, but it has little to do with altering someone else's behavior during one's lifetime.

Indeed, there is a time for giving, a time for giving in, and a time for giving up. It takes time, as well as effort, to discover and to determine what the most appropriate time is for the necessary kind of giving.

There are no hard and fast rules about what to do or what to say when we want to intervene in drug misuse. Obviously, different approaches work with different families and in different groups. We have to constantly remind ourselves that we have had a variety of experiences, using different approaches, to help children and peers make decisions about their drinking, smoking, and eating patterns. Sometimes we failed— whatever that means. But there is no instant success. Nor is there any guarantee for success. More often than not, we have been able to demonstrate that it is in a person's interests to satisfy his appetites and his needs in ways in which most others do. When we have been able to do this, it is because we offered alternatives that made sense to the person. They were achievable and acceptable to him, as well as satisfying.

What to do and what to say are very personal things. When we face these issues *im*personally, when we hide behind the facade of objectivity or the dramatic masks of guilt or rage, we are playing, not being. As trite as it may seem, where there is life there is hope. And where there is hope there is the potential for alternatives and solutions. The choice of what to do, how to do it, and when to do it is partly ours. We have to consciously decide our own role before we attend to the behavior of the person we want to help.

PROJECTS

1. Develop a role-playing situation with family members, friends, etc., in which you are a drug user seeking help, but you are not quite sure what kind of help. After about 15 minutes of this role playing, consider the following issues:
   (a) Did you feel that they were offering help in a way that you could use it?
   (b) From your perspective, were they responding to what you were doing and saying or to their notions of what you needed?
   (c) What demands were being made upon you for receiving help? Could you have met these demands?
   (d) As a potential "helper" in this situation, what were the factors that made it difficult or easier to offer your help?
   (e) What *proof* was demanded of the "drug user" that he really deserved help?
2. In a relatively small social situation, indicate that you are feeling uptight and ask if anyone has a tranquilizer. Note how many people offer you one.
3. Consider that someone you are much concerned about is taking drugs for other than medical reasons or may do so in the future. Develop a course of action with various alternatives or contingency plans. Note what the action is, what alternatives are related to it, what role the other person is to play, as well as your own role, and whether each of you is up to the demands of the roles that you have outlined.

   Action   *Alternative*   *Roles*   *Demands*
                                       Theirs   Yours

4. Remember and note the first time you did something that someone who was important to you (parent, friend, sibling) didn't like and let you know this. Did their reaction to your behavior effect what you were doing? And if so, why do you think it had an effect? Were there any common denominators from this event which you can utilize in making a functional response to a drug-related issue which presently concerns you?

BIBLIOGRAPHY

Anonymous, *Go Ask Alice.* Englewood Cliffs, N.J.: Prentice-Hall, 1971.

Barber, B., *Drugs and Society.* New York: Russell Sage, 1967.

Barnes, D. E., and Messolonghites, L., *Preventing Drug Abuse.* New York: Holt, Rinehart & Winston, 1972.

Bell, R. G., *Escape from Addiction.* New York: McGraw-Hill, 1970.

Cameron, D. C., "Youths and Drugs—A World View," *Journal of the American Medical Association,* vol. 206, pp. 1267–1271, 1968.

Castaneda, C., *The Teachings of Don Juan: A Yaqui Way of Knowledge.* Berkeley, Calif.: University of California Press, 1968.

Cohen, S., *The Drug Dilemma.* New York: McGraw-Hill, 1969.

Erikson, E., ed., *Youth: Change and Challenge.* New York: Basic Books, 1963.

Erikson, E., *Identity: Youth and Crisis,* New York: Norton, 1968.

Fort, J., *The Pleasure Seekers.* New York: Bobbs-Merrill, 1969.

Friedenberg, E., *Coming of Age in America.* New York: Random House, 1965.

Goldhill, F. M., *A Parent's Guide to the Prevention and Control of Drug Abuse.* Chicago: Regnery, 1971.

Group for the Advancement of Psychiatry, *Drug Misuse.* New York: Scribner, 1971.

Keniston, K., *Young Radicals, Notes on Committed Youth.* New York: Harcourt, Brace & World, 1968.

Lennard, H. B., and associates, *Mystification and Drug Misuse.* San Francisco: Jossey-Bass, 1971.

Louria, D. B., *Overcoming Drugs.* New York: McGraw-Hill, 1971.

Marin, P., and Cohen, A. Y., *Understanding Drug Use.* New York: Harper & Row, 1971.

National Coordinating Council on Drug Abuse Education and Information, *Common Sense Lives Here—A Community Guide to Drug Abuse Action.* Washington, D.C., 1971.

Watts, A., *The Joyous Cosmology: Adventures in the Chemistry of Consciousness.* New York: Pantheon, 1962.

Weil, A., *The Natural Mind.* New York: Houghton Mifflin, 1972.

Zinberg, N. E., and Robertson, J. A., *Drugs and the Public.* New York: Simon & Schuster, 1972.

CHAPTER 7

Education and Prevention

The welfare of the people has always been the alibi of tyrants.

Camus

Education and prevention are concepts as common in the field of drug abuse as apple pie, motherhood, and sin are in our general culture.

The strength and impact of drug-abuse education and prevention programs lie in their potential; their greatest weakness lies in their present actual use. Combined with treatment as it is currently generally practiced, education and prevention programs permit most of us to feel that we have little role in or responsibility for the American drug scene.

In order to understand what drug-abuse education and prevention mean, we had best understand what they presently are. We live in a culture which believes that man is a rational being. That premise leads us to think that if we present sufficient information to people, particularly youngsters, about the dangers of drugs and drug use, then the recipient of this knowledge will either not enter the drug scene, or else he will leave it.

The Temperance Movement was concerned about the spiritual-moral, physical-psychological dangers of drug use. The Temperance Movement effort led to the development of meaningless school programs. Most often, these consisted of a series of self-contained lectures which were generally given by the school nurse or the health/physical education teacher. One can only assume that their impact upon preventing or decreasing drug abuse was at best minimal, given the huge incidence of current drug use.

In recent years, the increase in drug misuse by every segment of our population has been paralleled by an increase in hysteria, even panic, and a demand for saving the youth of the nation. Thus, drug-abuse education has tended to focus on young people, leaving the over-thirty generation to fend for itself.

During the spring of 1970, representatives of every state met in Chicago to discuss and carry out President Nixon's plan to save the nation. The key idea of that meeting was the "multiplier effect." Each of the representatives was to return home and develop intensive training programs in their respective states for selected teachers, who were then responsible for developing less intensive training programs for other teachers during the fall of 1970. As the numbers of teachers being trained multiplied, the impact and scope of their training lessened, and then during the spring of 1971 they were to go forth and save the youth. In certain areas of America, sufficient money was available to save students from kindergarten through high school.

In other communities, there was only enough money to save schoolchildren from the seventh grade on. Youngsters who were not in school and oldsters long out of school would either have to save themselves or, if they succumbed to drug misuse, they could be saved through treatment.

And how were we going to save the students that we had money to save? Through films which were often scientifically inaccurate; through school surveys, lectures, and with the help of superficially trained teachers, inadequately trained health professionals, and law enforcement representatives, and the use and misuse of ex-addicts, against a general background of school policies, that call for the suspension and/or dismissal of suspected or actual drug-using students in order to contain their contagious influences.

How effective were these new drug-abuse programs? It is hard to tell at this time. Most new programs are variations of the old ineffective scare programs, with no built-in evaluation of their efficacy. Perhaps most significantly, most new education programs are not really *education programs*; rather, they are drug-abuse *training programs*. The distinction is a major one. There are places in our society for both kinds of program, but given the limitations in the scope of each, we should not mix them up if we seriously want to change the drug-misuse pattern in a given community at a given time.

Training assumes that a group of people with varying skills and abilities—a heterogeneous group—is brought to a given level of proficiency in the skill or topic they are being trained in. One result of this kind of process is to turn a heterogeneous group into a homogeneous one. We can do this with typing, driver safety, reading, math levels, etc. We can do this in drug abuse if our goal is simply the dissemination of facts and knowledge about drugs, drug laws, and any other area that has limited and clear factual boundaries.

Using various educational techniques, and even a number of gimmicks, we can feel somewhat confident that we have gotten the message across about the dangers of the drug life and the advantages of the nondrug life. Underlying this type of program is the strong and unproved assumption that, given the facts, a person will draw the correct conclusions and change or pattern his life on these facts. It should be fairly clear by now that man's behavior, particularly his appetitive behavior, is not necessarily based on an orderly progression of decisions based on avoiding danger. In fact, for adolescents, one might go so far as to suggest that information about dangers may induce or stimulate them to test themselves out with the hope of beating the danger—a type of adolescent Russian roulette.

Education, on the other hand, assumes that a group of individuals who are also heterogeneous will become active participants in a process which leaves them being heterogeneous. The individual will become increasingly aware of his present level of skills, abilities, interests, and aspirations as well as his potential ones—the alternatives open to him for every decision he makes spontaneously or which he has to make, and his role and responsibilities in the decision-making process as well as some of the consequences of the decisions and their associated behavior. This is a long way of saying that education permits the person to learn who he is and who he isn't.

This process occurs both formally and informally; it starts at birth and is completed at death. It may be significantly interfered with when the person's energy, time, and focus of attention are stopped by training. This is particularly so in the area of drug abuse. Emphasis on the dangers of drugs and the stereotypes of drug users will often neither permit nor challenge a person to consider what personally meaningful alternatives are available for him in a drug-oriented society, what some of the consequences to the alternatives are for him, and what his role might be in relation to drug abuse.

Drug-abuse education and prevention are processes; they are not panaceas. The way we interpret and carry out the various processes determines the types of programs that are developed. The success or failure of a given program is not really related to the program, although it may look that way. Rather, success or failure is related to the kind of process we choose and the assumptions underlying each process.

Current programs are generally based on the assumption that drug abuse is dangerous to the individual. These dangers are then felt to have a spin-off that is dangerous to the neighborhood and to society at large.

Under the best of circumstances, contemporary drug-abuse education and prevention may have limited success because it is haphazardly abstinence oriented. (Recreational drug use is only acceptable for society at large if the drugs are alcohol, tobacco products, and most foods.) The active drug abuser may call this hypocrisy.

By now the reader may be angry, confused, or depressed, depending upon his views on drug abuse and what usable, functional material he anticipated reading. The rest of this chapter will attempt to help turn anger into viable alternatives, confusion into meaningful concern, and depression into delineated, achievable roles and programs.

The concept "nondrug alternatives to drug abuse" can become merely another catchy phrase which most people can agree on, but which appears to be too abstract to grasp and use. After all, one of the advantages of an abstinence-oriented program is that it is simple and easily related to, even though it appears to be difficult to achieve. Abstinence means not using certain drugs in certain ways for certain reasons. Nondrug alternatives to drug abuse means that we have to come up with alternatives that are meangingful, achievable, acceptable, and flexible to satisfy the individual, his personal community, and society at large. Such alternatives have to be hand-tailored, whereas abstinence is, to a great extent, pretailored.

When we consider developing alternatives to drug abuse, we may be at a loss, because the task seems too huge beyond our individual mortal talents, energy level, and time commitments. This is the biggest barrier to overcome. Once we overcome it (and we can!), the development of alternatives to drug abuse takes on the coloration of a decision-making process.

This decision-making process must begin with our understanding what we ourselves and our society mean by drug abuse. The definitions are necessary if we are to know what we want to and what we actually can do regarding intervening in drug abuse.

For the sake of this chapter, drug abuse will be defined in three ways:

1. the abuse of current drug laws, mores, and rituals;
2. self-abuse;
3. abuse of others.

The first implies that the taking of certain drugs in certain ways for certain reasons runs counter to existing drug laws or conventionally accepted mores and rituals.

Self-abuse implies that by taking any drug to excess, the person is primarily harming himself in some way. The harm may result in either direct or indirect physical, psychological, social, or negative consequences to the individual regardless of how this behavior affects others.

Drug abuse of others implies that others in the drug user's life space are negatively affected by the existence of drug-abuse behavior. One example of this could be how the nonsmoker is affected by the smoker in close quarters.

One can immediately discern why many contemporary drug-abuse education and prevention programs fail. Their working definition of drug abuse, instead of being limited and clear, embraces too much all at once and is confusing.

Are current education programs primarily concerned with preventing laws from being broken, with how the drug abuser is harming himself or with how he is harming the rest of us? Would there be little need for educational programs if all drugs were easily and legally available? Would there be little need for educational programs for most of the population if we trained drug abusers how safely to use pharmaceutically pure substances, which we would easily make available? Would there be a need for programs if we isolated the drug abuser so that his behavior could only minimally affect the rest of us?

My own bias leads me to believe that there will still be a need for drug-abuse education and prevention programs because man's relationship to various chemical substances has always been unpredictable, unstable, and irrationally colored.

There will always be new laws, mores, and rituals to challenge and break, new substances to experiment with, and others who will feel adversely affected by substance-oriented behavior.

Once drug abuse is defined, the next task is selecting the focus of our intervention efforts as well as the possible sources of intervention. These decisions will again be arbitrary ones. Possible foci of intervention become:

1. the available drugs;
2. drug abstainers, either individuals who have never misused particular drugs, or individuals who have and are presently abstaining;
3. active drug users and misusers;
4. intervention agents: teachers, clergy, treatment agents, parents, peers, etc.;
5. the general community.

Defining our focus permits us to decide which areas have priority at which time.

The last step is to determine the *sources* of intervention. These include: Treatment, attitudes, media, culture, religion, laws, policies and procedures, politics, economics, research and education—at least 10 avenues for active intervention. Table 7-1 suggests that at the present time there are at least 15 cells of intervention with each choice, education being just one of the choices.

The reader may by now be feeling that he has been had. After all, anyone can create a chart, and charts aren't necessarily the most effective way of confronting ongoing social problems, nor even describing them. Perhaps this is true. But this chart is meant to permit the reader to consider what viable alternatives and roles are available for him as he determines what he can and cannot do to retard or minimize drug abuse. It is also meant to cut through the understandably common experience of what I can do about *a problem that professionals haven't given any significant direction in.* It is meant to remind us that we each have a significant role to play in educating about and preventing drug abuse, given our personal skills, energies, available time, and interests. It is meant to schematically present the fact that there is no simplistic single answer to a problem that is complex and multifaceted. Lastly, it is meant to remind us that as we go from box to box, if there doesn't appear to be something that we can do in one, there surely will be a box that can engage us productively. (See Table 7-1.) And if education or prevention isn't one's "bag," schemas can be worked out for any of the above 10 mentioned areas of intervention.

Table 7-1   A schema for intervening via drug-abuse education and prevention.

Focus of Effort	Abuse of Laws, Mores and Rituals	Self-Abuse	Abuse of Others
Drug			
Abstainers			
Active drug users and misusers			
Intervention agents			
General Community			

More specifically what can we do about drug-abuse education?

To start with, we must always remember that whatever we do is based on arbitrary decisions and must be hand-tailored to coincide with the needs of individuals and their community at any given time. Drug-abuse education and prevention must be a dynamic program and not a monument or an institutionalized edifice.

DRUGS

Focusing on Drugs Laws

The contemporary focus on drugs has led to passing a variety of laws which continue in increasing numbers to be broken. Many have suggested that drug laws should be made more lenient or, indeed, nonexistent. Without legal controls, there would be no drug abuse (in terms of breaking drug-related laws). The reality is that we would still set some kind of drug laws with a different set of arbitrary criteria. We would not necessarily permit 12-year-olds to buy tobacco products, alcoholic beverages, depressants, stimulants, or hallucinogens. Nor would we necessarily legislate their possession and/or use for recreational purposes. Drug laws are new only in that they have served to formalize social mores, rituals and customs. In that sense, education to prevent the abuse of drug laws may be a complete waste of energy, time, and concern.

Focusing on Self-Abuse

Throughout history we have searched for drugs to solve problems. We turned to heroin as a "cure" for morphinism. Presently, we are turning to methadone as a cure for heroin addiction. Since there are no chemical solutions to people problems—and to a great extent drug-related self-abuse is a people problem—drug education is missing the boat when we focus on the use of certain drugs or abstinence from other drugs as a way of combating drug abuse. From an educational-preventive perspective, we should be focusing on drugs by teaching respect for drugs—what they do and don't do. And we should tell it the way it is, what we know, and what we don't know about drugs. In fact, all of the reasons given for recreational drug use are achievable in other ways as well. We must remember that some desirable experiences, for most of us, will always remain elusive. Personal Valhallas are as unlikely to be induced by quick chemical action as they are to be achieved by any other quick technique.

Focusing on Abuse of Others

Perhaps the best effort that can be made in this area is to help the other person understand his own attitudes and stereotypes. In doing this, one of the goals should be to help him come to terms with the role he is playing in the current drug-abuse scene. For example, while it is not pleasant to be irritated by someone else's cigarette smoke or alcohol-induced abusiveness or to be physically or psychologically hurt by particular patterns of drug use, we reinforce all of these events when we accept our society's notion of *progress through chemistry*. In a sense, nonusers help to create the circumstances for their own abuse by playing a personally passive role vis-à-vis the available drugs and their use in their own community. One practical solution for preventing or minimizing the drug-related abuse of others is for these "others" to refocus their energies, time, and commitments away from our present drug orientation and become engaged in concerns, issues, and activities that are more central to the problems and pleasures of contemporary life. In practical terms, this means that we stop blaming what's wrong with our society on drugs and start developing ways of living life styles—that enhance our human qualities and aspirations.

ABSTAINERS

Abuse of Drug Laws

Drug-abuse education has the primary task of helping the abstainer understand his role vis-à-vis himself and those he feels concerned about and responsible for, regarding the variety of drug laws and rituals. He can be helped to understand that his personal decision to abstain may presently be in tune with laws and rituals, but that these laws and rituals may change. Likewise, he must be helped to understand that his abstinence status only relates to the drugs he is abstaining from and that he may have to reconsider his role in relation to other drug-related laws and rituals. For example, when empathizing with an anxious friend, does he suggest a tranquilizer? Will he permit a minor to smoke or drink alcoholic beverages?

In the previous section, drugs were the primary focus, and respect and knowledge of what drugs do and don't do were key issues. In this section, the key issue is the role and responsibility associated with rules.

Self-Abuse

Since abstinence as a concept is only related to specific drugs and rarely to a style of life, the abstainer can be helped to learn to be more tolerant of drug misusers. The less tolerant he is of self-abusers, the less likely are they to turn to him for help. The abstainer must understand that his decision is meaningful only for himself and is not necessarily appropriate for someone else. The fact that "I did it" doesn't mean that someone else can or should do the same thing. The abstainer shouldn't parade just his abstinence status, but rather make clear what it is about personal and community life that is sufficiently satisfying that it doesn't necessitate drug-related self-abuse. The distinction is an important one to make. Abstainers have a crucial role to play as people models, not as abstinence models. Drug-abuse education programs cannot just help them to see and learn this, but also how best to put this knowledge to appropriate use.

Abuse of Others

Not only can abuse of others be caused by active drug users, but abstainers are responsible for a fair share of this too. There surely are more important concerns than regaling others with our feat of abstinence. Indeed, the ex-addict may be able to play a significant role in helping others to minimize or even completely eliminate the drug-related abuse they have been experiencing. They can do this by pointing out some of the alternatives that are available.

Often, one of the consequences of being abused by others is that we may become habituated in this pattern. At times, so much of our energy may be negated in protecting ourselves that we continue to repeat or ritualize our own behavior and feel there is little else we can do. The abstainer can be taught how to translate his abstinence decision in ways that may be productive and usable by people who are caught up in a pattern of being abused. Sometimes just being told by someone else that "you don't have to put up with this" will be sufficient to get a person to reorganize his own life style.

ACTIVE DRUG USERS AND MISUSERS

Abuse of Drug Laws

Active drug users and misusers usually know that they are breaking drug-related laws, mores, and rituals. They, like anyone else, have the ability to rationalize what they are doing. Drug-abuse education may be most helpful for this group if it points out how the energies used in playing cops and robbers can be put to better use.

Self-Abuse

Once again the active drug misuser is more often aware of how he is abusing himself. Often he doesn't care or doesn't feel it's worth changing, or even that it makes sense to try. The major responsibility for drug-abuse education is to help the person to learn *trust* and *hope*, to enable him to reach out to others rather than to chemicals, to gain a respect for his physical, psychological, and social self, and to discover the available alternatives. In a sense, the major responsibility of drug-abuse education is to educate a person to consider new achievable identity roles which minimize self-abuse while maximizing the satisfaction of needs.

Abuse of Others

Abusing others may be pleasurable. Drug-abuse education surely has a role in pointing out the costs to everyone concerned when abuse of others is permitted or even reinforced. The active drug misuser can be helped to understand that as long as his behavior involves the abuse of others, then the mistrust that he is treated with, the general negative stigma associated with his drug status, and the anger and despair he is greeted with are very much associated with his being considered the originator of abuse.

If he desires to be responded to in a more positive and accepting manner, he must be helped to understand and then use those available alternatives that are not based upon his being a source of abuse to others. He must also be helped to understand that just because he begins to change, others will not immediately recognize, acknowledge, believe, or accept the changes. One of the sad realities of life is that it is quite easy to get tagged, but it is difficult to get untagged. Drug-abuse education has a significant role in communicating this message to the active drug misuser.

INTERVENTION AGENTS

Abuse of Drug Laws

Intervention agents, whoever they are, can be educated to understand that contemporary patterns of life have minimized the effect of drug laws upon patterns of drug use. Thus, whether laws are considered to be liberal or punitive, they cannot be looked to as a major force in changing or channeling man's appetitive behavior. On the other hand, intervention agents must be taught the current drug-related mores, rituals, and customs of the groups in the community that they are working with. It is not enough to know what drugs are being used and how they are being used. They must also learn the meaning attributed to that use and how much of that meaning is related to individuals per se and how much is related to and colored by the dynamics of the group that he is a member of or that he identifies with. Intervention agents must also be taught that drug-related mores and rituals most often change in terms of substitution of drugs and drug patterns rather than complete drug abstinence. They must be helped to understand how mores and rituals are reinforced as well as inhibited.

Lastly, most people who do not represent law enforcement feel that they have little or no role regarding the law other than respecting-agreeing or disrespecting-disagreeing with it. Intervention agents of all kinds need to be educated as to their possible roles and activities regarding drug-related laws, as well as why we have the kind of drug laws we do or, for that matter, any kind of drug laws.

Self-Abuse

Intervention agents must be educated to perceive and acknowledge the drug abuser as a dynamic being and not a static stereotype. Self-abuse may be minimized or completely eliminated when the person understands and then integrates for himself that it is in his own best interests to change his drug-oriented style of life. Drug-abuse education can help the intervention agent achieve this by getting him to accept that his focus must be on the value system as vested interests of the drug abuser and not on his own. What is good for the doctor, teacher, clergyman, or lay parent is not necessarily what is best for the patient, student, believer, or child at any given point in time. The intervention agent must be helped to understand that drug abuse is not simply a particular person using a particular drug or that abstinence is necessarily the only viable and appropriate solution for it. Obviously, it is also necessary to offer training in the use of specific educational and therapeutic techniques, how to communicate hope and trust, to present reality as it is, and to learn how to listen, hear, see, and understand.

Abuse of Others

The major role of intervention agents in this area is to teach them how they can best help others protect themselves from being abused and what role they play in being abused. For example, while people legitimately are concerned about drug-related crimes in their communities, someone must be able to point out to them that their continued purchasing of stolen goods from drug abusers not only reinforces the drug problem in their community, but also enhances the possibility of their being personally abused. A trained intervention agent can point out that the indiscriminate use of tranquilizers in response to our feelings about someone we care about who is using drugs is a poor model for the drug abuser. Likewise, believing every rationalization presented to us by a drug abuser rather than confronting him with our feelings and thoughts at the time may only serve to precipitate, if not reinforce, our being abused. Surely many more examples could be given by each reader. The point is that drug-abuse education can prepare a group of intervention agents not only to effectively intervene in the lives of drug abusers, but they must also be trained to help the rest of the population, who may be suffering for the pleasures of someone else's drug abuse. Someone must be available to help a non-abuser who is concerned about how he is being affected by someone else's drug abuse to deal with the general issue of "What do I do? What do I say?"

GENERAL COMMUNITY

Abuse of Drug Laws

If the community at large does not want its drug laws, rituals, or mores broken, it must be helped to decide whether these laws continue to be relevant to the changed drug and nondrug conditions they are living in. If the laws or rituals, the penalties associated with them, and the judicial or societal practices that are meant to sustain them are not in keeping with the needs or the dynamics of contemporary reality and if changes are desirable and/or necessary, the community must be helped to make appropriate decisions. Drug-abuse education can serve to point out available alternatives, the risks, costs, and advantages or disadvantages, and the roles to be taken by all who are involved. Active citizenry is an ongoing process and not a result of casual participation or isolated concern. In a sense, drug-abuse education should result in helping a community develop the kind of life it wants and deserves. Perhaps it is not a mere coincidence that drug abuse appears to be growing as man's insensitivity to man grows. When we make ourselves unavailable to another person, whoever he may be, using whatever rationalizations we use, we must keep in mind that the "other" person cannot just turn inward upon himself, but he can learn about chemical pleasure and solace. Progress through chemistry was not discovered by the media; it is merely packaged cleverly and reinforced by them because it apparently mirrors our desires.

Self-Abuse

Until we discover the gene for self-abuse, we can only assume that self-abuse is a style of life learned by some and condoned, if not reinforced, by society. Drug-related self-abuse is but one variation of this life style. The community at large can be helped to understand the role that it plays in creating the conditions that lead to a lack of self-respect and self-worth, to the mistrust if not disrespect for a variety of human feelings and needs, to a style of living that runs counter to the celebration of life, to the fear of spontaneity, and to the philosophy of "Nowism."[1] Drug-abuse education can help a community learn and come to terms with the fact that drug abuse, recreational drug use, or whatever term we ascribe to it does not grow or continue to exist in a vacuum. Drug-related self-abuse is one of the concomitants of the drug abuse that results from this kind of community life style that fosters it.

Perhaps the most obvious task that must engage drug-abuse education is to get across the notion that such behavior can be intervened with effectively. In this light, the role of education is to see to it that there exists the necessary, continuous, and appropriate delivery of care and education. Through such efforts, the drug-related self-abuser can be encouraged to seek out and test out those programs that do exist. He can learn that success, whatever that means, is possible and that failure occurs for now and not forever.

It should be quite clear by now that effective drug-abuse education is available. It can serve to mobilize meaningful rather than hysterical community interest. This concern must be translated monetarily and must serve to cut through stereotypy and self-fulfilling vested interests and attitudes. Otherwise, drug-related self-abuse is sure to continue. Surely, if it appears that it is not in the interest of the general community to offer viable programs and alternatives to the self-abuser, it is not in his interest to change his behavior.

[1]One's needs must be met immediately and at the time one experiences them. The past is over, we may never live to experience the future and, thus, we must experience as much as we can now and immediately so.

Abuse of Others

Perhaps the most relevant issue for drug-abuse education in terms of the general community is to point out what the needs or dynamics are of allowing a community life style which permits the abuse of many to be caused by the abusive behavior of many. Indeed, the abusive consequences associated with drug misuse, whatever its type, is but one example of the variety of abusiveness that most of us have been taught to accept and tolerate as well as to cause.

Drug-abuse education could serve as a model to help us understand our own roles as both causative agents as well as recipients of all kinds of abuse and point out some of the alternatives and their consequences in minimizing the occurrence of such behavior. The goal of minimizing, rather than total elimination, is being suggested as the outcome of education, because it may well be that abuse, experiencing it and inflicting it, may be part of the human condition.

This orientation is being suggested for other reasons as well. If we can learn that the common denominator is *general abuse*, with drug-related abuse being only one of the variations, we may be able to more easily move away from what seems like entrenched negative attitudes and stereotypes about drugs, drug users, and drug misuse. To do otherwise is to continue to make believe that we have little role in the reasons for the consequent patterns of drug use and misuse. Is it simply *they* who are abusing *us*? Should *they* be grateful for whatever *we* do for *them*? When we come to understand that abuse is generic, one kind not necessarily better or worse than any other kind, we may not as easily be able to rationalize our own behavior and that of our community. This may permit us to move away from scapegoating the drug abuser to beginning to come to terms with what's wrong that can be righted, what's right that can be improved, and what's just right that should be maintained.

It might appear to the reader that what's been presented is abstract philosophy when what is needed are answers. There are no answers until there are relevant questions. Relevant questions in the area of human behavior arise when we attempt to learn what our role and the role of our community and society play in reinforcing and/or inhibiting any pattern of behavior.

Specific programs were not spelled out for each cell for a very specific reason: They must be hand-tailored to the needs of given individuals and groups at a specific point in time. Drugs and drug abuse were not suggested as being primary foci of an educational effort, because it is felt that what should be taught is adaptation to life, the variations and alternatives that are available, and the consequences associated with the choices that are selected. It is not more information about drugs that we need; it is more information about learning who we are, who we are not, what effects our behavior has upon ourselves and others, and what we can do that are lacking.

In this sense, drug-abuse education is not the province of the drug-abuse expert. Rather, if it is to be taught, the teacher must be an expert in human adaptation. Where does one learn this? By living and evaluating and reevaluating what one has experienced, and then by translating this knowledge into teachable forms.

Drug-Abuse Prevention

As with drug-abuse education, we must be clear as to what we want to prevent. Whatever our decision, and it will be an arbitrary one, we must keep in mind that one of our guidelines must be minimal risk or negative consequences to everyone concerned. If the prevention effort in any way jeopardizes the focus of our concern, ourselves, or the general community, we must question and weigh its usefulness.

The issue is not simply what any given program is meant to prevent, but also what it is meant to reinforce. This is aside from the crucial issue of whether it is effective at all. Surely, no single prevention program is going to disengage or prevent people from the use and misuse of drugs. It may, however, be effective in reinforcing certain decision making, inhibiting others, and thereby altering and/or affecting patterns of use.

Indeed, it may be that the concept of drug prevention serves to confuse us in this area. What society, as a unit, and various individuals, who are concerned about drug abuse, may want is a *selection program*. The aim of this program would be to socialize the person into the then-present and acceptable drug choices. In this sense, prevention-selection would have as its mandate teaching people how to use drugs, under what circumstances, and for what meaning. For individuals who used the "wrong" drugs, under the "wrong" circumstances, and for "unacceptable" meaning, prevention could be focused not on the drug use but upon teaching how to minimize facets of self-abuse or abuse of others. It should be obvious by now that the reason we have to know what we are preventing is because the programs can be quite different depending upon the agreed-upon focus.

Who Is the Program For?

All too often we accept as a fact the myth that drug education and prevention programs should be aimed only at youngsters. This makes sense if we mean by this that the format of the program should be hand-tailored to the various needs of youngsters and that similar care will be made in tailoring programs for other kinds of groups.

Drug-abuse education and prevention programs are presently needed in every segment of our society. We can no longer continue to delude ourselves that one particular group is really the only one that is at risk. If we are alive, then we are actually or potentially involved in some form of drug use or misuse, which education could help avoid. The general rule of thumb might be—if it is not blatant, it's latent.

We must remember that drug-abuse education is not equivalent to passing educational statutes or other laws. It is the content of a program, who is responsible for it, its aims, and the techniques used that will determine its success or failure, and not whether it is mandated or not. All too often when we mandate programs, we assume that the law or edict will get the program off the ground and keep it running, that the law will cause significant changes in human behavior and maintain those changes. Obviously only people can do this—people who care, who are concerned, and who in the process of teaching are also intent upon learning.

Education is not a panacea, but neither is anything else. We should not, however, assume that we must do it because nothing else works. Drug-abuse education can only be one part of an effort that is based on offering options and alternatives to drug-oriented life styles.

Given all that has been said, done, and written about drug education and prevention, what can we do at the present time that is more than just a variation of what has already been done?

- We can choose to develop more effective ways of communicating with one another about many facets of the drug scene as well as contemporary living so that we listen rather than hear, talk with and not talk at.
- We can choose to create a climate of trust and mutual respect which will permit us to put the drug scene in a more realistic perspective, as being but one of the issues that need to be confronted.
- We can choose to translate "prevention" and prevention efforts from their present narrow boundaries to that of doing something about those factors that may induce drug-oriented ways of living.
- We can choose to learn to look at the "drug problem" in a more discriminating way by identifying the component parts.
- We can choose to teach ourselves and others how to adapt to a world of drugs and people, by teaching the most appropriate use of drugs as well as the meaningfulness of developing and maintaining mature relationships.

• We can choose to acknowledge, learn, and teach that there are no instant, lasting, or simplistic answers to the many complex questions and issues that drug use has already raised for individuals and communities, and the many more which have yet to be raised.

Drug behavior is not very different from other behaviors about which we are less hopeless and hysterical in our response, behaviors to which there are many entrances and many exits and in which we all play roles.

PROJECTS

1. Develop a model education program including written and visual materials. Decide on the goals of the program, whom the program is for, and what kinds of skills and abilities they will need to understand and use your program. Test it out in a dry run, with family members and friends, both youngsters and adults, and note what the areas of difficulty are.

Program Goals	Type of Materials	Abilities Needed	Difficulties Incurred

2. Attend a drug-education lecture in your community. Note the implicit and explicit content of the lecture in regard to:
   (a) How drug problems are defined?
   (b) How drug users are described?
   (c) What alternatives are offered to drug use?
   (d) What roles are suggested to members of the audience?
   (e) What roles are suggested to drug users?
   (f) Whether the actual or potential drug user you are most concerned about would have some of his needs met by the suggestions that are offered?
3. Get to know how many drug education and prevention programs are currently available in your community. Explore which of them has been evaluated to date and how this was done. In your considered opinion, do these programs accomplish what they say they are doing and can they be of help to you and the people you are concerned about?
4. At a drug-education lecture or program, take one of the following positions:
   (a) You are fed up with hearing about drugs. If the drug addict wants to kill himself, that's his prerogative. If he is a burden for the community, let's put him out of action.
   (b) Talking about drugs is a cop-out in that it camouflages other issues that have greater priority for us all; mention a number of political, economic, or social issues as examples.
   Note the type of response you get from the lecturer and the audience. Is their response conducive to building a program that is hand-tailored to the needs of your community? If you were thinking of stopping drug use or starting, would the lecture have had any effect on your decision? If it would, why is this so? And if it wouldn't, why wouldn't it?
5. Develop a drug-education talk without ever referring to drugs, drug use, or drug users.

BIBLIOGRAPHY

Barber, B., *Drugs and Society.* New York: Russell Sage, 1967.

Bejerot, N., *Addiction and Society.* Springfield, Ill.: C. C. Thomas, 1970.

Bell, R. G., *Escape from Addiction.* New York: McGraw-Hill, 1970.

Brecher, E. M., *Licit and Illicit Drugs.* Boston: Little, Brown, 1972.

Brown, B. S., *et al.*, "In Their Own Words: Addicts' Reasons for Initiating and Withdrawing From Heroin," *International Journal of the Addictions,* vol. 6, no. 4, pp. 635–646, 1971.

Castaneda, C., *The Teaching of Don Juan: A Yaqui Way of Knowledge.* Berkeley, Calif.: University of California Press, 1968.

Clark, W. H., *Chemical Ecstasy.* New York: Sheed and Ward, 1969.

Cohen, A. Y., "The Journey Beyond Trips: Alternatives to Drugs," *Journal of Psychedelic Drugs,* vol 3, no. 2, pp. 16–21, 1971.

Coles, R., *The Grass Pipe.* Boston: Little, Brown, 1969.

Coles, R., *et al.*, *Drugs and Youth,* New York: Liveright, 1970.

DeLone, R. H., "The Ups and Downs of Drug Abuse Education," *Saturday Review of Education,* pp. 27–32, November 11, 1972.

Drug Crisis: Schools Fight Back with Innovative Programs, Washington, D.C.: National School Public Relations Association, 1971.

Edwards, G., *Reaching Out: The Prevention of Drug Abuse Through Increased Human Intervention.* New York: Holt, Rinehart & Winston, 1972.

Einstein, S., and Allen, M., eds., *Student Drug Surveys.* New York: Baywood, 1972.

Einstein, S., *et al.*, "The Training of Teachers for Durg Abuse Education Programs: Preliminary Considerations," *Journal of Drug Education,* vol. 1, no. 4, pp. 323–345, 1971.

Erikson, E., *Identity: Youth and Crisis.* New York: Norton, 1968.

Fort, J., *The Pleasure Seekers.* New York: Bobbs-Merrill, 1969.

Glaser, D., and Snow, M., *Public Knowledge and Attitudes on Drug Abuse in New York State.* New York: New York State Narcotic Addiction Control Commission, 1969.

Goldhill, P. M., *A Parent's Guide to the Prevention and Control of Drug Abuse.* Chicago: Regnery, 1971.

Kalant, H., and Kalant, O. J., *Drugs Society and Personal Choice.* Toronto, Canada: Addiction Research Foundation, 1971.

Kaplan, J., *Marijuana—The New Prohibition.* New York: World, 1970.

Klerman, G. L., "Drugs and Social Values," *International Journal of the Addictions,* vol. 5, no. 2, pp. 313–319, 1970.

Leech, K., and Jordan, B., *Drugs for Young People: Their Use and Misuse.* Oxford, England: Pergamon, 1967.

Lennard, and associates, *Mystification and Drug Misuse.* San Francisco: Jossey-Bass, 1971.

Marin, P., and Cohen, A., *Understanding Drug Use: An Adult's Guide to Drugs and the Young.* New York: Harper & Row, 1971.

National Commission on Marijuana and Drug Abuse, *Marijuana: A Signal of Misunderstanding.* Washington, D.C.: U.S. Government Printing Office, 1972.

Nowlis, H., *Drugs on the College Campus: A Guide for College Administrators.* Detroit: National Association of Student Personnel Administrators, 1967.

Segal, M., "Drug Education: Toward a Rational Approach," *International Journal of the Addictions,* vol. 7, no. 2, pp. 257–284, 1972.

Vatuk, V. P., and Vatuk, S. J., "Chatorpan: A Culturally Defined Form of Addiction in North India," *International Journal of the Addictions,* vol. 2, no. 1, pp. 103–114, 1967.

Watts, A., *The Joyous Cosmology: Adventures in the Chemistry of Consciousness.* New York: Pantheon, 1962.

Weil, A., *The Natural Mind.* New York: Houghton Mifflin, 1972.

Zinberg, N. E., and Robertson, J. A., *Drugs and the Public.* New York: Simon & Schuster, 1972.

CHAPTER 8

Treatment: Who For? What For?

When man experiences that certain sequences of mental events lead to behavior which has, as a matter of fact, survival value, he calls such mental facts "right." It would be better, however, if instead of this word some neutral symbol were being used for those particular events; because the word "right" leads to the unfortunate notion that some combination of mental facts are intrinsically better than others . . .

Wolfgang Kohler

What is the proper duty of the physicians to create beds for people who do not want to be in them? Or to offer treatment—in or out of bed—to those who want it, and to those only?

Thomas S. Szasz

Someone discovers that a person we care about is misusing a particular drug or combination of drugs. The stereotypes we hold probably lead us to assume that it is a parent or adult making a discovery about teen-age drug use. But in our day and age, it would not be rare for the reverse to occur, particularly with those colorful ups-downs and tranquilizers. What does one do in such a situation? The most common response is to try and get the person into treatment. Makes sense, doesn't it? Perhaps not!

Attempts to alter the behavior of a drug user—by treating him—rest on these two assumptions:

1. the drug abuser is sick; and
2. if he goes through a series of processes under the direction of certain designated individuals, then the outcome is predictable, and we are justified in labeling this entire procedure "treatment" or "rehabilitation."

On paper, and perhaps in our minds, treatment of a drug abuser is fairly simple. A set of procedures or techniques is tailored to the strengths and

199

weaknesses of both the drug abuser and the various treatment agents who are responsible for his care. This is generally the way in which most of us perceive treatment of the drug abuser. If we want to describe the process a bit more, we might conclude that treatment is a process which:

1. is initiated with an evaluation of the person who is to be treated—the drug abuser or drug addict—noting both his strengths and weaknesses;
2. determines treatment goals, which should meet the criteria of *achievability, meaningfulness, acceptability,* and *flexibility* for the person being treated, and *acceptability* and *flexibility* for the person doing the treatment and for the community at large;
3. depends upon the selection and use of specific techniques which are effective for the selected goals, the drug abuser's status or state of being at the time, and the treatment agent's state of training;
4. pinpoints the range of responsibilities and roles of the person being treated, the treatment agent, and the community at large;
5. evaluates the results of this entire process, using understandable, agreed-upon criteria, rather than dramatic anecdotes;
6. includes *early case finding* and *prevention* as a core in this process, rather than as an afterthought to which we pay lip service.

Using this as a framework and diligently adhering to it should lead to positive results for both the drug abuser and the rest of us. If this is so, one could raise the question: Why do many programs treating the drug abuser throughout the world report such poor treatment results? This is an important issue when one is concerned about a friend or relative whom we want to "cure" through treatment.

The poor treatment outcome for many drug abusers is generally predictable given our present situation. Unfortunately, the usual treatment pattern is to offer verbal and chemotherapeutic techniques to visible drug abusers whose status (strengths and/or weaknesses) is rarely adequately assessed, who live in or have appointments at hastily put together programs, the goal of which is abstinence for all, and which more often than not employ staffs who are inadequately trained in the techniques they use, are often unaware of the complexities of the drug scene, who generally don't include hope in their vocabulary, and who have to contend with various community pressures that they are unprepared for.

The harsh reality of this description should make all of us wonder what factors in the contemporary treatment process lead to the drug abuser giving up drugs or changing his way of life at all.

If indeed we wish to alter the drug-taking behavior of others, we are obligated to critically evaluate each part of the treatment process, the assumptions underlying them, and the roles that we play in all of this. And this is a task for all of us, not only for professionals.

Basic to what we do in treatment is our definition of what is a drug. If our definitions are derived from socioreligious concepts or medical, legal, or scientific ones, this will affect the kind of treatment we offer. For example, the smoking and drinking, both casual and excessive, that occur among professionals at drug-abuse conferences are not perceived as problems. These same professionals who are trying to minimize drug abuse in our nation would resent being told that they have a drug problem and that they should be treated. This is an important point to keep in mind—while each of us may feel quite sure that someone we are concerned about needs treatment for some part of his behavior, that person may not feel the same way.

It is important, in each case, to determine just what the drug abuse is. Is the person abusing himself by using particular drugs, abusing others through his behavior and manner of support of his drug use, or abusing society's rituals, mores, and laws concerning drugs?

Unfortunately, once we decide we don't approve of certain drug behavior, we almost automatically feel the urge to intervene in the "drug abuser's" life as if what we were doing were both necessary and rational. More often than not, this behavior on our part results in the first piece of dishonesty in treating the "drug abuser." The reality is that we want the drug abuser to give up certain drugs *because we want him to.* Any other reasons are afterthoughts. This may not be a concept that is easy for most of us to accept.

The imputing of rational meaning to irrational and/or arbitrary considerations is not new or foreign to most of us. We arbitrarily decide at what age a youngster can purchase alcoholic beverages and tobacco products. We arbitrarily decide upon certain criteria for the distribution of contraceptive devices and knowledge about contraception. We arbitrarily decide the criteria enabling a person to vote or lose his right to vote. Each of us can surely add our own examples of the arbitrariness of most decision making. Perhaps if we were able to be more open and honest about our reasons for wanting someone that we care about to stop using drugs or not to start, we might accomplish this goal. We might not. Perhaps we can't be honest about our arbitrariness because we fear that direct communication will not result in what we would like to happen. While this may be so, it is equally evident that the traditional use of less than open and honest approaches has not resulted in significantly less drug abuse.

Around the turn of this century, it was felt that excessive drinkers and other kinds of drug users were immoral or amoral individuals. One assumed that such people were unable to handle their daily lives the way most others could, and thus they turned to drugs because of personal weakness and for illicit pleasure. The most obvious intervention for a moral condition is theologically and/or philosophically based. Whatever theoretical merit this approach may have held, it apparently had little effect on changing man's drug appetites. Perhaps if our forefathers (and ourselves) paid less lip service to morality, we could use our energies to permit the growth of viable ethical systems which would be based upon people turning to people rather than to things, both in times of pain and in times of pleasure.

The "immoral" perception of drug use soon changed into the criminal-deviant notion of drug abuse. This type of analysis leads to discussions about whether:

• drug users are involved in crime prior to their drug involvement;
• the drug user's crimes are against people or against property;
• drug abuse tends to reinforce an existent propensity for crime or whether it creates and causes it.

Many more such considerations can be added. Any and all of these issues resolve themselves in terms of legal action and reaction. The obvious treatment for criminals is punishment. Being modern, we call the process of removing the drug abuser from his mainstream of living "rehabilitation." This is what happens:

• The judicial system determines the length and the geographical locus of "rehabilitation."
• Other penal system representatives determine the focus of the rehabilitation and the status of the person being rehabilitated.
• And the general community, responsible for paying for this entire process, sees to it that only minimal funds are available. After all, since the drug abuser got himself into this mess, surely part of his treatment is for him to learn how to get himself out of it.

While some readers may question whether this description is too simplistic and too cynical, the reality is that judicially proscribed rehabilitation only focuses on *where* and *how long*. Rarely, if ever, does the court involve itself in *what* is actually made available for the drug abuser during his enforced treatment. That's a local decision.

At the same time as an increase in civil commitment procedures for drug abusers has occurred, the whole contemporary emphasis has been upon viewing drug use as equivalent to personal sickness. Professional, nonprofessional, and even groups best designated as unprofessional are viewing the use and misuse of all sorts of drugs as a symptom of individual psychopathology. Starting with this assumption, they then go on to suggest, to demand, and to offer the necessary types of verbal and/or chemotherapeutic techniques. The evidence for the necessity of treatment is both clear and logical:

• Who but a sick person would stick a needle into his arm?
• Who but a sick person would buy drugs illicitly and take a chance on being arrested?
• Who but a sick person would use drugs the contents of which he knows little of?
• Who but a sick person would take drugs whose consequences are unpredictable?

Each of us could certainly add more such rhetorical questions to this list. The trap, and there is one inherent in such rhetorical question, is that many kinds of people are involved in a variety of behaviors which appear to be bizarre, irrational, and illogical. Yet they may not be psychologically or socially sick, given the agreed-upon mores, rituals, and definition of health and illness of the time. Young children very often engage in the kind of play in which they turn and tumble until they are very dizzy and apparently enjoy this state. Are they sick? Another example is the one in which the perils of drug use are discussed, while smoking in a hallway which is improperly ventilated, after having consumed an excessively rich meal, washed down by alcohol—which is a typical drug-abuse conference scene.

The main point is that once we view a person who is using drugs as being a "sickee," we automatically fall into the trap of assuming and recommending treatment for him. The choice of using traditional or avant-garde modalities is but a minor variation after our initial perception of the person and his "problem."

Notwithstanding our legitimate concern for and interest in people we know who are using a variety of drugs casually or in a more committed fashion, we must begin to question whether treatment is always the most useful course. At the same time that we do this, we must not become hopeless about treatment outcomes. Surely we must recognize that offering a single treatment goal (abstinence), to a population of drug users that may vary greatly, through techniques whose effectiveness for a given person is not predictable, may not turn out too well. We should hesitate before we rush into treatment as a panacea.

Confronting this issue means that we, professionals and lay people, must become more aware of, and knowledgeable about, what kinds of people need and can use what kinds of treatment. Perhaps a major source of difficulty is that we continue to view the drug abuser as a particular kind of person whose actions and needs are quite distinct from our own. He is an "addict personality," a "passive-aggressive," a "drug-dependent personality," an "oral individual," a "retreatist," a "sociopath," etc. One could fill pages with the categories into which we self-righteously lump people who use drugs for other than conventionally approved reasons.

The so-called difficulties associated with treating the drug abuser became quite manageable when a treatment procedure is developed and adhered to which pinpoints the various necessary facets and when we acknowledge and remember that treatment is not equal to therapy. Treatment is an entire process; therapy is a specific technique.

This is not just a semantic distinction. The sad reality is that everyone being "therapied" these days may not be getting appropriate treatment, and everyone who supposedly is receiving treatment may not be involved in the most appropriate kind of therapy. Not only may the "patient" suffer because of this, but the rest of us may suffer as well. When the drug abuser's behavior doesn't change when he is in treatment, we may respond with a variety of inappropriate feelings and actions, and he or she may become increasingly more uptight, depressed, and hopeless, and may even turn to greater involvement with drugs.

Outlined below are those facets of treatment that must be understood if we ever hope to significantly challenge the contemporary drug scene.

EVALUATION

Evaluation is the first step in any proposed treatment procedure. Its effective use must include the assessment of the strengths and weaknesses of the individual in his past, present, and anticipated future. The evaluation must be broad enough to cover the person's adaptation in conventional, deviant, and drug-oriented areas of behavior. For effective treatment planning, we want a picture of a person, not a reinforcement of a stereotype. Evaluating the person and using relevant information about him that has been gathered from significant others in his life should help us to determine the following issues:

1. the type of intervention, including treatment, that is necessary if indeed any is necessary;
2. the immediate and long-term goals;
3. the areas to be focused on;
4. the roles and responsibilities of the treater and the treated;
5. the roles and responsibilities of ancillary community services;
6. the roles and responsibilities of significant others in the "patient's" life.

Obviously, this kind of assessment makes it more difficult for all of us to continue to believe that the cause of drug use and the solutions for it are the total responsibility of the "drug abuser" whose status we have conveniently changed into that of "patient." If treatment is needed and possible, and if it is of some potential use, the next obvious step in planning is the selection of appropriate goals. We must be quite clear in our own thinking, regardless of our legitimate concern for people we care about who are misusing drugs, and understand that not everyone is treatable at this point in time. This is not a unique situation. There are a variety of physical, psychological, social, educational, and vocational conditions for which we have no solutions. This has always been so. Just as we find a solution to a traditionally unsolvable problem or condition, new ones which seem to be unsolvable appear.

TREATMENT GOALS

Traditionally, abstinence from certain drugs has been the single goal that society has insisted on as being the only meaningful sign of cure from drug addiction or drug misuse. What is odd, particularly for America which prides itself on its pragmatism, is that we continue to insist on abstinence when very few drug abusers have ever been able to achieve it for any substantial length of time.

Whatever meaning we attribute to any goal, we surely must keep in mind that the specific goal is useful only if a person can achieve it. Experience as a therapist and a pragmatic outlook on treatment has led me to the following bias: Abstinence is a legitimate goal only if there are medical and/or psychiatric reasons that contraindicate continued drug use.

If the "alcoholic" has cirrhosis of the liver, he shouldn't be drinking. If he does, he will exaggerate his condition. If the "pot head" has paranoid reactions following his use of marijuana, he shouldn't be using that drug. If he does, he may increase his paranoid adaptation or maladaptation to life. Thus, abstinence can be a goal at times, and at other times it may be but one of a number of techniques through which treatment goals are achieved. The reason for this is simple: We can rarely change a person's drug behavior without changing other parts of his behavior. James Thurber caught the essence of this in one of his fables.

The Bear Who Let It Alone[1]

In the woods of the Far West there once lived a brown bear who could take it or let it alone. He would go into a bar where they sold mead, a fermented drink made of honey, and he would have just two drinks. Then he would put some money on the bar and say, "See what the bears in the back room will have," and he would go home. But finally he took to drinking by himself most of the day. He would reel home at night, kick over the umbrella stand, knock down the bridge lamps, and ram his elbows through the windows. Then he would collapse on the floor and lie there until he went to sleep. His wife was greatly distressed and his children were very frightened.

At length the bear saw the error of his ways and began to reform. In the end he became a famous teetotaller and a persistent temperance lecturer. He would tell everybody that came to his house about the awful effects of drink, and he would boast about how strong and well he had become since he gave up touching the stuff. To demonstrate this, he would stand on his head and on his hands and he would turn cartwheels in the house, kicking over the umbrella stand, knocking down the bridge lamps, and ramming his elbows through the windows. Then he would lie down on the floor, tired by his healthful exercise, and go to sleep. His wife was greatly distressed and his children were very frightened.

Moral: You might as well fall flat on your face as lean over too far backward.

The evaluation procedure permits the determination of which behavior can or *should* be changed. For some people, when drug use ceases and no plans are made to replace such behavior, a Pandora's box may be opened. This is particularly so if the initial drug use was an attempt at self-medication to hold down deeply disturbing thoughts and feelings. Since the drug abuser is the focus of the treatment, it is suggested that he should have an active role in goal-setting and know what responsibilities he has and doesn't have regarding the selected goals.

Various goal systems may be developed in order to meet the immediate and future needs of the different types of drug abusers being treated. The selection of a given goal must meet, at the very least, four criteria: *meaningfulness*, *achievability*, *acceptability*, and *flexibility*.

The goal must be meaningful to the person being treated, but not necessarily to the person doing the treatment. While adults have a responsibility in socializing both the young and their own peers, imposing one's values on others has rarely worked. If the goal is not meaningful to the "patient," why should he aspire to it? What's in it for him?

The goal should be achievable, because if it isn't the treatment process simply becomes a series of compounded frustrations. The frustration may lead to a self-termination from treatment, or perhaps the person may stop using a particular drug, only to commit himself instead to other drug and nondrug behaviors which can adversely affect himself and others.

Acceptability is a crucial concept, because the "patient" is unlikely to commit his time and energies to unacceptable goals. Likewise, the general community will predictably undercut any treatment goal that it feels is unacceptable.

Table 8-1   A proposed goal system for the treatment of drug abusers.

Palliation	Evaluation indicates that behavioral changes are unlikely because physical, mental, or social condition is too deteriorated. Palliation will permit minimizing of the pain the person is experiencing.
Disability limitation	Evaluation indicates that level of functioning has become increasingly inadequate through time. The goal is stopping the dysfunctional behavior before it gets worse.
Rehabilitation	Evaluation indicates that the person has functioned on a healthier level at other times in his life and the strengths to do so again are present. Rehabilitation will permit the person to return to a previous level of satisfactory functioning.
Maintenance plus	Evaluation indicates that the person is generally functioning on a satisfactory level but that he needs help in one or two areas. Maintenance plus will permit the individual to reinforce his present satisfactory functioning and will either limit his present dysfunctions or teach him viable alternatives to them.
Promotion	Evaluation indicates unutilized strengths and skills. Promotion will permit the individual to function on a level he has never functioned on before.

For example, although a good case for offering pharmaceutically pure doses of heroin to narcotic addicts might be made, we have been led to believe that this hard drug is so dangerous that it is unlikely that we could get most people to back such a nonabstinence goal. Likewise, we have been taught about the dangers of addiction so that it is seemingly impossible to get most professionals and lay people to agree to give methadone in daily doses to teen-age narcotic addicts. This type of treatment, called methadone maintenance, will be discussed in another section of this chapter.

Flexibility is needed to remind all of us that goals are manmade and, thus, can be changed by man whenever it is necessary. A commitment to a single goal system may make it difficult to do so. In fact, one might view treatment generally as a process which either creates and/or reinforces the flexibility to adapt in healthy personal ways to internal and external strengths, weaknesses, and pressures.

Achievement of a goal is obviously related to the choice of treatment modalities, the availability of these modalities and other resources that may be needed, the comprehensiveness of the care being offered, and the coordination of the treatment effort and the posttreatment effort. It's an eyeful to read, a mouthful to say, and, for man, it takes a lifetime to achieve. But then, again, so does living.

TREATMENT MODALITIES

The correct choice of treatment can only be based upon whether or not the specific technique chosen relates favorably to the achievement of the selected goal. At this point in time, it is impossible to predetermine which goals are best achieved with particular treatment modalities. In the future we may be in a better position to make this kind of determination. Although this continues to be a key difficulty in treating the drug abuser and in predicting the outcome of treatment, we should not blame this difficulty entirely upon the "patient."

Although an assessment of the patient cannot, by itself, allow us to predict which technique will "cure" the patient and which one won't, it can and must give us other important information. The choice of a specific modality obviously should be based on considering whether the person has the ability to benefit from it, let alone partake of it. Likewise, too little consideration is given to the availability of staff, professional or paraprofessional, who have the necessary expertise with a particular technique to implement and utilize it effectively. Professional schools rarely, if ever, prepare the future therapist or treatment agent to work with drug abusers. Most often such training is obtained inadequately on the job, and this makes it difficult to determine and study what adequate treatment is. The paraprofessionals, which mainly consist of ex-addicts, have little more than their "ex" status to fall back upon as they treat others.

Indeed, it is strange that while the public moans about poor treatment outcome, it does little to see to it that the treatment tax dollar is used as effectively.

Surely, if any of us were on a table being rolled into an operating room and overheard the surgeon say to the nurse: "Funny thing, Nurse Smith, I never even worked on a cadaver," we would do something to protect ourselves. But then again, we are we and they are drug abusers.

Hope, a necessary ingredient for taking a chance on changing one's way of adapting, is not one of the core courses taught to professionals in their schools of training, or to paraprofessionals in their schools of hard knocks. Without the communication of hope, the treatment process ultimately may become a series of technical movements, which may lead to playing at life, not living it or learning from it.

Aside from training, another consideration regarding treatment modalities is the meaning imputed to them by both the professional and lay public. Many believe that if we change a person's status from drug abuser to patient by putting him into some form of verbal therapy in which he gains some insight, significant behavioral changes should be forthcoming (most specifically, drug abstinence). Gaining knowledge and experiencing insight do not necessarily lead to their productive use, as many people who have been in verbal therapy for years can attest. We learn from knowledge and experience by taking a chance on changing our usual behavior and by assessing the results. We take the necessary chance because we come to believe or are helped to believe that when all things are weighed, it's in our best interests to do so.

We often forget that getting a person to take a chance may not necessarily be appropriately associated with a specific verbally based therapy. The verbal therapies include individual and group therapies. They range from analysis to counseling, from traditional group therapy to encounter groups to psychodrama and may take many minutes to many hours for any given session. Marathon sessions, a recent form of group therapy, may go on for days with time out for food and sleep. Verbal therapies demand that the person being treated be word oriented rather than action oriented and that he be able to tolerate anxiety as he seeks insights into his behavior. For many people, including drug abusers, particularly those from low socioeconomic groups, life has come to be defined in terms of action and not words. For others, most often the professional therapist, life is almost entirely word oriented. When he's not reading or writing, he's listening. When the patient is action oriented and the therapist is word oriented, they are often unable to reach a common understanding. When this occurs, the difficulties of arranging a therapeutic relationship often preclude any useful outcome.

Another barrier to effective verbally based therapy occurs when the patient can't tolerate his anxiety and he turns to drugs as self-medication to allay a variety of discomforting feelings and thoughts.

Underlying the use of chemotherapeutic techniques in the treatment of the drug abuser may be the unrealistic notion that there are chemical solutions to maladaptive sociopsychological behavior. Chemotherapeutic techniques are used separately as well as in combination with verbal techniques. The former techniques are essentially used to stop the person's involvement in his drug misuse. If he is too anxious, depressed, etc., medication may be given to him to take the edge off these disabling feelings and thereby permit him to effectively utilize verbal therapy. By prescribing drugs that alter moods or reactions to drug experiences, the therapist can relieve the drug abuser's physical and psychological distress or provide him with an opportunity to discover how his behavioral patterns relate to his drug misuse.

In recent years certain drugs have been used as substitutes for the illegal narcotics that addicts use. Methadone and cyclazocine are two such drugs. The former is a synthetic long-acting narcotic; the latter is a narcotic antagonist. Methadone, whose effects last for at least 24 hours (there is now an experimental form which lasts 72 hours), is prescribed so that an addict can be assured that he will not be "sick" when heroin is not available, so that he need not continue to be involved in illegal behavior, and so that he can engage himself in conventional living. Cyclazocine prevents the narcotic addict from experiencing a high when using narcotics. We assume that if the person doesn't feel high from his drugs, while taking our medicine, he will eventually learn to stop relying on drugs and return to an acceptable way of life. This theory is based upon the notion that the addict's drug use is constantly reinforced or conditioned by his pleasurable high and by his activity in a drug-oriented daily way of living. When he can no longer feel the high, the assumed conditioning process that maintained the drug habit and orientation should begin to break down.

Both of these types of drugs are relatively new, and there has been what is best described as a bandwagon attempt to offer them as solutions to *our contemporary increasing drug-problem scene.* We must keep in mind that these drugs "do" specific things related to narcotic use. We must also remember that a great many people use more than one drug at a time.

Actually, the important issue is not which chemotherapeutic technique is the best—after all there are no "magic" drugs. We often easily forget that a major task in treating the treatable drug abuser is to help him to turn to others, to people, rather than to drugs to meet his everyday needs. He may already be sufficiently committed to medication, although it's of the self-prescribed variety.

In our concern for drug users, we may become seduced into thinking that a therapeutic drug or technique will place a person in the mainstream of conventional living. This is doubtful—particularly if he never lived there before or if the present inhabitants are reluctant to invite him in. Obviously, no medicine or other technique will decrease deviant behavior if conventional behavior has little meaning for the drug abuser.

Equally obvious is the fact that treatment modalities have, as do the human beings treated by them, distinct limitations. Success with both the techniques and the persons being treated depends upon our knowing the specifics of these limitations.

Another critical issue is that without the continuous delivery of the appropriate services as they are needed, treatment becomes just a meaningless term and not a meaningful process. Someone must take responsibility for the delivery of care. One can think of such a person as a "case manager" whose task is to see that whatever is supposed to be done is done and if it isn't, to know why it isn't as well as who should be doing what. If someone doesn't take responsibility for all of this, the drug abuser is bound to be blamed for the inefficiency and ineffectiveness of the treatment system.

In fact, one of the most destructive traps we can fall into is to believe that if the drug-abusing patient gets better (gives up his drugs), then he is a good and motivated patient who is able to profit from the professional expertise and skill offered to him. We cured him. If, however, he continues drug use, this is clear evidence that he is unmotivated, a poor treatment risk, who cannot profit from our skill. Strangely enough, no one assesses the kind of motivation present in the *treatment agent* and what his therapeutic skill really is.

Table 8-2 Etiology of the nonmedical use of drugs and some derived consequences.

I Model	II Process for drug adaptation	III Theoretical assumptions about types of drug users	IV Activity level for nondrug adaptation	V Preferred treatment agent	VI Successful treatment outcome
Biochemical, physiological, genetic	Biochemical deficit, Genetic predisposition	Homogeneity	Minimal to nil	Biochemists Geneticists	An arrested biochemical disorder (ex-addicts, recovered alcoholics)
Psychoanalytic development of personality	Regressed or fixated psychosexual development (oral addict personality)	Homogeneity	Moderate to maximally active	Psychoanalysts	Sublimated oral personalities or more mature psychosexual personality development
Learning	Conditioning	Homogeneity	Minimal to maximally active	Behavioral therapists	New nondrug overt behavioral adaptations (conditioned ex-addicts)
Environmental	Retreating from external milieu via drugs	Homogeneity	Minimal to nil	Builders, urban planners, etc.	Drug users or nonusers in better environment
Psycho-sociological ("burning out")	Not given	Homogeneity	Moderate to minimally active	None, self-change	Tired ex-addicts and/or socially acceptable drug substitutors
Altered states of consciousness	Normative need culturally determined	Heterogeneous	Moderately to maximally active	None specifically, self-change possible	Substituted altered states of consciousness (drug or nondrug related)

TREATMENT REEVALUATION

Constant evaluation and reevaluation is necessary in any treatment process. It is obviously necessary to know if the most appropriate choice of goals, treatment techniques, treatment agents, and ancillary services have been made for the particular patient.

From a goal perspective, treatment can be terminated once goals have either been achieved or not achieved, unless new goals are set. Goals should help to point us in the direction of where we are heading. If we are not going there, if we appear to be waylaid or even going in the opposite direction, why continue on the same road? Although it is important to know why we are lost, we may not be able to learn why this is so at the time. If this is so, it's better to cease a potentially frustrating effort than to make believe that all that is needed is more effort. An honest assessment leaves hope for tomorrow; whereas dishonesty may lose the traveler altogether. Pushing a patient who has achieved his set goals into further efforts immediately may fit into the American dream of constant and ongoing production. But we must come to recognize that there is a time to work and a time to rest, a time to learn and a time to integrate and actively enjoy the products of our efforts. Actively communicating the message that there is always a tomorrow may be one of the most fruitful antidotes to the devastating effect of contemporary Nowism.

Reevaluation permits us to maintain or change treatment techniques, given changes in goals, the skills of the patient and treatment agent, and the attitudes, laws, and policies in the community.

If a person who was crawling the walls with anxiety, and was given tranquilizers to help cut through the anxiety, now finds he can manage his anxieties without medication, it is obviously time to change treatment techniques. If a patient has become so adept with therapy language that he now hides his uncomfortable thoughts and feelings behind words and phrases, it may be time to move him into other types of therapy or treatment. If the therapist feels more and more that he has been taken in by a particular drug abuser and manifests what we call "negative countertransference," it may indeed be a time for change for everyone concerned.

FOLLOW-UP EVALUATIONS

After termination from treatment, follow-up must occur. Unfortunately, termination these days is too often arbitrarily decided upon. Termination is simply that point in time in which the treater and the treated decide that their treatment relationship should end because little benefit will continue to accrue to the patient. Part of termination might include referral for treatment to someone else for the same or a different form of treatment.

In a follow-up evaluation, the patient is revisited, and gives an accounting of his daily behavior and adaptive abilities so that he and we can decide if the whole treatment process was worthwhile. For most conditions, the procedure of follow-up is an attempt to determine if the person (1) is in some way healthier than he was prior to treatment, (2) is feeling a bit more comfortable, or (3) is holding his own.

In following up drug abusers, three areas have come to be focused on: present use of specific drugs, present educational and/or vocational status, and present involvement with the law.

Underlying this focus is often the stereotype that a bonafide drug abuser uses illicit or licit drugs for the wrong reasons, doesn't work in a productive and legitimate sense, and must be engaged in criminal behavior.

If our concern about changing the life styles of drug abusers is to have any meaning at all, it and the follow-up process should have little to do with verifying stereotypes. Rather, it should result in learning what a former patient's present functioning is like, given his present strengths and weaknesses weighed against his former ones, as well as against a background of available resources.

From the former patient's perspective, follow-up should help pick up the necessary clues as to whether further intervention is necessary. If it is, what kind, with what goals, and which treatment agents?

From the treater's perspective, follow-up should permit a clear assessment of whether the treatment was effective and what it was about the entire process that caused or prevented a positive treatment outcome. Obviously, there is much that we can learn from evaluating a negative treatment outcome.

From the community's point of view, a key question that must be answered is: Was it all worth it? With an increasing number of problems that the public must face and with less and less tax money available for these various problems, we have the right to know if we are wasting money and effort.

It may be a considerable attainment for a person to have given up his use of drugs and even his illegal behavior. But if he remains a burden to his society—a parasite—and if his abilities remain unchanneled for the good of his community, the general public may legitimately ask whether all of their treatment efforts and their concern were worth it.

Obviously, this type of analysis pinpoints an important issue in assessing the treatment of a drug abuser. Whose criteria are to be used for assessment? The values that one places upon human life, functioning, productivity, and community participation will vary given different perspectives. The point to remember is that similar dilemmas are present in the treatment of other physical, psychological, and social conditions; the use and misuse of drugs are not a unique behavior necessitating unique solutions.

The necessary components for successful treatment are not always present, but when they are, treatment for the drug abuser is as possible for him as it is for anyone else who needs and can use treatment. Obviously, there may be difficulties in treating anyone. We must not overlook the possibility that those mortals who treat drug abusers may, themselves, at times feel a lack of hopefulness in their own lives. They may also feel bogged down in professional and personal adversities which they cannot turn into successful outcomes. There are, no doubt, times that they, too, will experience the boundaries of their life space as constricted, with only minimal alternatives for daily functioning being available or experienced. This is not a description of doom-gloom. Rather, it is a reminder that mortal man treats mortal man for better and for worse.

What we need at this time is not specific techniques for drug abusers. We desperately need to develop, discover, or perhaps rediscover techniques and rituals to help people—drug abusers, abstainers, and those in between—to take a chance on nondrug options for experiencing life. Treatment is only one of the options. If we are to retard the apparent increase in the use and misuse of drugs, we may find ourselves developing new professions. These might include *hope communicators, adversity-to-success specialists,* and *alternative analysts.*

Obviously, this decade will be one of more drugs, and surely it will be one of more people. But whether more people will be using and misusing more drugs will have little to do with the difficulties or successes of treating the drug abuser.

Rather, it will have much to do with understanding, in a real way, the difficulties and pleasures of life and how best to experience both.

PROJECTS

1. Visit a drug-treatment center and tell them that you are concerned about a friend or relative using drugs. Ask them for suggestions for helping the person. Considering their response, note:
   (a) Is their response a hopeful one?

(b) How do they describe their form of help?

(c) What is it about their program that turns you on or turns you off?

(d) Are your concerns listened to with sensitivity?

(e) Can the program meet the many needs of a drug user or is it a fragmented program?

2. Get to know how many treatment programs are currently available in your community. Explore which of them has been evaluated and how this was done. In your considered opinion, do these programs accomplish what they say they are doing and can they be of help to you and to the people you are concerned about?

3. Volunteer your services to a drug hotline in your community. Keep a log of the kinds of requests for help that arise. Are drugs central to them or are there other common denominators?

4. Acquaint yourself with the procedure that your school system has devised for the treatment of or referral for treatment of a student drug user. If there is a set of procedures, evaluate whether

(a) it meets the needs of a schoolchild?

(b) it jeopardizes the student?

(c) it meets the needs and abilities of the school system?

(d) it jeopardizes the school?

(e) specially trained and qualified school staff are involved in it?

(f) there is a role for student involvement in it?

If there is no existing set of procedures, indicate your concern about this and note what response you get. What are the difficulties in developing such a program?

BIBLIOGRAPHY

Austin, B. L., *Sad Nun at Synanon.* New York: Holt, Rinehart & Winston, 1970.

Barten, H. H., *Brief Therapies.* New York: Behavioral Publications, 1971.

Birnbaum, M., "Sense about Sensitivity Training," *Saturday Review,* vol. 52, pp. 82, 83, 96–98, November 15, 1969.

Blum, and associates, *Horatio Algers Children.* San Francisco: Jossey-Bass, 1972.

Brayer, H. O., and Cohen, A. Y., "Parent Approaches to Teen and Subteen Drug Abuse," in J. C. Bennett and G. D. Demes, eds., *Drug Abuse and What We Can Do About It.* Springfield, Ill.: C. C. Thomas, 1972.

Brown, C., *Manchild in the Promised Land.* New York: New American Library, 1970.

Burris, D. S., *The Right to Treatment.* New York: Springer, 1969.

Burroughs, W., *Junkie.* New York: Ace, 1953.

Burton, A., ed., *Encounter.* San Francisco: Jossey-Bass, 1969.

Caldwell, V. W., *LSD Psychotherapy.* New York: Grove, 1968.

Casriel, D., *Daytop.* New York: Hill & Wang, 1971.

Child Study Association of America, *Your Child and Drugs.* New York: Child Study Press, 1971.

Cross, J. N., *Guide to the Community Control of Alcoholism.* Washington, D.C.: American Public Health Association, 1968.

DeRopp, R. S., *Master Game: Pathways to Higher Consciousness Beyond the Drug Experience.* New York: Dell, 1968.

Duncan, T. L., *Understanding and Helping the Narcotic Addict.* Philadelphia, Pa.: Fortress, 1965.

Edwards, G., *Reaching Out: The Prevention of Drug Abuse Through Increased Human Interaction.* New York: Holt, Rinehart & Winston, 1972.

Einstein, S., ed., *Methadone Maintenance.* New York: Marcel Dekker, 1971.

———, ed., *The Non-Medical Use of Drugs: Clinical Issues.* New York: Institute for the Study of Drug Addiction, 1972.

Einstein, S., and Garitano, W., "Treating the Drug Abuser: Problems, Factors and Alternatives," *International Journal of the Addictions,* vol. 7, no. 2, pp. 321–331, 1972.

Ford, D. H., and Urban, H. B., *Systems of Psychotherapy.* New York: Wiley, 1964.

Friedenberg, E. Z., *Vanishing Adolescent.* New York: Beacon, 1959.

Frykman, J., *A New Connection.* San Francisco: Scrimshaw Press, 1971.

Goldhill, P. M., *A Parent's Guide to the Prevention and Control of Drug Abuse.* Chicago: Regnery, 1971

Gross, H., *The Flower People.* New York: Ballantine, 1968.

Harris, J. D., *Junkie Priest.* New York: Pocket Books, 1964.

Hoffman, H. von., *We Are the People Our Parents Warned Us Against.* New York: Fawcett World, 1969.

Hoopes, N., ed., *Who Am I: Essays on the Alienated.* New York: Laurel Leaf, 1969.

Kramer, J., "Controlling Narcotics in America, Part I and II," *Drug Forum,* vol. 1, no. 1, pp. 51–70, 1971; vol. 1, no. 2, pp. 153–168, 1972.

Laing, R. D., *The Divided Self.* New York: Pantheon, 1969.

Laurie, P., *Drugs: Medical, Psychological and Social Facts.* Middlesex, Great Britain: Pelican-Penguin, 1971.

Menninger, K., *The Vital Balance.* New York: Viking, 1963.

Meyer, R., *Guide to Drug Rehabilitation: A Public Health Response.* Boston: Beacon Press, 1972.

Proceedings, Third National Conference on Methadone Treatment. Washington, D.C.: U.S. Government Printing Office, 1971.

Proceedings, Fourth National Conference on Methadone Treatment. New York: National Association for Its Prevention of Addiction to Narcotics, 1972.

Rachman, S., and Teasdale, J., *Aversion Therapy and Behavior Disorders.* Coral Gables, Fla.: University of Miami Press, 1969.

Report of the Canadian Government Commission of Inquiry into the Non-Medical Use of Drugs, *Treatment.* Ottawa, Canada: Information Canada, 1972.

Roszak, T., *Making of a Counter Culture.* New York: Doubleday, 1969.

Slater, P., *The Pursuit of Loneliness.* Boston: Beacon, 1970.

Solomon, L. N., and Berzon, B., eds., *New Perspectives on Encounter Groups.* San Francisco: Jossey-Bass, 1972.

Stafford, P. G., and Golightly, B. H., *LSD: The Problem-Solving Psychedelic.* New York: Award Books, 1966.

Szasz, T., *Law, Liberty and Psychiatry: An Inquiry into the Social Uses of Mental Health Practices.* New York: Macmillan, 1963.

The President's Commission on Law Enforcement and Administration of Justice, *Task Force Report, Narcotics and Drug Abuse.* Washington, D.C.: U.S. Government Printing Office, 1969.

Thurber, J., *The Thurber Carnival.* Middlesex, Great Britain: Penguin, 1945.

Watts, A., *This Is It and Other Essays on Zen and Spiritual Experience.* New York: Macmillan, 1967.

Weisman, T., *Drug Abuse and Drug Counseling.* Cleveland, Ohio: The Press of Case Western Reserve University, 1972.

Wittenborn, J. R., *et al.*, ed., *Drugs and Youth.* Springfield, Ill.: C. C. Thomas, 1969.

Yablonsky, L., *Synanon: The Tunnel Back.* New York: Macmillan, 1965.

Zborowski, M., *People in Pain.* San Francisco: Jossey Bass, 1969.

CHAPTER 9

Politics and Drug Use

Demanding a policy of "brutal honesty" in dealing with the drug problem, Governor Rockefeller today proposed that all convicted "pushers" of hard narcotics and violent addicts receive mandatory life sentences with no possibility of parole . . . . Joseph Zaretzki of Manhattan, the Senate minority leader, said, "Well, if that doesn't do it, I don't know what will." The narcotics proposals—the only ones that drew applause in the Governor's State of the State message—brought hearty nods from various legislators on both sides of the aisle. But others were left frowning or smiling incredulously.

The New York Times [1]

Many politicians and drug users have one major thing in common. They both use drugs. The latter actually uses the chemical; the former uses drugs as an issue. At this point in time, it's difficult to tell which type of use is more dangerous for the community or for individuals.

The relationship between man's chemical appetites and politics is not a new one, particularly when economics is added. It has been suggested that the famous *Indian Hemp Commission Report*, which was published in 1894 in seven volumes, was motivated by the British in an attempt to push Scotch whiskey over cannabis products. The hope was that the report might demonstrate that Scotch whiskey, which could yield a sizable tax revenue, and which was much more expensive than cannabis, was less dangerous than cannabis. The report was unable to demonstrate this. Sadly enough, the alcohol-marijuana debate is still with us and is still being used by political leaders.

Former Vice-President Spiro Agnew raised this question again in a speech to law-enforcement officers in 1970. The essence of his logic was that since most nations have permitted the consumption of alcoholic

[1] Copyright © 1973 by *The New York Times* Company. Reprinted by permission.

beverages for centuries and have controlled the use of cannabis products that alcohol must be safe and marijuana dangerous.

The primary issue at stake in this argument is not its validity or lack of validity. Rather, it is that during a time when people are much concerned about the problems of day-to-day living, a national policy maker chooses to engage our energies over an issue which has little actual national priority. And this has been the gist of the relationship between politics and the use and misuse of drugs. Most often the drug issue is a red herring, a smoke screen raised by the political leader in power or the candidate aspiring to power, which more often than not is guaranteed to protect him from taking a stand on vital issues.

For example, over the past decade, there has been concern about the increasing incidence of crime, particularly crime in the streets. This is a legitimate concern that affects us all. Our streets, parks, and highways are no longer safe for us. Politicians continue to tell us that the increase in crime is due to the addict. This becomes easy enough to believe. The addict has to support his habit; there are more addicts, more crime, so it must be his fault.

The day before the gubernatorial elections in New York, a group supporting Governor Rockefeller had a full-page advertisement in *The New York Times* which showed an arm with a needle in it. The background scene did not look safe. The message noted that if his opponent was elected, "they" would be on the streets of New York. The conclusion that the reader was asked to draw was that if the governor was reelected, the streets would be safer. But the streets were becoming unsafe while he was governor. But who has the time or desire to think about logic and reality when fiery rhetoric and well-done layouts trigger off our anxiety.

Actually, his opponent was no better in abusing drugs as an issue. He promised that if he was elected he would institute a new two-week cure. Since he wasn't elected, New York has not been able to benefit from this unknown cure.

One would think that voters would learn not to be seduced by the politics of drugs. In 1970, four years later, during the next gubernatorial elections, the following TV commercial regarding drugs was used:

> A warning to dope pushers in New York State. Governor Rockefeller has increased the maximum penalty for selling hard drugs to life imprisonment. And now, pusher, when you're caught, it can be for keeps. You've messed up a lot of people's lives. And Governor Rockefeller will do all he can to see to it that you'll regret it for the rest of yours.

The message is short and to the point. But apparently it had very little effect on pushers or on the growth of drug use in New York State. And it is quite doubtful that this message helped many New Yorkers find a reasonable and achievable way of coming to terms with drug use in their family or their community. And if the reader works from the assumption that political statements are not to be believed anyway, just what statements concerning drugs and whose statements is he willing to believe?

In the midst of all of this, national leaders have been assassinated; sociologists have reminded us that violence has been part of America's heritage, and the GI has been involved in massacres. Is this all due to drug use? Some people may believe this. At a national drug-abuse conference held at Rutgers University, I was standing next to a federal law-enforcement agent when it was announced that Senator Kennedy had been assassinated. The agent became visibly upset and then spontaneously said, "Some junky must have done it." He was not being facetious.

When Lieutenant Calley was being tried for the Mai Lai massacre, it was suggested that he may have been under the influence of marijuana. Oddly enough, the press rarely mentions that commandoes, such as the Green Berets, are issued their own supply of amphetamines, a drug which has been associated with paranoid behavior. Of even greater mystery is that the media did not present the facts concerning the use of drugs by GIs in Vietnam until it became impossible to hide. Their drug use was blamed on the Viet Cong by American politicians. But how does one explain photographs in *Life* magazine of Vietnamese youngsters selling drugs to our soldiers.

But political leaders have a way of explaining things. In the United States many of our problems were the result of youngsters who willingly turned on, tuned in, and copped out. Overseas, our soldiers were seduced by Oriental wiles to try drugs. And anyhow, the extent of GI drug use was only between 4 percent and 15 percent. Those are small numbers. But very few people raised the mathematical issue of how much is 4 percent of 300,000 soldiers, let alone 15 percent of this number.

Between the statistics and the rhetoric, there isn't much time or, perhaps, even desire to raise key issues such as what is there about our present society that results in both young and old moving away from it and often turning to various drugs?

So what does all of this have to do with our concerns about Jimmy or Mary using drugs? What is at stake is that our political leaders continue to lead us to believe that if we can point out who is at fault for whatever is ailing us, the condition will go away. But the issue is not *who* is at fault, but *what* is at fault. And most political leaders understand this since they patented and revised the political game called "Tag the Person and Avoid the Issue."

No doubt each of you could add more *do's* and *don't's* to this list. But it is not simply a bigger list that we need. What we need is the kind of elected and appointed officials who will stop exploiting the drug issue so that the Johnnies and Marys we care about can not only get help that they need for their drug misuse, but also that they can carry on with the more vital issue called living. And living a meaningful life is really what going beyond drugs is all about. And this is a legitimate expectation that can be made of political leaders. When we had to cope with just existing, we couldn't afford the luxury of elected political leaders. Now that we have gone beyond existing, we have a right to demand that our leaders help make life meaningful, hopeful, and easier and not more difficult, irrelevant, and hopeless. In practical terms this means that the next time a politician says he has the solution to the drug problem and will offer it once he is in office, ask yourself if you want a patent medicine-man as your elected official.

And when a political aspirant lists as one of his credentials "narcotics fighter" (which was done in Newark, New Jersey), ask him about his record. It may be irrelevant to the real battles of life.

And when a candidate states that he is for helping the addict, find out where he stands with people and not stereotypes.

And when a politician relates drug use to crime, sexual ones, promiscuity, evil, and other deviant behavior, trace his political record to determine what he has done to make it possible to celebrate life.

And when a politician asks you only for your money and your vote, find out what the hidden costs are. One of these costs may be an aggravated drug condition.

The personal and community problems that are associated with drug use are significant ones. We should be able to expect of our political leaders one crucial trait—leadership. Regarding the contemporary drug mess that we are in, this means that they will:

1. take the necessary time to study the various facets of the drug scene;
2. delineate the crucial underlying issues that reinforce drug use;
3. suggest alternatives that are meaningful, achievable, and acceptable;

1. not become instant drug experts;
2. not camouflage issues with empty words and meaningless deeds;
3. not offer slogans in lieu of viable alternatives;

4. give careful consideration to the development of education and treatment programs that can be evaluated;
5. relate contemporary drug issues to more generic common denominators such as the problems and pleasures of living;
6. help determine and offer meaningful roles in combating drug-related issues to their constituents;

7. help to pinpoint and dispel drug related mythology;
8. help us all to go beyond drugs.

4. not lend their position and prestige to programs that have not or cannot be evaluated;
5. not isolate out drug issues and drug users as being unique and separate from other concerns and other people;
6. not reinforce the dangerous notion that only drug experts and politicians have a role in combating today's drug scene;
7. not reinforce, disseminate or initiate new drug related mythology;
8. not lead us in circles which start with drugs and end with drugs.

This is not meant to be an empty assertion. There are many nations in which political, military, and business leaders are intimately involved in deriving profit from the growth, manufacture, and distribution of drugs.

In an article in *The New York Times* headed "Asians Doubt that U.S. Can Halt Heroin Flow" (8/11/71),[2] the following associations were made:

1. "The trading networks (for opium) are so firmly established and their links with Government and military officials who provide protection and tolerance so close that the Burmese Government is believed to be resigned to its inability to act and the Thai and Laotian Governments at a loss on how to carry out their new found desire to act."
2. Remnants of the Chinese Nationalist armies that sought refuge in Burma after the communist victory in 1949 dominate 80 percent of the opium traffic in the Shan State. These groups pick up raw opium from growers and traders and may even refine the opium. They then convey the opium in well-protected caravans.
3. Major General Ouane Rathikane has "never denied allegations that he is in charge of opium traffic in Laos." General Ouane was commander of Laotian armed forces.

When confronted by the allegation of his being an opium kingpin, the general responded: "It's been going on for a long time. Why stop now? If we stop, the foreigners will take it over. Why let the Chinese have it? I am not stealing the State's money."

[2]© 1971 by *The New York Times* Company. Reprinted by permission.

4. A newly appointed Laotian ambassador to a European country had to be recalled for "consultation" before he presented his credentials. On his arrival at his post, his baggage was found to contain 60 kilograms of white heroin.

All of this was in one article. Again, the issue is not that some men can and will profit from the appetites of others. Rather, it is that if we permit our leaders to fall short of being leaders, we can only blame ourselves for the growth of today's drug problem. And as we know, blame, in and of itself, will be insufficient to correct what has to be corrected.

Perhaps what is needed is for us to work with the Johns and Marys we care about and change drug use from a rabble rousing political issue into a soluble social concern. Can it be done? Can you afford for it not to be done?

PROJECTS

1. Acquaint yourself with the views of one of your political leaders regarding the
   (a) causes of drug misuse
   (b) solutions to today's drug scene.
2. Collect election campaign statements made by a politician and then evaluate them. Are they concrete and can they be tried? Or are they empty rhetoric?
3. Assess what position your district attorney has taken regarding drug treatment and drug education.
4. At a drug-education lecture or program, take the position that the drug scene can't be adequately handled by the average citizen because it is a political issue. Note the type of response you get from the lecturer and the audience. Is their response generally one of "you can't fight City Hall"? Is the general group tone one of "let's find somebody, aside from ourselves, to tackle the drug problem"? Attempt to get them to see that they have a viable role to play.
5. Become part of a group of citizens or organize such a group in an attempt to remove drugs as an issue from the political arena. Note the problems that you experience in doing this.

BIBLIOGRAPHY

Blum, R., "Legislators and Drugs," in R. Blum and associates, eds., *Society and Drugs.* San Francisco: Jossey-Bass, pp. 245–247, 1969.

Brecher, E. M., *Licit and Illicit Drugs.* Boston: Little, Brown, 1972.

Kaplan, J., *Marijuana: Report of the Indian Hemp Drugs Commission, 1893–1894.* Baltimore: Waverly, 1969.

King, R., *The Drug Hang Up.* New York: Norton, 1972.

Kramer, J., "Controlling Narcotics in America, Part I & II," *Drug Forum*, vol. 1, no. 1, pp. 51–70, 1971; vol. 1, no. 2, pp. 153–168, 1972.

Lennard, H. B., and associates, *Mystification and Drug Misuse.* San Francisco: Jossey-Bass, 1971.

Lindesmith, A. R., *Addiction and Opiates.* Chicago: Aldine, 1968.

McCoy, T., *The Politics of Heroin in South East Asia.* New York: Harper & Row, 1972.

Morris, H., and Hawkins, G., *The Honest Politician's Guide to Crime Control.* Chicago: University of Chicago Press, 1970.

Ross, M., "Alcohol Versus Pot," *24 Magazine,* vol. 1, no. 1, pp. 26–31, January 1971.

Szasz, T. S., "Drugs and Politics," *Transaction,* pp. 4, 6, January 1972.

Terry, C. E., and Pellens, M., *The Opium Problem.* New York: Bureau of Social Hygiene, 1928; Montclair, N.J.: Patterson and Smith, 1971 (reprint).

Zinberg, N. E., and Robertson, J. A., *Drugs and the Public.* New York: Simon & Schuster, 1972.

CHAPTER 10

Economic Aspects and Drug Use

An Illinois drug firm shipped up to 15,000,000 pep pills over a ten-year period to a post office box for a drug store in Tijuana, Mexico. The address was the 11th hole of the Tijuana Country Club golf course.

News Item

Presentations about today's drug scene rarely deal with the economic factor. And when they do, the focus is almost always on the illegal economics of drug behavior. After we read about the burglaries, forgeries, muggings, etc., or the latest drug arrest, we are obviously brought back to the criminal aspects. It is as if we couldn't remove ourselves from the *criminal-sick* oversimplification of drug misuse. If we really want to effectively minimize current drug appetites, we shall have to move away from this unproductive approach. And it is unproductive because it gets us nowhere. One way of beginning to do this is to take a very critical look at the economics of drug use.

To begin with, we shall have to acknowledge that there are two economic components: *the legal and the illegal.*

LEGAL COMPONENTS

Half in jest and half seriously, Dr. Jerome Jaffe, President Nixon's former advisor on national drug problems, once said that there were two major ways left to make much money in America: saving drug users and creating them. Indeed, one of the major legal components of today's drug scene is the money spent on treatment and education. Professional, nonprofessional, and, unfortunately, some very unprofessional people and groups are quite prepared to take care of a community's or individual's treatment needs. One just has to consider the variations of inpatient and outpatient treatment programs that are presently asking for public support. Federal, state, and local agencies are being asked for funding. So are

227

private foundations, large corporations, and neighborhood stores. Most often it is for money, but many are asking for merchandise. Some rehabilitation centers collect money door to door, while others in large cities collect money on the streets. Some inpatient centers receive partial public support because their members are on public assistance. The fact is that millions of dollars of tax money go into drug-treatment efforts.

There are many dilemmas inherent in these funding procedures.

1. Almost all programs receive inadequate funding to carry out what they feel is their answer to today's drug problems.
2. Almost all programs have no extramural built-in evaluation so that the public is unable to decide whether the funding should be continued or dropped.
3. Most treatment programs spend a good deal of time and energy in trying to achieve financial stability, when their time and energy should be spent in doing treatment.
4. Private practitioners often charge what appears to be exhorbitant fees for consultations and treatment in an area in which few have been adequately trained.
5. When programs have not achieved the stated goals that they should have, more public funds are invested—based on the American myth that with enough funds, all problems become soluble. New York City is an example of this kind of logic. Having spent $17,000,000 during one fiscal year (1969–1970) with little success, the budget of their Addiction Services Administration was doubled for the next year.

Surely you could add to this list. What is at issue is that more and more public funds are being used for the treatment of drug misuse without many of us considering this as being a significant element in today's drug scene. And it is an increasingly important and large element. When we or our families are affected by the drug scene, we may feel that insufficient funds are available for treatment in our community. We may want funds for a "rap center," or an anonymous telephone help-line. They all cost money. And the question we have to ask ourselves is whether these services are relevant to today's drug problems.

For example, narcotic detoxification becomes much less costly if it's not done in a hospital, and yet there continues to be a cry for more hospital beds for heroin detoxification.

At issue then is whether we simply go along agreeing with the expenditure of public funds for the treatment of drug misuse, take the opposite position, or take the time to discover whether adequate funds are being relevantly used. And this is only one part of the "legal" component of today's drug economics.

Another one is the growing area of testing for drug use. More and more corporations are insisting upon testing potential employees as well as those already working for them. These tests have cost up to $10 for each person tested. The tests are not always reliable. They raise the issue of whether one can be fired or not hired in terms of a "guilty urine" if a person can fulfill his job responsibilities.

The drug-related research that continues to be funded is yet another area of economic consideration. Examples of this include the development and testing of chemotherapeutic techniques such as methadone maintenance, seeking the active ingredients of drugs such as marijuana and scientifically studying their effects, developing and evaluating materials and programs for drug-prevention efforts, and evaluating and developing drug-effect testing programs.

A difficult question about this research concerns its pertinence to the daily drug-related problems that we all face. If, for example, research should determine, after great expenditures, that marijuana is relatively safe or dangerous (whatever that means), will that discovery alter a parent's anxiety about his child's actual or potential marijuana use? Would such knowledge necessarily change the parent's behavior toward his child? Would it change yours? This is not an empty question. Has the proved statistical association between smoking cigarettes and cancer and emphysema significantly altered parent-child relationships in the United States or, for that matter, has it altered our national level of health? (See Figs. 10-1 and 10-2.)

One of the biggest economic components of the legal drug scene is the production, distribution, and sale of drugs and the taxes thus generated. Drugs are a big business. Pharmaceutical companies expend millions of dollars to test the safety of new drugs before they are mass-produced. More money is spent in getting physicians to use new approved drugs. And life is made longer and less painful for many of us. From a scientific perspective, it would appear that the investment has paid off. But has it from a social, ethical, and philosophical perspective?

It would seem that many of us have deprived ourselves of experiencing and learning from vital emotions because of the availability of instant chemical solutions. And yet we don't complain about this. We do become irate about someone stealing an object of ours to support his drug habit. But who would become irate about the vast amounts of money spent that could result in our feelings' being stolen? Sounds bizarre, you may think.

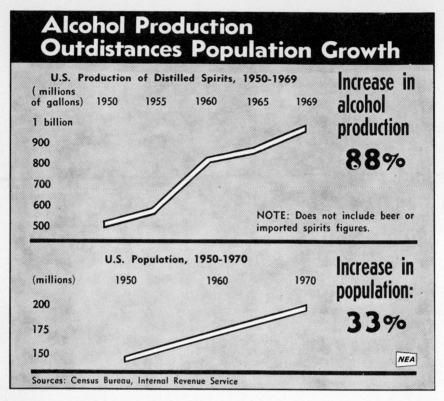

Alcohol Production Outdistances Population Growth

U.S. Production of Distilled Spirits, 1950-1969

(millions of gallons)   1950   1955   1960   1965   1969

1 billion

900

800

700

600

500

Increase in alcohol production

88%

NOTE: Does not include beer or imported spirits figures.

U.S. Population, 1950-1970

(millions)   1950   1960   1970

200

175

150

Increase in population:

33%

NEA

Sources: Census Bureau, Internal Revenue Service

Fig. 10-1   Alcohol production outdistances population growth. (Reprinted by permission of Newspaper Enterprise Association Inc.)

But perhaps not. The pharmaceutical industry and the medical profession have known for some time now that amphetamines are necessary for only three conditions: narcolepsy, hyperkinesis, and some weight-reduction problems. These three conditions in no way necessitate the massive amphetamine production that exists in the nation. One can only assume that the production continues for legal economic considerations. But why do we take these drugs—assuming we don't suffer from these three conditions? (See Fig. 10-3).

Part of the answer to that has to do with advertisements, and part with entertainment. Both of these institutions help to mold the roles that we take on in daily living. Both of these institutions have tended to become more drug oriented in recent years. Ironically enough, our purchases of products permit more drug-oriented advertisements to occur, and we pay

	1950	%	1955	%	1960	%	1965	%	1970	%	1971
PRODUCTION											
Cigarettes (millions)	391,956	28.9	412,309	22.77	506,127	11.12	562,368	-0.03	562,153	4.07	585,056
Cigars (millions)	5,468	6.69	5,834	18.93	6,937	28.08	8,883	10.18	7,979	-1.39	7,868
Tobacco (1000 lb)	235,189	-15.33	199,120	-11.58	176,059	-3.77	169,409	-3.19	163,992	0.32	164,529
PER CAPITA CONSUMPTION											
All products (pounds)	12.29	-2.44	11.99	-1.41	11.82	-2.62	11.51	-15.38	9.64	-1.65	9.48
Cigarettes (number)	3,522	2.12	3,597	15.97	4,171	2.08	4,258	-6.41	3,985	1.38	4,040
Cigars (number)	53	3.77	55	10.91	61	14.77	70	-14.28	60	-5.0	57
Tobacco (pounds)	1.50	-5.35	1.22	-18.86	0.99	-11.11	0.88	-5.68	0.83	-1.2	0.82

SOURCE: *U.S. Statistical Abstracts 1972.*

Fig. 10-2   The production and consumption of tobacco products in the United States 1950–1971.

	1950	**1955**	**1960**	**1965**	**1970**	**1950–1970**
Aspirin (1000 lb)	11,110	15,092	23,553	29,089	35,170	222.22
%		35.97	56.17	23.52	20.92	
Barbiturates (1000 lb)	688	864	852	972	1,003	72.46
%		25.44	-1.38	13.98	3.29	
Tranquilizers (1000 lb)	0	ᵃ	1,164	1,583	1,206	3.6 ᵇ
%				36.10	-23.86	
Vitamins (100 lb)	3,455	6,139	11,063	16,297	22,915	714.28
%		78.12	80.64	47.39	40.65	
Alcohol (1000 proof gallon)	313,535	411,840	518,724	658,641	673,727	114.94
%		31.44	25.97	27.02	2.29	
POPULATION	154,233,234		183,285,009		207,976,452	
%		18.86	13.47		34.96	

ᵃWith heed to avoid disclosing figures for individual producers.
ᵇ1960–1970.

SOURCE: *U.S. Statistical Abstracts 1972.*

Fig. 10-3 The production of various chemicals contrasted with the U.S. population growth.

232

to hear and see drug-oriented plays, films, and skits. (See Fig. 10-4.) One might assume that if there were less of this permitted, there would be less drug taking. That would be difficult to prove. How does one explore whether advertisements and entertainment create and reinforce drug use or simply mirror this behavior? Perhaps a more appropriate economic question might be whether this same money couldn't be better spent on more relevant nondrug advertisements and more mind-and-soul-expanding nondrug entertainment which is satisfying to all concerned?

When the treatment is over and the clean and dirty urines have been collected and the research data are coded on cards and what has been produced is advertised, sold, and distributed, there still remains a large legal economic component of the drug scene—the law-enforcement sector. The police, attorneys, judges, probation and parole officers, jail and prison guards have to be paid. Jails and prisons have to be maintained and expanded. Trials have to be carried out, and we pay. And we continue to pay public funds for a law-enforcement process which has yet to demonstrate that it is capable of retarding, let alone holding the line on, today's drug scene.

These various economic factors are just some of the legal components of today's drug culture. They are important to acknowledge because in doing so we remind ourselves that we play a role in the growth of drug-oriented behavior.

ILLEGAL COMPONENTS

As I was writing this chapter, a friend of mine told me that as far as he was concerned, if drug users weren't involved in crime, he wouldn't be too concerned about today's drug scene. His personal concern was over his children being robbed and his father having twice been mugged. This position is quite understandable, even though it permits many of us to make believe that "the drug problem" is simply someone we don't know who takes drugs and supports this behavior illegally.

The illegal component of drug economics includes:

1. the various costs to the community for stolen property,
2. the development of a resale system for stolen goods to nondrug-using segments of the population,
3. the profits derived from the sale of illegal drugs,
4. the payoffs to law-enforcement officers to prevent arrests, and

	1960	1965	1969	1970	1971	
Alcoholic Beverages (1000)	62,276	69,781		65,412		Newspapers
%		12.06	-6.26			
Beer & Wine (Millions)		20	0	20	26	TV excludes national regular spot advt.
%					30.03	
Beer & Wine (Millions)			56	67	78	TV spot advt.
%			19.64		16.42	
Beer, Wine, Liquor (Millions)	51	70		98	88	Magazines
%		37.31	25.77		-10.20	
Cigarettes (1000)	31,907	8,314		16,504	0	Newspapers
%		-74.07	99			
Tobacco Products & Supplies (Millions)		145		160	14	TV excludes national/regular spot advt.
%			10.35		-91.74	
Tobacco Products & Supplies (Millions)			40	51	5	TV spot advt.
%			27.54		-90.9	

Smoking Materials (Millions)	26		42		65		118	Magazines
%		61.72		54.94		81.96		
Drugs/ Remedies (Millions)			144		211		204	TV excludes national/ regular spot advt.
%				46.72		-3.31		
Drugs/ Remedies (Millions)				73		86	96	TV spot advt.
%				20.57		11.62		
Drugs/ Remedies (Millions)	29		41		38		38	Magazines
%		41.49		-7.32		0		

SOURCE: *U.S. Statistical Abstracts 1972.*

Fig. 10-4   The costs of advertising various chemical substances in the United States 1960–1971.

235

5. the use of profits derived from the drug scene to enter legitimate businesses (the nonchemical phenomenon of dirty money being turned into clean money).

One could combine the first two factors and tentatively conclude that those communities that have a large street-addict population may have a vested interest in their drug problem. A fairly recent study done in Baltimore (O'Connor, *et al.*, 1971) has suggested that the sale of property stolen by addicts is indeed a "secret domestic Marshall Plan for the poor."

It may also be a blessing in disguise for the business world. Many people benefit by it. Insurance rates go up. Merchants charge more. And in an odd way, many of the poor get something out of it. While the poor may make up a disproportionate number of the victims, they also may make up a disproportionate number of the buyers of stolen merchandise. Bombarded constantly by the media message that who you are depends on what you have, they are ready to buy.

And there are many items to buy. In many inner cities, the neighborhood merchant charges too much, and the fancier merchant isn't too receptive to every kind of customer. But the local addict is willing to take orders in the morning for delivery in the afternoon. Even the best of stores don't deliver as quickly, and their prices are no match. And many products are for sale, including high grades of meat (a "cattle rustler" is a drug user who steals meat from a store and sells it at much lower prices). But it is not only the poor who buy from the drug user. After all, a bargain is a bargain. And this becomes a key issue which we often tend to overlook. If someone has to steal to support his drug habit, he has to sell these goods. And those of us who buy these goods are reinforcing not only a criminal system, but a drug-oriented way of living as well.

Related to this is an odd consequence of preaching the American ideal of owning objects. If the poor can't legitimately purchase things or as many things as they have been led to believe are important, and they have the opportunity to do so from illegitimate sources, they may do so.

A sociologist working in Spanish Harlem in New York reported the following incident. A few days before Easter Sunday, he was interviewing some people on a street where he was known. The interview was abruptly interrupted when a known addict rushed by with a selection of expensive white dresses for children. They were being offered for three dollars each. Within minutes all of them were bought up with no questions asked. Actually, no questions were necessary. The price and the source were already known. Now, if the adults buying the dresses, many of whom were on public assistance, had asked for more money that month, many questions would have been asked. And if the request for more money had been granted, it would have come from tax money. But if no questions are asked, everyone appears satisfied. Tax payers aren't out too much money; the poor can get their bargains; and both groups can focus on the drug addict as a major source of problems in their life. Indeed, the Baltimore group may be right in suggesting that the addict is more than tolerated by his community because of his central role in implementing this local Marshall Plan.

The relationship between the police and the drug scene is relatively new. But it is one that should concern us all. In an article titled "The Pusher-Cop: The Institutionalizing of Police Corruption," Fred J. Cook noted that "gambling graft is no longer the chief source of corruption in the Police Department—now it is narcotics. And gambling graft is to narcotics graft as the dime is to the dollar . . ."

The article noted that many officials are becoming aware of this, but that it is difficult to do anything about it because the police, just like most other groups of people, attempt to protect their own. Often this is done because there is a fear that an open scandal would create even greater problems than the original incident. Unfortunately, we are by now all too aware of the devastating effects that denial and fear of scandals regarding drug use may have on families and communities. Perhaps the most devastating statement in Cook's article[1] is the comment by Joseph Fisch, chief counsel for the New York State Commission of Investigation: "Corruption cannot exist without the 'honest' cop. When the honest cop will not inform on his crooked partner, he creates the climate that lets the dishonest cop operate with impunity. Every time corrupt conditions are exposed, the police will yell that every man in the department is being blackened and their families are being hurt; but is it fair to ask, if they are honest, where were they when all of this was going on? They can't have it both ways. No corruption can exist on a widespread basis without fellow officers being aware of it. It is the honest cop who can stop it—but not if he adopts the code of silence and turns his back. The whole attitude in the department has to be changed so that the dishonest cop will actually fear the honest one. Until that happens, the police have only themselves to blame."

[1]Quotations from article used with permission.

And as long as we permit the "pusher-cop" to become an increasing factor in today's drug economics, we have only ourselves to blame.

The profit derived from the sale of illegal drugs is enormous. A kilo (2.2 pounds) of unadulterated heroin bought at $7000 may yield a profit of $250,000 or more when adulterated and sold on the streets. Not only is there much money to be made this way, but the sale of illegal drugs involves the development of a system which includes roles for many kinds of people. And the fact is that some of the people fulfilling these roles have never had the feeling that conventional work roles were available for them or achievable by them.

At the present time, a United States importer may purchase through a courier a kilo of 80 percent pure heroin in Europe for $5000 to $7000. By the time the importer has gotten the kilo, farmers have grown and harvested the opium poppy and sold it into a distribution system that has changed the raw opium into pure heroin. The quality of this heroin is tested by scientific instruments or by an addict or tester using experimental cuts.

The kilo is sold to a *kilo connection* for $20,000. He adulterates the heroin with milk sugar, quinine, and mannite which now results in two kilos. The cutters' preference determines the proportions of ingredients used for cutting. This adulterated heroin is now sold to *ounce men* or *connections*. Each of the units are cut resulting in two units, and each ounce is sold for $700. From this point on, the aggregate weight of each unit is reduced at each subsequent level of distribution.

The ounces are bought by the *dealer in weight*, who usually makes three units from each one, selling each one for $500 per ounce. The new unit is called a *piece* or street ounce. He is also the first person in this system who really risks being arrested.

The piece is bought by the *street dealer* who makes two units from each one. The cutting results in *bundles* consisting of twenty-five $5 bags, each piece being cut into seven bundles which sell for $80 each. The street dealer, who may himself be a heroin user, may also package half-bundles (ten $5 bags) which sell for $40 each or half-loads (fifteen $3 bags) which sell for $25 each.

The *juggler* is the person from whom the average user buys. He is almost invariably a drug user himself. Buying the bundle for $80, he sells each bag for at least $5. This enables him to support his own habit. But it also means that he puts himself in the most jeopardy. He can not only be arrested for sale and possession of drugs, but he may also be robbed by his own customers. He is also most likely to fit the stereotype of our conception of the drug addict (See Table 10-1).

Table 10-1   Distribution of heroin to the heroin user.[1]

Distributor	Price Per Unit	Adulteration	Percent of Heroin	Net Profit Per Unit	Rate of Return on Investment (percent)
Importer	$5000 per kilo	None	80	$15,000	300
Kilo connection	$20,000 per kilo	2	40	$20,000	100
Connection	$10,000 per kilo	4	20	$14,500	145
Weight dealer	$700 per ounce	12	6.7	$1500	114
Street dealer	$500 per piece	24	3.3	$620	124
Juggler	$80 per bundle	?	?	$45	56

[1]Reprinted from Preble E., and Casey J. J., "Taking Care of Business," *International Journal of the Addictions*, vol. 4, no. 1, pp. 1–24, 1969, by courtesy of Marcel Dekker, Inc., N.Y.

Other distribution systems have evolved for the sale of other drugs. The important issue is that each system does permit for various roles to be filled, which is in sharp contrast to the number and types of roles that are available for the ex-addict or, for that matter, for nondrug-using young adults in our society.

Obviously more information is needed in order to understand how both the legal and illegal components reinforce or inhibit drug use, how they affect the state of scientific knowledge, the attitudes and values of professional and lay community, and the development and operation of treatment programs and public policy. But affect these areas they do. And we permit them to do so.

PROJECTS

1. Carry out a small survey exploring how many of your friends and relatives have ever purchased stolen merchandise. Ask them if they ever considered that this might be reinforcing the contemporary drug scene.
2. Request information from your local school board about how much money is budgeted and spent on drug education. Dividing the number of students into the amount, do you feel that adequate funds are being made available?
3. Acquaint yourself with the amount of money that is being spent by your state or federal government on treatment for drug abusers as well as the "official" number of drug abusers. Does it seem too little, too much, or just right?
4. Ask your local pharmacist for an estimate of the number of prescriptions he fills in an average week for sedatives, tranquilizers, and amphetamines. Ask him how much this equals in dollars.
5. Including alcohol, tobacco products, and medicines, how much did your family spend on these substances last year and what percentage was this of the family's net income?

BIBLIOGRAPHY

Cook, F., "The Pusher Cop: The Institutionalizing of Public Corruption," *New York Magazine*, August 16, 1971.

Erickson, E., "The Social Costs of the Discovery and Suppression of the Clandestine Distribution of Heroin," *Journal Political Economy*, vol. 77, pp. 484–486, 1969.

Fernandez, R. A., "The Clandestine Distribution of Heroin, Its Discovery and Suppression: A Comment," *Journal Political Economy*, vol. 77, pp. 487–488, 1969.

Koch, J. V., and Grupp, S. E., "The Economics of Drug Control Policies," *International Journal of the Addictions*, vol. 6, no. 4, pp. 571–584, 1971.

Kunnes, R., *The American Heroin Empire: Power, Profits & Politics.* New York: Dodd, Mead, 1973.

McCoy, T., *The Politics of Heroin in South East Asia.* New York: Harper & Row, 1972.

Moscow, A., *Merchants of Heroin.* New York: Dial, 1968.

O'Connor, G., *et al.*, "The Drug Addiction Business," *Drug Forum*, vol. 1, no. 1, pp. 3–12, 1971.

Peleggi, N., "Drug Pushers," *New York Magazine*, January 8, 1973.

Preble, E., and Casey, J. J., Jr., "Taking Care of Business," *International Journal of the Addictions*, vol. 4, no. 1, pp. 1–24, (Marcel Dekker, Inc., N.Y.), 1969.

Regush, N. M., *The Drug Addiction Business.* New York: Dial, 1971.

Stazzone, S.J., "Blue Collar Pushers," *The New York Times*, p. 31, February 17, 1973.

Stewart, W. W., ed., *Drug Abuse in Industry.* Miami, Fla.: Halos and Associates, 1970.

Trice, H., *Alcoholism in America.* New York: McGraw-Hill, 1967.

Yurick, S., "Political Economy of Junk," *Monthly Review*, vol. 22, pp. 22–37, December 1971.

CHAPTER 11

Legal Control Efforts

The degree of civilization in a society can be judged by entering its prisons.

Fydor Dostoevski

During America's early period of legal attempts to control the use of narcotics, many physicians stopped prescribing for their addict patients. The courts had ruled that prescribing narcotics to addicts without attempting to cure the addiction was not sound medical practice. (The reader must keep in mind that to date there is no such thing as a medical cure for addiction. People change their drug-oriented lives for other styles of life when they feel that it has meaning for them to do so and when they sense that they can do so.) This court ruling was, in many ways, the beginning of the removal of the physician as a treatment resource for addicts in his community. The creation of 44 narcotic clinics throughout the country in 1919 was not sufficient to meet the needs of the addict or his community. These clinics had little direction, purpose, or knowledge upon which to base their administrative decisions. They were essentially based on the simple and logical notion that if addicts are given daily doses of drugs their needs are taken care of, and they will not supplement their drug supply from other sources. The closing of the clinics appeared to be even less well thought out than their opening. The last clinic was closed because it was the last clinic.

The relationship between drug laws and treatment remains essentially the same today as it was during the clinic era. To avoid the impact of the law, one should be treated. And as a result of treatment, one should have less involvement with the law. What is obviously wrong with this simple way of thinking is the assumption that law enforcement and/or treatment can significantly alter drug-related legal entanglements.

One of the key cases in America's drug law history occurred in 1922.

The Behrman Case prevented physicians from legally supplying narcotics to addicts for self-administration. But it really did more than that. It was interpreted as meaning that the maintenance of addiction was forbidden. Perhaps of even greater significance, it helped to reinforce the growing notion that addicts were not to be treated as outpatients. The social message was becoming much clearer for all concerned: fewer physicians, no clinics, no maintenance, no outpatient status. The addict was to change his behavior and become more in tune with newly passed laws, but this should be accomplished away from his community. The reader might stop to consider whether we have changed our response to the addict in 50 years, particularly in the reader's community.

The penalty structure of drug-related laws increased, and by 1937 marijuana was also brought under legal control. Table 11-1 pinpoints some of the key dates and issues in America's drug laws. During these last five decades, we have continued to oscillate between extending the law to include more drugs and more drug-related issues, with severer penalties, as well as to discriminate between various drugs and drug-related issues with a lessening of penalties. And these oscillating laws have done little to help the concerned adult or youngster to better understand the drug scene.

The United States Public Health Service Hospitals at Lexington, Kentucky, and Forth Worth, Texas, were established in the mid-1930s to care for addicts imprisoned for crimes as well as addicts who voluntarily sought treatment. A question we must continue to ask ourselves and our legal policy makers is whether legislated rehabilitation is possible. After all, even the omniscient Lord didn't add an 11th amendment: "Thou shalt get well." An even more difficult question is whether a parent wants his child incarcerated for rehabilitation when we are not at all sure that the available treatment meets the needs of the child.

We permitted the introduction of the concept of mandatory minimum sentences while differentiating among drug possession, drug sales, and drug sale to minors. We even permitted the introduction of the death penalty for sale to a minor. And the drug scene continued to increase. We tightened the drug controls in 1966 by including sedatives, stimulants, tranquilizers, and hallucinogens. Limitations were placed on who was legally permitted to handle them; careful record keeping by physicians, pharmacists, and manufacturers became mandatory. Renewals of prescriptions were limited to five, and prescriptions could not be renewed or dispensed after six months from the date of issue by the physician.

The drug scene continued to increase. Part of this may have had to do

Glossary

A-head: an amphetamine user.

Abstinence syndrome: *see* withdrawal syndrome and physical dependence.

Acapulco gold: high grade of marijuana, somewhat gold in color, supposedly grows in the area of Acapulco, Mexico.

Acid head: frequent user of LSD.

Addict: stereotype of a drug misuser often synonymous with junkie.

Addiction: a physiological state resulting from continued use of narcotics, barbiturates, or alcohol which is manifested by physical withdrawal symptoms and the achievement of drug tolerance.

Administration (drug): the process of introducing a drug into the body (e.g., swallowed, inhaled, injected).

Adverse reaction: a drug reaction which is unpleasant or harmful psychologically and/or physiologically.

African black: a grade of marijuana grown in Africa; *see* marijuana.

Agent: law-enforcement officer; also buster, bull, fed, fuzz, the heat, the man, plant, pig, narco, Sam, uncle, whiskers.

Agonies: withdrawal symptoms usually in early stages; *see* withdrawal.

Alcoholic cardiomyopathy: impairment of pumping function of the heart muscle due to toxic effects of alcohol.

Amenorrhea: absence of menstrual periods.

Amped: "wired" on crystal (methamphetamine); stems from the original methedrine.

Amphetamine-barbiturate combinations: *see* French blues, greenies, amphetamines.

Amphetamines: stimulants that increase the activity of the nervous system; used medically to relieve narcolepsy, hyperkinesis, and/or to reduce weight.

259

Ampules: small glass vials in which pharmaceutical methamphetamine was sold.

Amytal: registered trade name for amobarbital, a barbiturate; *see* barbiturates.

Analgesic: pain relieving.

Anesthesia: the loss of feeling or sensation; and may imply, with general anesthetics, a loss of consciousness.

Antagonist (drug): a drug which blocks or counteracts certain effects of another drug.

Antifreeze: heroin; *see* heroin.

Antihistamine: a drug used to combat allergies.

Aphrodisiac: sex-drive stimulant.

Arsenal: an addict's or pusher's supply of drugs.

Artillery: equipment for injecting drugs; *see* works.

Babysit: to guide a person through his drug experience; *see* guide, guru.

Back up, back track: blood which is allowed to come back into the syringe during intravenous injection.

Bag: small packet of narcotics.

Bang: to inject drugs.

Barbiturates: the most commonly abused depressants (sedatives).

Barbs: barbiturates; *see* barbiturates.

B bee: a penny match box volume, now a measure of marijuana approximately that size.

Bennies: benzedrine (amphetamine sulphate in tablet form).

Bent out: under the influence of LSD.

Benzedrine: amphetamine sulphate.

Bhang: a grade of marijuana found in India; *see* marijuana.

Big chief: mescaline.

Big D: LSD 25, usually referring to the original Sandox pharmaceutical.

Big John: police.

Big man: someone high up or at the top in a drug-selling ring; *see* pusher.

Bi-guy: bisexual person.

Bindle: a packet of narcotics.

Bit: a person's specialty, pastime, or favorite drug; a prison sentence.

Black beauty: biphetamine caps.

Blackbirds: amphetamines; *see* amphetamines.

Black mote: marijuana cured with sugar or honey.

Blank: bag of nonnarcotic powder sold as a regular bag; low-grade narcotics.

Blasted: under the influence of or high on drugs; *see* hopped up.

Blast party: group of marijuana smokers smoking together.

Blocked: under the influence of a drug—alone or in combination with alcohol; *see* drug experience.

Blood alcohol level: the concentration of alcohol in the blood (usually represented in percent by weight).

Blow a stick: to smoke a marijuana cigarette.

Blow one's mind: break from reality.

Blow the vein: the use of too much pressure when injecting into a weak or sclerosed vein causing it to rupture.

Blow your mind: to experience severe mental effects from a hallucinogenic drug, such as LSD.

Blue acid: LSD.

Blue angels, bluebirds: a barbiturate, Amytal.

Blue cheer: LSD.

Blue devils: a barbiturate, sodium Amytal (sodium amobarbital); also blue angels, bluebirds, blue heaven, blues.

Blue heaven: a barbiturate, Amytal; *see* blue devils.

Blues: a barbiturate, Amytal; *see* blue devils.

Blues and reds: *see* rainbows.

Blue velvet: a mixture of paregoric (a preparation which contains opium) and antihistamine (a drug used to combat allergies).

Bogart a joint: to salivate on a marijuana cigarette; to retain and not share a marijuana cigarette.

Bombita: vial of desoxyn, an amphetamine; amphetamine-heroin injection.

Boo, bu: marijuana.

Boost: to shoplift, steal.

Booster: a drug taken to cause another drug to take effect; shoplifter.

Booting: be jacking off; *see* jacking off.

Bottle: a quantity of tablets or capsules, usually 1000.

Boxed: jailed.

Boy: heroin; *see* heroin.

Bread: money.

Break the needle: to attempt to break or drop the narcotic habit; *see* withdrawal.

Brewery: a place where drugs are made, bought, or used.

Brick: a kilogram (2.2 pounds of marijuana).

Brody: feigned illness to obtain drugs from a doctor.

Broker: a dealer in drugs.

Brought down: depressed feeling following elation from drug use.

Browns: amphetamines.
Bu: *see* boo.
Bull: law enforcement agent.
Bull dike: female homosexual assuming masculine role.
Bummer: an unpleasant drug experience.
Bundle: twenty-five $5 bags of heroin.
Burn: to cheat someone, selling him something different from what he thinks he is buying.
Burning out: the cessation of drug use after many years because the drug user is tired of the efforts he must put in to continue his drug habit.
Busted: to be arrested.
Buster: law enforcement agent.

C: cocaine.
Caballo: heroin.
Can: approximately an ounce of marijuana.
Candy: barbiturates of cocaine.
Cannon: the addict's hypodermic syringe; *see* works.
Cap: a packet of heroin; gelatine capsule used to package powdered drugs; also person's head.
Cardiovascular: pertaining to the heart and blood vessels.
Cartwheels: benzedrine (amphetamine sulphate); the usual tablet is white with a scored crisscross, hence the nickname.
Central nervous system(CNS): the portion of the nervous system consisting of the brain and spinal cord.
Champed: drug user who will not reveal his supplier, even under pressure.
Charge: marijuana.
Charged up: under the effects of narcotics; high or under the intoxicating influence of drugs.
Charlie: cocaine.
Chasing the bag: seeking the best available bag of heroin.
Cheese eater: informer.
Chicago green: dark green marijuana said to be the same as variety popular in Chicago.
Chief: LSD.
Chillum: a clay pipe used in India to smoke ghanja (about halfway between hashish and marijuana in strength).

Chip: irregular drug use; *see* dabble.

Chippy: irregular drug user.

Chloral hydrate: a barbiturate.

Chistmas tree: dexamyl, green and white capsule containing a barbiturate and a stimulant.

Chromosomes: threadlike materials in the nucleus of a cell which contain the genes (i.e., the factors responsible for hereditary transmission).

Chronic: persisting over a long period of time.

Chuck: to eat excessively while undergoing withdrawal.

Cibas: Doriden, a sedative, hypnotic.

CNS depressant: substances that depress the central nervous system.

Cocaine: a stimulant obtained from a plant grown on slopes of the Andes.

Codeine: an opiate derivative used as a pain killer and in cough medicines.

Cognitive: psychological processes involved in perception, thinking, reasoning, etc.

Coke habit: small narcotics habit.

Cokie: a cocaine user.

Cold turkey: abrupt withdrawal from narcotics without medication.

Come down: the ending of a drug experience.

Connection: dealer in drugs; may either be an ounce man or, in street slang, the person the drug user buys from.

Contact high: to experience the effects of a drug without having taken it, by simply being in the presence of those who are under the influence.

Control group: a group of subjects as similar as possible to the experimental subjects (and exposed to all the conditions of the investigation) except for the experimental variable or treatment being studied (compare experimental group).

Cooker: a receptacle in which drugs are heated prior to intravenous injection.

Cook up a pill: to smoke opium; also to dissolve a pill in a spoon for injection.

Cop: to buy narcotics.

Co-pilots: amphetamines.

Cop to: to admit.

Cotic: a narcotic.

Cotton: the piece of cotton used to filter the dissolved narcotic after it has been "cooked." Addicts often reuse this material, saving it for a time when they are unable to secure drugs. When soaked in water, such material yields a weak solution.

Count: the quality of a drug.

Courage pills: barbiturates.

Crash: to go to sleep.

Crash pad: a place to crash.

Cristina: methamphetamine.

Croaker: unscrupulous doctor who sells or prescribes drugs to illicit drug users.

Cross-dependence: a condition in which one drug can prevent the withdrawal symptoms associated with physical dependence on a different drug.

Cross-tolerance: a tolerance developed to drugs other than the specific drug taken.

Crutch: *see* roach clip.

Crystal: methamphetamine, hydrochloride, speed.

Cubehead: a frequent user of LSD.

Cut: to adulterate narcotics with a nonnarcotic, such as milk sugar.

Cyclazacine: a narcotic antagonist used in the treatment of narcotics addiction.

Dabble: to "chip" or take small amounts of drugs irregularly.

Dagga: South African term for marijuana.

Dealer: a seller of drugs.

Dealer in weight: third person adulterating heroin, making three units of each one.

Deck: small packet of heroin.

Delirium: a condition (usually of relatively short duration) characterized by excitement, confusion, incoherence, illusions, delusions, and sometimes hallucinations.

Delusion: a belief which exists in spite of contrary reason or evidence which would normally be considered sufficient to change it.

Dependency: the same as habituation but used with moral and philosophical overtones.

Depersonalization: a state in which a person's sense of his own, or his body's reality or existence is weakened or lost.

Depressant: a drug which depresses or decreases bodily activity. Depressants may be classified according to the organ or system upon which they act. The terms "CNS depressant" and "sedative" are often used interchangeably.

Desoxyn: methedrine; *see* bombita.

Det: dimethyltryptamine derivative, a hallucinogenic drug.

Dexedrine: dextroamphetamine sulphate.

Dexies: dexedrine (dextroamphetamine tablets or capsules).

Dig: to understand.

Dike: female homosexual.

Dime bag: $10 worth of drugs.

Dimethoxy 4: a hallucinogen.

Dimethyltryptomine: a hallucinogen.

Dirty: with drugs in the system, therefore unable to pass a test, also unsterilized (needle for injection).

Ditch: the inside of the elbow which has two large veins.

DMT: dimethyltryptomine, a hallucinogenic drug.

Dollar: $100.

Dollar bill: $100.

Dollier: dolophine, methadone.

Dolls' pills: amphetamines, barbiturates, or a combination of these two drugs.

Dolophine: methadone.

Dom: dimethoxy 4, methylamphetamine, a hallucinogenic drug, same as STP.

Doper: anyone who uses drugs.

Doriden: cibas.

Double trouble: Tuinal, a combination of two barbiturates.

Do up: to inject a drug into a vein.

Downer: depressant, or any sedative-type drug.

Dreamer: morphine; a person who is never in touch with reality.

Drop: to take a drug by mouth.

Drop a cap: to swallow an LSD capsule.

Drop a dime: to telephone the police in order to inform on someone.

Drop out: to renounce conventional society.

Dropped: arrested.

Dropper: homemade syringe, using an eyedropper.

Drug: any chemical substance that alters the structure or functioning of a living organism.

Drug experience: being under the influence of a drug.

Drug misuse: use of the drugs for medically and socially unacceptable reasons.

Drug use: use of drugs for medically and socially acceptable reasons.

Drying out: detoxification after excessive and continuous use of alcohol.

DT's: delirium tremens; withdrawal symptoms from alcoholism.

Dust: cocaine.
Dynamite: heroin of exceptional purity.

Eating: taking a drug especially by mouth.
Eighth: one-eighth ounce of heroin.
Electric Kool Ade: punch containing LSD.
Embolic pneumonia: inflammation of the lung resulting from obstructions of the small blood vessels of the lung.
Endocarditis: infection or inflammation of the surface of the heart chambers and heart valves.
Equipment: items used to prepare and inject a dose of drugs, usually heroin; includes bent spoon or bottle cap for dissolving drug-containing powder, matches, hypodermic needle, eye dropper, and cotton.
Etiology: the basis for or cause of a disease or condition.
Euphoria: a feeling of well-being or elation sought by drug users and sometimes found the first few times that certain drugs are taken.
Explorers' club: group of LSD users.
Eye opener: first injection of the day.

Factory: equipment or instruments for injecting drugs.
Famine: a lack of available drugs resulting from a raid by the police on a supply.
Farmer: someone naive about drugs.
Far out: terrific, wonderful, fantastic, amazing.
Fatty: a fat or thick marijuana cigarette.
Fed: law enforcement officer.
Feed bag: a container of narcotics.
Feed store: a place where drugs can be purchased.
Fifteen cents: $15.
Fine snuff: marijuana in good quality; also heroin of good quality.
Fink: informer.
Fix: an injection.
Fixated: to remain at or return to an earlier or more immature level of personality development.
Flake: cocaine.
Flake out: lose consciousness from misuse of drugs.
Flash: the intense "orgasmlike" euphoria experienced immediately after an intravenous injection, usually of speed, heroin, or cocaine.

Flashback: the unpredictable phenomenon of undergoing again the effects of LSD weeks or even months after last use of the drugs.

Flattened: an addict in stupor resulting from overdose.

Flea powder: low quality or weak drugs.

Floating: *see* hopped up.

Fly agaric: a hallucinogenic drug from the poisonous mushroom *amanita muscaria*. It was originally used on fly paper.

Focus: drug solution ready for injection.

Football: oval-shaped amphetamine tablets.

Freakout: acute anxiety reaction usually referring to a bad LSD experience.

French blue: amphetamine-barbiturate pill.

Fresh and sweet: just out of jail.

Frises speedball: 50 percent heroin, 50 percent cocaine with a dash of LSD.

Front to: give someone drugs on credit for him to sell and then pay the wholesaler back.

Fruit salad: a variety of capsules or tablets contributed by group members and shared by all.

Fuzz, fuzzy: police; law enforcement officer.

G: a paper funnel placed at the end of an eyedropper, used to inject heroin.

Garbage: very weak heroin.

Gasket: anything that can be placed on the small end of an eyedropper to prevent leaks between the dropper and the hub of the needle, most commonly a torn corner of a dollar bill.

GB's: abbreviation of goofballs.

Get off: the "orgasmic" feeling right after injecting a drug, also feeling the effect of a drug on one's mind.

Gimmicks: *see* outfit.

Gluey: glue sniffer.

Go: a deal.

Gold dust: cocaine.

Good go: fair quality of drugs received for one's payment.

Good people: one who can be trusted with drugs.

Goods: drugs.

Goofball: *see* goofer.

Goofer: barbiturates.

Grass: marijuana.

Grasshopper: marijuana smoker.

Greenies: amphetamines.

Greezy addict: an addict who takes any drug available whenever it is available.

Ground control supervisor: guide in an LSD session.

Grow head: opium smoker.

G. shot: a very small dose of drugs, used to stave off sickness until a full dose can be taken.

Guide, guru: a person who gives guidance or support during a psychedelic experience.

Gum: opium.

Gun: hypodermic needle for "shooting" drugs.

H: heroin.

Habit-forming (drug): a drug which may produce dependence (usually psychological) in certain users in certain circumstances.

Habituation: a psychological condition resulting from the continued use of addicting and nonaddicting drugs; the user craves the drug.

Habituation (drug): usually implies (1) a desire (but not a compulsion) to continue drug use, (2) little or no tolerance, and (3) no physical dependence.

Hallucination: a vision or sensation without objective reality.

Hallucinogens: one way of classifying drugs such as LSD, mescaline, STP, DMT, DET, marijuana.

Happening: a psychedelic event or show.

Hard stuff: morphine, heroin.

Harry: heroin.

Hawk: LSD; *see* LSD.

Hay: marijuana.

Head: usually a positive term, referring to someone who uses drugs in a "cool" way, mostly referring to LSD and marijuana users.

Head shop: store that sells accessories for using drugs.

Hearts: amphetamines.

Heat: police.

Heavenly blues: morning glory seeds; *see* hallucinogens.

Heroin: an opiate, derivative of the opium poppy; a pain killer.

High: under the effect of narcotics; the state of mind produced by a drug.

Hippie hepatitis: hepatitis associated with the use of methedrine and amphetamine.

Hit: single dose of any drug.

Hog: benactyzine or PCP tranquilizerlike drugs.

Hold: to have an illegal drug in one's possession.

Hooked: addicted.

Hopped-up: drugged, "high," being under influence of a drug.

Horrors: terrifying dreams and hallucinations "caused" by LSD and other hallucinogenic drugs.

Horse: heroin.

Hot: wanted by the police.

Hot shot: an injection of poison often used in place of the drug, possibly given to informers; fatal dose of drugs.

Hung up: unable to obtain drugs, depressed, let down, disappointed.

Hustle: to prostitute.

Hydrochloride: an amphetamine; speed.

Hype: narcotics addict.

Hypersplenism: overactivity of the spleen, which may result in bleeding, infection, anemia.

Hypertension: elevation of blood pressure above the normal range; prolonged hypertension may result in serious heart disease, kidney failure, or stroke.

Hypnotic: sleep inducing.

Hypo: narcotics addict.

Ice cream habit: off-and-on use of drugs.

Idiots' pills: *see* cibas.

Illusion: a false or misinterpreted sensory impression. The individual is usually aware of the unreal qualities of the perception (compare delusion, hallucination).

Indian hemp: inaccurate term popularly used to describe all forms of cannabis.

Instant Zen: LSD; *see* LSD.

J: marijuana cigarette.

Jacking off: repeatedly allowing blood to reenter the outfit; the practice carries sexual implications.

Jelly babies: amphetamine pills; *see* amphetamines.

Jive: marijuana.

Joint: marijuana cigarette; also prison, penis.

Jolly beans: amphetamine pills.

Jones: a drug habit.

Joy pop: infrequent injection of narcotics; to inject small amounts of drugs intramuscularly or subcutaneously.

Joy powder: heroin.

Jug: ampule of liquid drug; also multidosage container.

Juggler: person the addict generally buys from, usually an addict himself.

Juice head: an alcoholic.

Junk: heroin.

Junkie: narcotics user.

Karma: fate; *see* Nirvana.

Key: *see* kilo.

Kick: to break the drug habit; *see* withdrawal.

Kilo: 2.2 pounds.

Kilo connection: the first person to adulterate heroin; he generally makes two kilos from each kilo.

King Kong pills: *see* cibas.

Kit: *see* outfit.

Ky.:   U.S. Public Health Service Hospital, Lexington, Kentucky, a narcotics treatment center.

Lady in white: heroin; derives from the fact that many users feel married to the drug.

Latency: the period of inactivity between stimulation and the response or reaction to that stimulus.

Layout: *see* outfit.

Leapers: amphetamines.

Lemonade: *see* garbage; poor heroin.

Lid: one ounce of marijuana.

Lid poppers: amphetamines.

Lift: the temporary escape from mental depression given by some drugs.

Load: thirty $3 bags of heroin.

Loco weed: marijuana.

Love weed: marijuana.

LSD: lysergic acid diethylamide, a hallucinogenic drug.

Lyseric acid: a hallucinogen.

Machinery: *see* outfit.

Macking: pimping.

Magic mushroom: psilocybin, a hallucinogenic drug (from *psilocybi mexicana*, a mushroom containing the drug).

Mainliner: drug user who injects directly into veins.

Maintaining: keeping constant a certain level of drug effects.

Man: law enforcement officer.

Manicure: to clean and prepare marijuana for smoking.

Mannite: a product from the ash tree used in adulterating heroin; a mild laxative.

Marijuana: a substance, often classified as a psychedelic, which is derived from *cannabis sativa*.

Mary Jane: marijuana.

Match box: small amount of marijuana, enough for about 5 to 8 joints.

Mayo: hard drugs.

MDA: methylenedioxyamphetamine, a hallucinogenic drug.

Menorrhagia: excessive menstrual bleeding.

Mescaline: a hallucinogenic drug.

Meth: methamphetamine hydrochloride, speed.

Methadone: a synthetic narcotic used to alleviate pain in terminal illness, to withdraw narcotic addicts, and legally to maintain heroin users.

Meth freak, meth head: person who uses speed regularly.

Mexican: term for marijuana.

Mexican brown: brown-colored heroin, from Mexico.

Mickey Finn: chloral hydrate, a sedative hypnotic.

Mike: a microgram—one millionth of a gram—used to measure the dosage of LSD.

Mint weed: marijuana substitute, usually parsley flakes impregnated with PCP or another sedative drug.

Miss: when the needle accidentally slips out of, by, or through the vein, so that the drug is injected into the surrounding tissue.

Miss Emma: morphine.

Monkey: expensive drug habit.

Morphine: opiate derivative, used medicinally as a pain killer.

Mud: opium.

Mule: one who sells or transports drugs for a regular peddler.

Muscle, muscle pop: intramuscular injection of a drug, done to conceal needle marks, to prolong the effects of the drug, or because of inability to find a usable vein.

Mushroom: *see* magic mushroom.

Nail: hypodermic needle.

Narco: narcotics detective.

Narcoland: the fanciful world of addicts.

Needle freak: one who delights in using a needle intravenously and will "shoot" almost anything, from peanut butter to potent drugs.

Needle friend: one who has a hypodermic.

Needle habit: person who enjoys the act of injecting himself more than he enjoys the drug experience.

Nembies: barbiturates, Nembutal.

Niacinamide: an antidote for LSD, used to interrupt a bad trip.

Nickel bag: $5 worth of drugs.

Nimby: *see* nembies.

Nirvana: the state of freedom from Karma; the extinction of desire, passion, illusion, and individual consciousness; the attainment of rest, truth, and unchanging being.

Nodding: to be somnolent and lethargic when under the influence of drugs.

Nonmedical use of drugs: use which is not indicated or justified for generally accepted medical reasons, whether under medical supervision or not.

O: opium.

O.D.: overdose of narcotics, may be lethal.

Off: no longer under the influence of drugs.

On the nod: state of nodding.

Opium: derivative of the opium poppy from which many pain killers are derived.

Oranges: *see* dexies.

Ounce man: second man to cut or adulterate heroin.

Outfit: paraphernalia needed to use drugs; syringe, needle, etc.

Overamped: on too large a dose of speed.

Overcharged: under the influence of an overdose of narcotics.

Pain-prone addict: individual who generally has become addicted in an attempt to treat physical pain of undetermined origin.

Panama red: a high grade of marijuana from Panama.

Panic: a scarcity of drugs.

Paper: *see* bag.

Paranoia: a condition characterized by delusions of persecution and/or grandeur; in severe instances paranoia may be considered a sign of psychosis.

Paregoric: an opium derivative.

PCP: sernyl (phencyclidine), an animal anesthetic with a strong sedative effect; stems from "peace pill."

Peace pill: *see* PCP; can also be benactyzine.

Peace weed: *see* mint weed.

Peaches: *see* dexies.

Peanuts: barbiturates.

Pentabarbital: a barbiturate.

Peyote: small cactus that contains mescaline, a hallucinogenic drug.

PG: paregoric.

Pharmacology: the scientific study of the effect of drugs on the living organism.

Phennies: phenobarbital, a barbiturate.

Phenobarbital: a barbiturate.

Physical dependence: a physiological state of adaptation to continuous use of a drug (normally occurring after the development of tolerance) which results in a characteristic set of withdrawal symptoms, often called the abstinence syndrome, when administration of the drug is stopped.

Physiology: the scientific study of biological functions in the living organism.

Pick up: a new customer for drugs; a shot of narcotics usually given to another addict as a gift or favor.

Piece: one ounce of narcotics.

Piece of stuff: one ounce of heroin, approximately ten spoons.

Pig: policeman.

Pill freak: person who will take almost any kind of pill indiscriminately and does it to an extreme.

Pill head: one who takes pills for kicks.

Pinks: *see* reds.

Pin shot: an injection made by using a pin or other sharp instrument to make a wound into which the end of the medicine dropper is directly inserted.

Pipe: large vein.

Placebo: an inactive drug or medication which is pharmacologically unrelated to any drug which would cause what the drugs user reports experiencing.

Plant: an undercover narcotics agent or policeman pretending to be a drug user so as to gain leads or suspects; stash of drugs placed on a person to make him vulnerable to arrest.

Plastic hippie: part-time hippie.

Point: hypodermic needle.

Poison: a drug in a quantity which exceeds the amount the body can tolerate without damage or injury; any drugs can be poisonous if the dose is high enough.

Pop: to inject a drug subcutaneously.

Potentiation: an overall effect of two drugs taken together which is greater than the sum of the effects of each drug taken alone.

Pot head: frequent user of marijuana.

Primary addict: person who begins drug use early in his life, generally during adolescence.

Psilocybin: a hallucinogen obtained from a Mexican mushroom.

Psychedelic: mind expanding, mind manifesting.

Psychological or psychic dependence: a condition in which a person depends upon something (e.g., a drug) for satisfaction or a feeling of well-being.

Psychology: the scientific study of behavior and the mind.

Psychomotor: pertaining to muscular activity or behavior associated with certain psychological functions; psychomotor tests usually measure such things as muscular coordination, behavioral skills, etc.

Psychotropic (or psychoactive) drugs: those drugs that alter sensation, mood, consciousness, or other psychological or behavioral functions.

Pulmonary fibrosis: increased scar tissue in the lung that is either localized or generalized.

Pulmonary hypertension: elevation of pressure in blood vessels of the lung.

Purple hearts: phenobarbital, a barbiturate.

Pusher: narcotics seller.

Quill: folded match box cover used for sniffing narcotics through the nose.

Rainbows: Tuinal capsules, a combination of two barbiturates.

Rainy day woman: marijuana.

Rap, rapping: conversation; to converse; conversing.

Reader: prescription.

Red birds, red devils: *see* reds.

Reds: Seconal (secobarbital), a barbiturate.

Reefer: a marijuana cigarette.

Reenter: return from a trip.

Reverse tolerance: a condition in which the response to a certain dose of a drug increases with repeated use.

Ride shotgun: protect someone who is selling drugs.

Rig: *see* outfit.

Rip off: to steal, also a theft.

Roach: butt of a marijuana cigarette.

Roach clip: something used to hold marijuana; most often made by the marijuana user.

Rope: marijuana.

Roses: benzedrine, a stimulant.

Sam: federal narcotics agent.

Satch cotton: cotton saturated with heroin.

Scag, scat: heroin.

Schizophrenia: a group of naturally occurring psychotic disorders generally becoming manifest in late adolescence or early adulthood. (Contrary to popular belief, this term does not refer to "split" or "dual" personality.)

Schmeck: heroin.

School boy: codeine.

Score: to obtain drugs.

Script: a doctor's perscription.

Secky: Seconal capsules.

Secobarbital: a barbiturate, reds.

Seconal: a barbiturate.

Secondary addict: person who begins drug use in adulthood, generally in reaction to some trauma.

Septicemia: the absorption and circulation of bacteria and their toxins in the blood system.

Set: the psychological state or disposition of an individual which affects his subsequent drug experience. Such factors as the expectations, motivations, and attitudes may be important factors in determining drug effects.

Setup: combined use of alcohol and barbiturates.

Shit: primarily heroin, but can refer to any drug.

Shooting gallery: place where addicts congregate to shoot up.

Shoot up: to take an injection.

Shorts counts: misrepresentation of a great weight of drugs, generally heroin, in a given unit.

Shot: an injection of drugs.

Simple Simon: psilocybin, a hallucinogenic drug.

Single blind: an experiment in which the subject does not know which particular treatment (e.g., the identity or dose of a drug, or a placebo) is being given. The researcher is aware of these experimental factors at the time of the test in a single blind design.

Skin pop: injecting drug beneath the skin.

Smack: heroin.

Sniffing, snorting: sniffing narcotics or other drugs through the nose.

Sodium amobarbital: a barbiturate; *see* blue angels, blue birds, blue heaven.

Spaced: in a floating state, not quite in touch with reality while under the influence of a drug.

Speed: methedrine, an amphetamine.

Speedball: a simultaneous injection of a stimulant and a depressant; originally a mixture of heroin and cocaine.

Speed demon, speed freak: street classification of methedrine user.

Spike: hypodermic needle.

Splash: *see* speed.

Spoon: one-sixteenth ounce of heroin.

Stash: cache of narcotics.

Statistically significant: a measurement or score which is highly unlikely to have occurred by chance alone and might therefore be attributed to some specific nonrandom factors.

Stimulants: stimulating substances such as cocaine, amphetamines.

STP: DOM, a hallucinogenic drug; initials are thought to stand for serenity, tranquility, and peace.

Straight: a feeling of well-being after a shot of drugs.

Street addict: stereotype of the overt addict, akin to the skid row bum of alcoholism.

Strung out: continuously dependent on a drug; addicted.

Stuff: narcotics; heroin.

Sugar: powdered narcotics; also LSD.

Swing man: drug supplier.

Tai: opium.

Tall: good.

Tea: marijuana.

Teratagenic: producing physical defects or abnormalities in the offspring factors during pregnancy.

THC: tetrahydrocannabinol, marijuana's active ingredient.

Tie: anything that can be wrapped tightly around the arm to make the veins pop out, thus facilitating injection.

Tolerance: the taking of increased drug doses as the body accustoms itself to the presence of drugs in its system to achieve what was originally experienced from lesser doses.

Toy: smallest container of prepared opium.

Toxic: a damaging or disrupting drug effect (often used to describe symptoms of poisoning). All drugs have toxic effects if the dose is high enough.

Track marks: from repeated injection along the same vein.

Tuinal: a barbiturate; amobarbital plus secobarbital.

Twist: marijuana.

Uncle: law enforcement agent.

Uppers, ups: stimulants.

Up tight: tense, anxious, frightened.

Valley: *see* ditch.

Vibrations: nonverbal communication.

Wake-up: morning shot of a drug; also amphetamine.

Whiskers: law enforcement agent.

Whites: benzedrine pills.

Wired: strongly under the influence of a stimulant.

Withdrawal: to break a drug habit. Depending upon type of drug used, there may be specific types of physical and/or psychological symptoms when the addicted or habituated person does not have his drug.

Withdrawal syndrome (or symptoms):   a characteristic set of adverse physiological and psychological symptoms which occur after the development of physical dependence, when the regular administration of the drug is stopped (or its effect inhibited by an antagonist); also called the abstinence syndrome.

Works: equipment used for injecting drugs; syringe, needle.

Yellow jackets, yellows: Nembutal (pentabarbital sodium) capsules.

Yen: craving for drugs.

Yen hack: instrument used for smoking opium.

Yonked: highly under the influence of a drug.

Young blood: young person starting to use marijuana.

Yo-yo phenomenon: the process of sequential injection of barbiturates and stimulants, particularly amphetamines.

Resources

INFORMATION RESOURCES

A selected list of national, governmental, professional, educational, law enforcement, service, religious, and youth organizations working in the area of drug-misuse information dissemination.

Addiction Research Foundation of Ontario
33 Russell St., Toronto 179, Ontario, Canada   (416) 595–6056

American Association of Colleges of Pharmacy
850 Sligo Ave., Silver Spring, Maryland 20910   (301) 585-0011

American Association for Health, Physical Education, and Recreation
1201 16th St., N.W., Washington, D.C. 20036   (202) 223-9400

American Association of Poison Control Centers
Nebraska Master Poison Control Center, Children's Memorial Hospital
44th and Dewey Ave., Omaha, Nebraska 68105   (402) 553-3400

American College of Apothecaries
7758 Wisconsin Ave., N.W., Washington, D.C. 20014   (202) 657-2055

American College Health Association
2807 Central St., Evanston, Illinois 60201   (312) 491-9775

American Council on Alcohol Problems, Inc.
119 Constitution Ave., N.E., Washington, D.C. 20002   (202) 543-2441

American Medical Association
535 North Dearborn St., Chicago, Illinois 60610   (312) 527-1500

American Nurses Association
10 Columbus Circle, New York, N.Y. 10019   (212) 582-7230

American Orthopsychiatric Association
1790 Broadway, New York, N.Y. 10019   (212) 589-5690

American Pharmaceutical Association
2215 Constitution Ave., N.W., Washington, D.C. 10019   (202) 628-4410

American Psychiatric Association
1700 18th St., N.W., Washington, D.C. 20009   (202) 232-7878

American Public Health Association
1015 18th St., N.W., Washington, D.C. 20036   (202) 467-5053

American School Health Association
American School Health Bldg. P.O.B. 416, Kent, Ohio 44240   (216) 678-1601

American Social Health Association
1740 Broadway, New York, N.Y. 10019   (212) 245-8000

American Society for Pharmacology and Experimental Therapeutics
9650 Rockville Pike, Bethesda, Maryland 20014   (301) 530-3200

B'nai B'rith (CVS)
1640 Rhode Island Ave., N.W., Washington, D.C. 20036   (202) 393-5284

Boy Scouts of America
North Brunswick, N.J. 08903   (201) 249-6000

Center of Alcohol Studies
Rutgers University, New Brunswick, N.J. 08903   (201) 932-2190

Child Study Association of America
9 East 89th St., New York, N.Y. 10028   (212) 369-6300

Committee on Drug Addiction and Narcotics, National Academy of Sciences—
National Research Council, Division of Medical Sciences, Washington, D.C.   (202) 393-8100

Drug Abuse Council
1828 L. St., N.W., Washington, D.C.   (202) 785-5200

Drug Abuse Research and Education (Project D.A.R.E.)
760 Westwood Plaza, Los Angeles, California 90024   (213) 825-0020

Food and Drug Administration, Dept. of Health, Education, and Welfare
Parklawn Building, 5600 Fishers Lane, Rockville, Maryland 20852   (301) 443-3170

Food and Drug Directorate, Dept. of National Health and Welfare
Tunney's Pasture, Ottawa 3, Ontario, Canada   (613) 992-5567

Institute for the Study of Drug Misuse
111 5th Ave., New York; N.Y. 10003   (212) 777-1000

Institute for the Study of Drug Dependence
Chandos House, 2 Queen Ann St., London, WIMOBL England   (01) 580-2518

International Council on Alcohol and Addictions
Case Postale 140, 1001 Lausanne, Switzerland   (021) 296485

International Narcotic Enforcement Officers Association
178 Washington Ave., Albany, N.Y. 12210   (518) 463-6232

Narcotic Education Foundation of America
5055 Sunset Blvd., Los Angeles, California 90027   (213) 663-5171

National Alcohol Beverage Control Association
Suite 1640, 5454 Wisconsin Ave., N.W., Washington, D.C. 20015   (202) 654-3366

National Association for Mental Health
10 Columbus Circle, New York, N.Y., 10019   (212) 747-7800

National Association for Prevention of Addiction to Narcotics
175 5th Ave., New York, N.Y. 10010   (212) 260-2750

National Association of Pharmaceutical Manufacturers
101 Park Ave., New York, N.Y. 10017   (212) 683-1700

National Association of Social Workers
2 Park Ave., New York, N.Y. 10016   (212) 686-7128

National Bar Association
5440 Cass Ave., Suite 405, Detroit, Michigan 48202   (313) 833-0060

National Board of YWCA
1030 15th St., N.W., Washington, D.C. 20005   (202) 223-6595

National Catholic Youth Organization Federation
1312 Massachusetts Ave., N.W., Washington, D.C. 20005   (202) 659-6664

National Clearinghouse for Drug Abuse Information
5600 Fishers Lane, Rockville, Maryland 20852   (301) 496-7171

National Clearinghouse for Smoking and Health
5401 Westbard Ave., Bethesda, Maryland 20016   (301) 496-7921

National Coordinating Council on Drug Education
Suite 212, 1211 Connecticut Ave., N.W., Washington, D.C. 20036   (202) 466-8150

National Council of State Pharmaceutical Association Executives
6619 White-Henry Stuart Building, Seattle, Washington, 98101   (206) 624-4818

National Council of the Churches of Christ in the United States of America
475 Riverside Drive, New York, N.Y. 10027   (212) 870-2200

National Council on Alcoholism
2 Park Ave., New York, N.Y. 10016   (212) 889-3160

National Council on Crime and Delinquency
Continental Plaza, 411 Hackensack Ave., Hackensack, N.J. 07601   (201) 488-0400

National District Attorneys Association
211 East Chicago Ave., Suite 1204, Chicago, Illinois 60611   (312) 944-2667

National Institute of Mental Health
5600 Fishers Lane, Rockville, Maryland 20852   (202) 655-4000

National Safety Council
425 North Michigan Ave., Chicago, Illinois 60611   (312) 527-4800

New York Narcotic Addiction Control Commission
Stuyvesant Plaza, Albany, N.Y. 12203   (518) 474-2121

North American Association of Alcoholism Problems
1130 17th St., N.W., Washington, D.C. 20036   (202) 628-1585

Pharmaceutical Manufacturers Association
1155 15th St., N.W., Washington, D.C. 20005   (202) 296-2440

Student American Medical Association
2635 Flossmoor Road, Flossmoor, Illinois 60422   (312) 785-4540

Student American Pharmaceutical Association
2215 Constitution Ave., N.W. Washington, D.C. 20037   (202) 628-4410

Student Association for the Study of Hallucinogens
638 Pleasant St., Beloit, Wisconsin 53511   (608) 362-8848

U.S. Bureau of Narcotics and Dangerous Drugs
1405 Eye St., N.W., Washington, D.C. 20537   (202) 382-5551

U.S. Department of Defense
1117 North 19th St., Arlington, Virginia 22209   (703) 694-5023

U.S. Jaycees
P.O. Box 7, Tulsa, Oklahoma 74102   (918) 584-2481

U.S. National Student Association
2115 S. St., N.W., Washington, D.C. 20008   (202) 387-5100
U.S. Office of Education
400 Maryland Ave., S. W., Room 2102, Washington, D.C. 20202   (202) 655-4000
Your State Department of Health

JOURNAL RESOURCES

Addictions
  Addiction Research Foundation of Ontario
  33 Russell St.,
  Toronto 179, Ontario, Canada
Original articles on drug misuse, alcoholism, smoking, and gambling.

Alcoholism
  Institute for the Study and Treatment of Alcoholism
  Zagreb, Yugoslavia
Original articles on alcoholism, its treatment, and prevention in English
and other languages.

Bulletin of Narcotics
  World Health Organization, Division of Narcotic Drugs
  Palais des Nations
  Geneva, Switzerland
Original articles on various facets of drug addiction, the pharmacology of
drugs, and the treatment of narcotic addiction.

Drug Forum
  Baywood Publishing Co.
  43 Central Drive
  Farmingdale, New York 11735
Original articles and book reviews on the treatment, education, and other
forms of drug-abuse intervention.

International Journal of the Addictions
  Marcel Dekker, Inc., Publishers
  95 Madison Ave.,
  New York, New York 10016
Original articles and reprints from other journals and book reviews on
theoretical, clinical, and experimental aspects of drug misuse, alcoholism, smoking, gambling,
and overeating.

Journal of Drug Education
  Baywood Publishing Co.
  43 Central Drive
  Farmingdale, New York 11735
Original articles on every phase of drug education.

Journal of Drug Issues
325 East Gaines St.,
Tallahassee, Florida 32304
Original articles on drug misuse.

Journal of Psychedelic Drugs
STASH Press
638 Pleasant St.,
Beloit, Wisconsin 53511
Original articles on psychedelic drugs.

Labyrinth
Orba Information Ltd.
418 Saint Sulpice St.,
Montreal 125, Ontario, Canada
Weekly abstracts of drug-related material in journals, magazines, and newspapers.

Psychopharmacology Bulletin
National Clearinghouse for Mental Health Information
National Institute of Mental Health
5454 Wisconsin Ave.,
Bethesda, Maryland
Abstracts and short articles on the psychopharmacology of drugs.

Quarterly Journal of Studies on Alcohol
Center of Alcohol Studies
Rutgers University
New Brunswick, New Jersey
Original articles, book reviews, and abstracts on alcoholism.

The British Journal of Addiction
E. & S. Livingstone
5 Bentinck St.,
London WIM, 5 RN, England
Original articles and book reviews on various facets of drug addiction and
alcoholism.

The Journal
Addiction Research Foundation of Ontario
33 Russell St.,
Toronto, 179, Ontario, Canada
Monthly original articles and news reports on various aspects of drug misuse
and alcoholism.

Toxicomanies
Office for the Prevention and Treatment of Alcoholism and Other Addictions
Edifice Sainte-Foy
969, Route de l'Eglise
Quebec 10 e, Quebec, Canada
Original articles in French on drug addiction and alcoholism.

BOOK RESOURCES

Becker, H. S., *Outsiders: Studies in the Sociology of Deviancy.* New York: Free Press, 1963.

A systematic study of marijuana users which points out some of the causes for use and some of the problems of the user. The major thesis is that marijuana use is considered deviant behavior because this label is applied to it by society, not because deviance is an inherent quality of the marijuana user.

Blum, R., and associates, *Society and Drugs,* vol. 1; *Students and Drugs,* vol. 11. San Francisco: Jossey-Bass, 1969.

This two-volume series presents an overview of the various factors that are needed to understand the use and misuse of various psychoactive drugs. From an historical review to the present patterns of drug use, the reader is helped to understand the changing patterns of drug use by various segments of society.

Brecher, E., *Licit and Illicit Drugs.* Boston: Little, Brown, 1972.

This major contribution to the drug literature is the Consumer's Union report on both licit and illicit drugs. Each of the drugs covered is presented within a historical perspective, and myths and drugs are delineated according to what they do. A great emphasis is placed on drug laws, policies, and attitudes. This report includes a series of recommendations that concerned citizens should be aware of.

Brotman, R., and Freedman, A., *A Community Mental Health Approach to Drug Addiction.* Washington, D.C.: U.S. Government Printing Office, 1968.

Views drug misuse as a community problem whose diminution and control necessitate the mobilizing of all relevant community forces.

DeRopp, R. S., *The Master Game: Pathways to Higher Consciousness Beyond the Drug Experience.* New York: Dell, 1968.

Written by a biochemist, this book explores the various avenues available to man to achieve the highest possible levels of consciousness, and thereby to go beyond drugs.

Einstein, S., *The Use and Misuse of Drugs: A Social Dilemma.* Belmont, Calif: Wadsworth, 1970.

A public health perspective of the nonmedical use of drugs. A short and concise overview of the various factors that affect today's drug scene.

Einstein, S., and Allen, M., *Student Drug Surveys.* Farmingdale, N.Y.: Baywood, 1972.

A collection of papers presented at the First International Conference on Student Drug Surveys (1971) which focuses on the rational of doing surveys, the consequences for all concerned, and a number of survey reports.

Group for the Advancement of Psychiatry, *Drug Misuse: A Psychiatric View of a Modern Dilemma.* New York: Scribner, 1971.

A short overview of facts and gaps in knowledge related to the nonmedical use of drugs with recommendations to change the current identification with "progress through chemistry."

King, R., *The Drug Hang Up.* New York: Norton, 1972.

A comprehensive review of the history of drug laws in the U.S.A. and how they came about.

The author's central thesis is that man's appetites should not be controlled by external forces as long as no one is making a profit from such behavior.

Laurie, P., *Drugs, Medical, Psychological and Social Facts.* (A Pelican Book) Middlesex, England: Penguin, 1971.

Based on interviews and literature research, this book focuses on the pharmacological uses and social effects of drug use and misuse.

Lennard, H. C., and associates, *Mystification and Drug Misuse: Hazards in Using Psychoactive Drugs.* San Francisco: Jossey-Bass, 1971.

Sets forth the thesis that today's drug scene must be understood in terms of the mystification of drugs. Accuses the mass media, pharmaceutical industry, medical profession, and the youth culture of creating the belief that everyday experiences can best be handled through drugs.

Marin, P., and Cohen, A. Y., *Understanding Drug Use: An Adult's Guide to Drugs and the Young.* New York: Harper & Row, 1971.

Focuses on the various meanings of a child's drug use. The book's central concern is to help parents and other adults understand drug use and to develop realistic alternatives to it.

National Commission on Marijuana and Drug Abuse, *Marijuana a Signal of Misunderstanding.* New York: New American Library, 1972.

This official report of the National Commission separates out facts from fiction, points out gaps in knowledge about the effects of marijuana, and makes recommendations for social policy.

Taylor, N., *Narcotics: Nature's Dangerous Gifts.* New York: Dell, 1963.

A humorous but earnest history of the use of various plant derivatives for pleasure and for escape from daily living.

Terry, C. E., and Pellins, M., *The Opium Problem.* Montclair, N.J.: Paterson and Smith, 1971.

An accurate historical and critical review of drug use and misuse in the United States from the time of the 13 colonies to the closing of the 44 drug maintenance clinics.

The Canadian Government Commission of Inquiry, *The Non-Medical Use of Drugs: An Interim Report.* Middlesex, England: Penguin, 1971.

Based on interviews, government hearings, and a literature search, this governmental report is an exhaustive review of what drugs do and don't do, as well as various theories explaining the nonmedical use of drugs.

The Canadian Government Commission of Inquiry, *Treatment.* Ottawa, Canada: Information Canada, 1972.

The most up-to-date and concise overview of treating the nonmedical user of drugs with particular reference to acute medical intervention.

Weil, A., *The Natural Mind.* New York: Houghton Mifflin, 1972.

Develops the thesis that man's need to get high is basic to his existence and that both young and old utilize various techniques to do this. Drugs are obviously only one of the available options. This book suggests that the need to get high is an attempt to remove ourselves from straight, clock-watching rationality, which we perceive as normal consciousness. The reader is urged to examine the concept of stoned thinking.

SUGGESTED RESOURCE DIRECTORY

Telephone
Number

Telephone
Number

HOSPITAL NUMBERS

Administrator _____

Anesthesiologist (on call) _____

Psychiatrist (on call) _____

Neurologist (on call) _____

Clinical Laboratory _____

PUBLIC AGENCIES

City and/or County Offices:

Drug Coordinator _____

Social Services _____

Mental Health _____

Public Health _____

Coroner_____

Toxicologist _____

Methadone Treatment
Center _____

Police

(include neighboring cities)

_____

_____

_____

OTHER HOSPITALS

_____

_____

_____

COMMUNITY RESOURCES

Acute Detoxification
Center _____

Crisis Intervention Team _____

Clergymen
(include main denominations)

_____

_____

_____

_____

Halfway Houses _____

Drop-In Centers _____

Free Clinics _____

Hot Line or

Emergency Switchboard _____

Alcoholics Anonymous_____

Other Self-Help Groups _____

_____

_____

_____

_____

_____

_____

_____

Index